OXFORD W

COLLE

ARTHUR RIMBAUD was born in Charleville, north-eastern France, in 1854, the second of four children. His mother came from a local farming family. His father, an army officer, abandoned the family six years later. At school the gifted, precocious Rimbaud was exceptionally successful. From a very early age he was writing poems, initially in Latin. By his teenage years he had outgrown his restricted life in provincial Charleville and had run away on a number of occasions, to Paris and to Belgium. In 1871 he formed a liaison with Verlaine. The two young poets soon fled Paris, living for many months in London. During all of this period Rimbaud was writing poetry. In 1873 Verlaine shot and wounded him, and their relationship ended. Rimbaud then spent some weeks writing the only work he saw through to publication, *A Season in Hell*, an account in prose and verse of his hopes for a new poetry, and their defeat. He completed the prose poems of *Illuminations*, begun before *A Season*. In 1875, however, aged 21, Rimbaud abandoned poetry altogether in disillusioned disgust and turned his back on everything in his former life. His remaining sixteen years were spent mainly out of France, the last years mostly in the Horn of Africa, where he worked as a trader. A tumour on his right knee forced him back to France, where the leg was immediately amputated. Still planning to return to Africa, he died of cancer in Marseilles in 1891 at the age of 37. The first edition of Rimbaud's complete poems appeared in 1895; all his known work was published in 1898, edited by his brother-in-law.

MARTIN SORRELL is Reader in French and Translation Studies at the University of Exeter. His monograph *Francis Ponge* was published by Twayne in 1980; his bilingual anthology, *Modern French Poetry*, by Forest Books in 1992; *Elles: A Bilingual Anthology of Modern French Poetry by Women* was published by the University of Exeter Press in 1995; his *Paul Verlaine: Selected Poems* appeared in Oxford World's Classics in 1999. He also translates plays for stage and radio, and has written original stories and plays for BBC radio.

OXFORD WORLD'S CLASSICS

For over 100 years Oxford World's Classics have brought readers closer to the world's great literature. Now with over 700 titles—from the 4,000-year-old myths of Mesopotamia to the twentieth century's greatest novels—the series makes available lesser-known as well as celebrated writing.

The pocket-sized hardbacks of the early years contained introductions by Virginia Woolf, T. S. Eliot, Graham Greene, and other literary figures which enriched the experience of reading. Today the series is recognized for its fine scholarship and reliability in texts that span world literature, drama and poetry, religion, philosophy and politics. Each edition includes perceptive commentary and essential background information to meet the changing needs of readers.

OXFORD WORLD'S CLASSICS

ARTHUR RIMBAUD

Collected Poems

Translated with an Introduction and Notes by
MARTIN SORRELL

UNIVERSITY PRESS

OXFORD
UNIVERSITY PRESS

Great Clarendon Street, Oxford OX2 6DP

Oxford University Press is a department of the University of Oxford.
It furthers the University's objective of excellence in research, scholarship,
and education by publishing worldwide in

Oxford New York

Athens Auckland Bangkok Bogotá Buenos Aires Cape Town
Chennai Dar es Salaam Delhi Florence Hong Kong Istanbul Karachi
Kolkata Kuala Lumpur Madrid Melbourne Mexico City Mumbai Nairobi
Paris São Paulo Shanghai Singapore Taipei Tokyo Toronto Warsaw

with associated companies in Berlin Ibadan

Oxford is a registered trade mark of Oxford University Press
in the UK and in certain other countries

Published in the United States
by Oxford University Press Inc., New York

First published as an Oxford World's Classics paperback 2001

British Library Cataloguing in Publication Data

Data available

Library of Congress Cataloging in Publication Data

Data available

ISBN 0–19–283344–8

1 3 5 7 9 10 8 6 4 2

Typeset in Ehrhardt
by RefineCatch Limited, Bungay, Suffolk
Printed in Great Britain by
Cox and Wyman Ltd.
Reading, Berks.

For Liam, Bethany, Rachel, and Katie

I'd have liked to show children blue-water
Dorados, golden fish and fish that sing
(Rimbaud)

CONTENTS

COLLECTED POEMS

Poems, 1869–1871

Poems from Album Zutique

The Stupra

Last Poems

A Season in Hell

Illuminations

INTRODUCTION

Rimbaud: Life and Legend

Rimbaud is the stuff of legend. A short, intense life, always on the edge, and brought to an early, agonizing end; the consistent refusal to take easy options; the astonishing firmness of will; the deliberate deregulation of the senses; the drugs; the homosexual phase; the arms-dealing in Africa; the slave-trading (unsubstantiated); above all, the astonishing precocity of major poetry written by the age of 21; the subsequent rejection of this poetry—these realities have combined to give Rimbaud a mythic status which, ironically, would have appalled him.

The significant facts[1] are these: Arthur Rimbaud was born in 1854, in Charleville, north-eastern France, hard by the Belgian border. He was the second of four children. In 1860 his father, an army officer, abandoned them to the less-than-tender mercies of a mother who did not or would not understand the precocious, poetic Arthur. Rebellion seethed in him, but for years he remained the model schoolboy, clever and hard-working. At a very early age he began to write verses, initially in Latin. His brilliant solitude was relieved by the arrival, in 1870, of a young teacher, Georges Izambard, a devotee of poetry. Before long came the first of Rimbaud's three significant flights from Charleville into Belgium and on to Paris, where he met—and quickly scorned—some of the most influential poets of the day. Aged scarcely 18, he took the poet Verlaine away from his young family and the two went to live together in London. Their turbulent relationship came to a dramatic end some two years later, in 1873, when Verlaine shot Rimbaud, wounding him in the wrist. For a while after that Rimbaud alternated spells on the family farm at Roche, writing some of his major work, with journeys to various places in Europe, undertaken in large part on foot. The last, and longest, phase of Rimbaud's life, the sixteen years up to his death, was spent almost entirely outside France, in improbable places,

[1] The numerous biographers of Rimbaud do not always agree about certain factual details. While developments in scholarship have cleared up some mysteries, others remain, and may never be resolved.

doing unlikely work, his back turned resolutely on family, friends, and poetry. Instead, his major concern became to develop trading possibilities in new African markets. However, thanks to his routine disregard for his physical well-being, a tumour that had developed in his right leg rapidly deteriorated, until he had to be brought in agony from the Horn of Africa to France, where the diseased leg was amputated. Still believing he could soon return to Africa, he died in Marseilles in 1891 of a generalized cancer. He was 37.

Early Poems

Rimbaud's life as a poet was meteoric. It was over in just a few years, roughly from his early teens to the age of 21. As there are problems in giving precise dates for some of his poems, to talk of phases might seem invidious. Nevertheless, what does mark his earliest poems is an amount of imitation and pastiche, of his great, immediate predecessor Baudelaire and of other, lesser contemporaries of the Romantic and Parnassian schools. However, these aspects of his writing disappear as his own poetic voice, audible in fact even in his first poem, becomes more distinctive. Whatever other voices echo in 'Orphans' New Year Gifts', Rimbaud's own is the loudest. The subject-matter, the unblinking, intelligent gaze, and above all the sadness, hurt, and latent anger are his. Together, they sound the first notes of the song of exclusion he was to sing throughout his writing, and to continue in a different key after he had left poetry behind for good.

In this substantially autobiographical poem, from its title onwards Rimbaud sets himself apart. It is tempting, and probably justified, to attribute in part his 'orphan' status to his family life. Biographers are agreed that *la mother*, as Rimbaud was to call her, was severe and cold. Vitalie Rimbaud (*née* Cuif) had such darkness in her soul that, late in life, she had herself lowered into the family tomb, between the corpses of Arthur and his sister Vitalie, in order to get a foretaste of what was to come. But life for an abandoned wife with children would have been difficult in mid-nineteenth-century Charleville, whose narrow provincialism Rimbaud later satirized in poems such as 'To Music'. Certainly, though, Madame Rimbaud was insensitive to Arthur's needs, and she nurtured only an austere conformity and piety in her children. Did Rimbaud love or forgive his mother? His

sinister nickname for her—'the mouth of darkness'—suggests not. Hence the pain which so marks a litany of poems, not only of loneliness but also of rage against women (tempered, it must be added, by sympathy for their historically low and abused situation—see 'First Communions', for example).

In the first thirty or so of his poems the effects of rage and desolation take artistic shape, and form themselves into a poetic vocation. Against the background misery at home and the boredom of Charleville, and then, after mid-1870, the Franco-Prussian War and the collapse of the discredited Second Empire, Rimbaud wrote a succession of poems which collectively stand as an indictment of repression of every kind. Whether the subject be politics ('The Blacksmith', 'Caesars' Rage'), social life ('Customs Men, Seated'), war ('Dead of '92', 'Asleep in the Valley'), or women ('Nina Answers Back', 'Venus Emerging'), Rimbaud's gaze searches out hypocrisy, self-interest, small-mindedness, injustice. Driven by his nature and experience, his imperative became to reject the old life and to find a new way of being—utterly lucid, rigorously honest—and to be attained by new love: love must be reinvented, as he says in *A Season in Hell.* Whatever the full meaning of that love might be (it has mysterious and mystical qualities), Rimbaud knew that it could not be found unless he broke the old ties. In 'Seven-Year-Old Poets', that muscular, unsettled poem of 1871, written just before his third flight from Charleville, not only did he confront himself and his mother with brutal directness, but, in the last, splendid line, he prophesied adventure, departure for a new life: 'thinking | Violent thoughts of getting under sail.'

Visionary Poetry

The year 1871 was a crucial one in France's history, and marked a turning-point in Rimbaud's life. Against a backcloth of national defeat, reactionary politics, and brutal repression,[2] he produced some of his most important writing, including 'Drunken Boat' and

[2] After France's defeat in the Franco-Prussian War, elections in February produced a National Assembly with a Royalist majority. With tensions rising in the capital, the government removed to nearby Versailles, while republican Parisians set up a Commune, based on socialist ideals, to resist the government. It was short-lived, destroyed by the Versaillais troops in a campaign which culminated in the notorious 'Week of Blood'.

two letters in which he enunciated his vision of a new poetry. By the autumn of that year, he was in Paris, offending social and poetic correctness and beginning to turn his back on the old life. His early phase was over. Ahead lay the sojourn in London with Verlaine, the years of vagrancy, and the towering prose poetry of *A Season in Hell* and *Illuminations*.

Rimbaud got 'under sail' when his poetic vision became fully defined, and he understood that poetry has nothing to do with easy pleasures and recreation but must be a total way of living in the world—or, as Yves Bonnefoy terms it, an ascesis.[3] What this involved was the discipline to reach and abide in the deepest, most authentic level of the self, however shocking and unacceptable this might be to oneself or others. For all that Rimbaud considered himself a pagan of inferior race who hated Christianity, the great life-denying force of our culture, his instincts were not wholly dissimilar to those of religion. Poetry for him was the hope of charity, albeit a hope on which he cast the gravest of doubts in the final section of *A Season in Hell*.

It is in the two so-called 'Letters of the Visionary' that Rimbaud sets out his new concept of poetry. Written from Charleville in May 1871, the first of these is addressed to George Izambard and outlines Rimbaud's central concern of how one is to become a poet. He says that he has unashamedly adopted the position of a cynical outsider, the drop-out who refuses to work or to conform to society's rules, but who will rather scrounge his sustenance from friends, for whom in return he will perform unspecified services. He implies that he can fulfil his obligations to society by becoming a *true* poet, as opposed to those who hold up their subjectivities for admiration. The target here is the Romantic poetry of the earlier part of the century, whose solipsistic modes still largely prevailed decades later. By contrast, Rimbaud wants to write 'objective' poetry, becoming what he terms a 'workman'—a concept which recurs throughout his work, and which might appear paradoxical given his contempt for labour as traditionally defined. His idea of the poet's work entails idleness, vice and depravity. The implied rationale is that this approach is essential if he is to reach a state in which objective poetry can be written: for this is, not a poetry of objects, but one in which the poet

[3] Yves Bonnefoy, *Rimbaud par lui-même* (Paris: Seuil, 1961, 1994).

transcends the psychology of the self and overcomes egoism, either deliberate (as in Romanticism) or unintended. Here we come to the key word: Rimbaud declares that he is 'working to become a visionary' (*voyant*). Anticipating Izambard's puzzlement, he adds that he neither can nor will explain the term. But he does go on to speak of the unknown (*l'inconnu*), objective poetry's aim, which can only be attained by the 'systematic disordering of *all the senses*' (his italics). Prophetically, he concedes that great suffering will be involved, and must be accepted. He goes on to assert that it is wrong to say: 'I think.' We should say: 'I am being thought' (*on me pense*). Rimbaud's analysis culminates in the extraordinary claim that 'I is another' (*Je est un autre*).

This is the heart of the matter, and the point is developed much more fully in the second letter, written to his friend the minor poet Paul Demeny. Rimbaud's apparent bad grammar says that the self, the 'I', is neither stable nor properly recognized by the subject, the experiencing 'I'. Setting himself against the psychological orthodoxy of a reliable, fixed self, Rimbaud's idea may be interpreted in at least two ways: first, that the self is indeed a meaningful entity, but has been forever wrongly conceived and understood; or secondly, that the self is so fragmented that to posit its indivisibility is wishful thinking. These two interpretations may amount to the same thing in the end, but to the extent that they are discrete the second is the one conventionally accepted, and it looks forward to some recent theories about the mind and the brain. It also leads to a third possible interpretation, to be discussed later.

In the second 'visionary' letter Rimbaud amplifies his assertion that 'I is another' with a metaphor which smacks of the alchemy which reputedly interested him for a while. 'If copper awakes as a clarion, it is in no way its fault.' The implication is that the 'I' is not what it thinks, and can be transmuted magically into other things. Indeed, Rimbaud then confirms this idea unambiguously by declaring that he is a witness to the birth of his own thought, which he watches and listens to. Then, choosing a musical analogy, he completes his argument by claiming that he has merely to touch his bow and the whole symphony stirs in the depths and leaps up. In other words, the self, the selves which inhere in the 'I', are both vaster than we know and unavailable to us by conventional means.

Rimbaud then claims that only the *true* poet can reach the

unknown 'I', and only do so by means of what he calls, in another celebrated phrase, 'the systematic disordering of the senses'. Here lies the route to the visionary state, and if it smacks of a reckless abandonment to the pleasure principle—as it has too readily been regarded by some of Rimbaud's later 'disciples'—in fact it requires that discipline, that ascesis which was pointed to above. Rimbaud is not granting a licence for self-indulgence. For all the drugs, drink, sex, and rebelliousness—he was still only an adolescent 16 when he wrote these letters—his life at this stage was scarcely comfortable, and it became progressively more demanding and austere. He goes on to say that the disordering (*dérèglement*) of the senses involves all forms of love, suffering, and even madness. Metaphorical poisons have to be absorbed and distilled, the awful tortures of mind, soul, and body welcomed, if the goal, the unknown (*l'inconnu*), is to be reached, a condition which Rimbaud equates with ultimate, objective truth. The punishing road to the unknown can be trodden only by 'horrible workers'.

If this visionary programme sounds mystical and impractical, the extraordinary fact is that from mid-1871 Rimbaud did his best to put it into action in his life and his writing. A matter of weeks after the two letters were written he was in Paris, having sent some poems to the young and rising poet Paul Verlaine, obtaining in return an invitation from him to come to the capital. From that time on, Rimbaud's life would become uncompromisingly rootless, anti-bourgeois, removed from the ususal considerations of money, comfort, and status. His poetry was about to show the most extreme results of a deliberately disordered imagination.

It is in one of the poems of that period, the celebrated 'Drunken Boat', that the visionary ideal and, prophetically, its failure are made flesh with astonishing brilliance. A wild poem in strictly measured form, 'Drunken Boat' was written when Rimbaud had not so much as glimpsed the ocean. Its account of a dream-voyage through uncharted seas, undertaken by an empty boat whose crewmen have all been killed, is an extended metaphor for the poet's discovery and ultimate loss of new light, new colour, new sound—in short, the new vision. As in Joseph Conrad's story *Heart of Darkness*, the journey through unknown waters is a journey into the depths of the self. At the start of the poem the boat frees itself from any European association, represented by the cargoes of Flemish wheat and

English cotton. Now that the crewmen are dead the boat is able to go where it will. Some stanzas further on, in a lovely line, the boat tells us that it is bathing in the Poem of the Sea; there now begins a sustained account of the voyage in the most vivid tones imaginable. A new world is discovered, of reefs, rocks, rainbows, glaciers, fish, sea-horses, Leviathans, moons, and suns . . . Rimbaud's imagination works at fever-pitch to create an unprecedented dreamscape. The adventure is the disordering of the senses, the dream is the vision itself, the unknown that can only become real once the poet-boat has slipped the moorings of the ego.

The poem is also, however, the recognition of failure, the sad acknowledgement that the vision has not been sustained. The first signs come in the middle of the poem, when the boat announces with regret that it would have liked to show the wonderful golden fish to children (and, incidentally, we are reminded of the neglected children of Rimbaud's first poem). It is not to be. In one of the saddest moments in all of Rimbaud's work, the boat concedes not just that the dream is over, but that it, and the poet, have come full circle and must now accept what perhaps was always their destiny, their selfhood, their 'I', reintegrated into the old pre-visionary, fallen world:

> If I want Europe, it's a dark cold pond
> Where a small child plunged in sadness crouches
> One fragrant evening at dusk and launches
> A boat frail as a butterfly in May.

The poem then closes in abject desolation, for if the poet-boat is resigned to the old order before *dérèglement*, it is also quite devoid of energy and will, and is haunted by prison-ships looking down with terrible eyes, a lingering image of crime and punishment reminding us that issues of guilt and redemption are never far from the surface in Rimbaud.

Rimbaud can be more enigmatic, more closed in his meaning, but nowhere does he astonish as much as in 'Drunken Boat'. This poet of visions, this hurt, angry boy-genius, unleashes torrents of the most dynamic imagery and vocabulary, stretching the French language as far as it will go. His poetry abounds in coinages and neologisms as it struggles to keep pace with the vision that is always running ahead and threatening to vanish. Language bursts

out of abstraction and floods the senses. Another famous poem, 'Vowels', turns the five sounds into colours, reminiscent of that neurological phenomenon known as synaesthesia, of which Baudelaire gives some idea in his celebrated 'Correspondances' sonnet.[4] By the time of 'Drunken Boat', Rimbaud's poetry is as blinding as those suns which are a hallmark of his work, his language resembling a high-voltage electrical circuit, overloaded, as Iris Murdoch has put it,[5] to the point where it fuses and explodes in spectacular constellations.

'Drunken Boat' was among Rimbaud's last poems in verse, a constraint which ensured that the forms of his writing at least remained orthodox in appearance. However, in view of his impatient search for new expression it was predictable that he should reject formal limitations, and from around 1872 adopt the much looser-looking structures of the so-called prose poem, and indeed of discursive prose itself.

A Season in Hell

The summer of 1872 finalized the break with Rimbaud's old life, for at that point, after some desultory months spent initially in a disappointing Paris and then with family in the Ardennes, he returned to the capital in July, only to decide to leave France, inviting Verlaine to accompany him. Making a choice he was later intermittently to regret, Verlaine abandoned his young wife and new baby to join Rimbaud in what became a picaresque adventure played out largely in London, and interrupted by occasional homecomings to France, and to Belgium. The saga of dire poverty in cheap boarding-houses came to its infamous end in Brussels in July 1873, when Verlaine shot Rimbaud, wounding him in the wrist—the desperate attempt of the terminally weak poet to detain the far stronger, impatient younger man who was already becoming remote from him. Rimbaud had grown sick of Verlaine's vacillations, and there is good reason also to suppose that he had tired of homosexuality, ultimately just one among others of his *voyant*-inspired experiments, a considered *dérèglement*, and serving only to reaffirm the old, bitter lesson about

[4] In synaesthesia an effect normally received through one of the senses is experienced directly through another. Thus, in Baudelaire's sonnet perfumes *sound* as soft as oboes.

[5] Iris Murdoch, *Sartre*.

the failure of love.[6] By the time of the shooting incident, Verlaine was of no further interest to the unforgiving Rimbaud, either as a lover, a poet, or as a human being worthy of respect. Verlaine ended up in prison, while Rimbaud returned to the family farm in Roche, near Charleville and wrote the only book he ever saw through to publication, *A Season in Hell*.

For a long time the majority opinion was that this work must have been Rimbaud's last piece of creative writing, his farewell to the old life, old loves, old aspirations, old poetry, so bitterly does it sever all attachments to everything that had gone before. But in the light of the latest evidence most scholars are now certain that the prose poems of the *Illuminations* were written before and after *A Season*. Absolutely reliable dating and an understanding of Rimbaud's precise intentions remain just out of reach, but the indications are that *A Season* was not intended to repudiate *all* poetry so much as the poetry which he himself had created up till then. Whether or not *Illuminations* should be included in this condemnation is a moot point. But in one of *A Season*'s most telling sections, 'Second Delirium: Alchemy of the Word', Rimbaud appears to distance himself from a too-exalted ambition for poetry, indeed, from any ambition at all. Its very title suggests the failure of alchemy, whereby poetic language should have provided the key to unlock the final door on to the radiant kingdom of truth. The first line speaks of the story he is going to tell of 'one of my madnesses', which, he adds later, threatened his health. That madness was a sustained hallucination, in which he saw a mosque in the place of a factory, or coaches rolling through the sky, or a drawing-room at the bottom of a lake. Rimbaud chastizes the visions and himself: 'I thought I could invent a poetic language accessible one day to all the senses.' He scoffs at some lines he once wrote:

> Found again. What?
> Eternity.
> The sea lost
> In the sun

pre-echoing the resolution claimed by the very last words of *A*

[6] There is no evidence that Rimbaud had homosexual relationships after Verlaine. On the contrary, he is known to have had at least one lasting, heterosexual liaison in Africa. He wanted, also, to start a family of his own.

Season. He has been, he says, a buffoon. The poetry of vision is a farce. If *A Season in Hell* is the diary of a farcical failure, ironically defeat is conceded in beautiful writing, short and cryptic verses such as the lines just given. Other examples are 'Song from the Highest Tower', a poignant lament for lost possibilities, and one of his great songs of yearning; and 'Four a.m. in Summertime', not only a metaphor for the stubborn endurance of the poetic quest, but also an expression of Rimbaud's sympathies with workers—whose ranks, as the 'Letters of the Visionary' made clear, he will never join. *A Season in Hell* is not only critical of certain poetic enterprises: it reveals as well a contempt for society, for its damaging institutions and its politics which feeble-minded and vicious men shape, and which shape them.

A Season closes with a section pertinently entitled 'The Impossible'—and here Rimbaud appears to have run out of options. The young poet resembles more a spiritually bereft adult than a lad of 18. On the verge of silence, however, he goes on, and completes the great collection of prose poems *Illuminations*. Then, up to his death, will come the years in which he all but disappears, glimpsed intermittently in matter-of-fact letters home, eighteen years of a gruelling odyssey halfway round the world, and during which apparently he writes not another single line of poetry.

Illuminations

How any of *Illuminations* can have been written after the apparent impasse of *A Season in Hell* may seem puzzling. There is a persuasive view that this sequence of prose poems—only two are in verse, free verse at that—expresses the final disorganization of an 'I' so multi-faceted that it has become too brittle to survive. It and its visions must shatter. The darkness of Rimbaud's ultimate silence looms even more than in *A Season*. The title *Illuminations* itself has more than one possible meaning. Verlaine said that it should be taken in an English sense of coloured plates; illuminated manuscripts suggest themselves too. Beyond this, however, 'illumination' also denotes something more abstract, a revelation, an insight or flash of understanding, the moment when a truth is brilliantly revealed, only to vanish as quickly—similar to what James Joyce meant by the name 'epiphany'.

However they are defined, the *Illuminations* come as close as

anything in Rimbaud to vision. In writing which dances on a tightrope strung between coherence and chaos, there comes into being a bedazzlement of events and moments, people and apparitions, dissolving as quickly as they appear, as if each illumination was like a waking dream. In trying to find a unifying thread throughout these pieces, we can have recourse to what I mentioned earlier as the third interpretation of this assertion 'I is another', one that focuses on the concept of authorship. Conventionally poetry, like all writing, recognizes implicitly that there is a gap between what is put forward—the subject-matter—and the intelligent self which puts it forward—the writer as an autonomy. Even a poem's most startling images show that a creative imagination has organized the material, put it into a language shared by all. This is how Rimbaud's poetic language works in the verse poems, even in the most visionary, such as 'Drunken Boat'. Here, in *seeing* the visions the boat is a commentator *on* them. But in at least some of the poems in *Illuminations* it is not the case that the visions manifest themselves *to* a beholder; rather, it is as though the vision were *in* the beholder, and the beholder *in* the vision. Thus, 'I is another' might mean that 'I'—an identity which stands apart—is in fact organically part of 'the other'. Subject is object, and the desired objective poetry has been found. Taken in this way Rimbaud's thinking becomes more recognizable, his preoccupation with the duality of self and non-self linked to a tradition of philosophical enquiry stretching back at least to Descartes.

If *Illuminations* represent Rimbaud's hugest ambition, they also hint at failure and the silence to come. Beyond the exhilaration of their visions, many pages are as sad, if not as sharply angry, as some of *A Season in Hell* or the verse poems: 'Tale', for example, or 'Dawn', the account of an adventure which unfolds as a metaphor for the new poetry.[7] As so frequently in Rimbaud's work, this piece opens to the confident promise of new light. The 'I' figure, the poet-persona, has embraced the dawn. The 'I' united with the dawn, therefore the sun, and by extension creation itself, is synonymous with the confidence that objective and subjective worlds are one. The first line is the poem's high point; what follows is the account of how that point supposedly was reached. In a wonderful sequence which recreates the sheer magic of dawn's arrival, Rimbaud weaves into the

[7] See C. A. Hackett's absorbing analysis of 'Aube', in P. H. Nurse (ed.), *The Art of Criticism*, listed in the Bibliography.

textures of astonishment some ominous hints that the adventure in fact did not happen at all. The second half of this tightly structured poem in prose makes clear the awesome reality of the dawn's size, its strength and speed, all of which turn out to have been too much for the 'I'. Significantly, towards the end 'I' has turned into a beggar trying vainly to keep pace with the fast-growing dawn. And, claiming to have tied up the dawn goddess in her own veils, 'I' confesses to having done no more than to feel only a *fraction* of her immensity. The final line, perfectly balancing the first and yet opposing its softness with its own shrill vowels, tells of a bitter defeat. Rimbaud now distances 'I' as a third person, 'the child' who wakes at noon to find, naturally, that dawn has gone. The visionary poet, then, believes that in his dream of wrestling the dawn to the ground and losing himself in her he has glimpsed the new poetry. But the metaphor says that this is an illusion from which Rimbaud must awake.

Beyond Poetry: Rimbaud's Legacy

When the journey towards the visionary goal finally ran out of road, Rimbaud's restlessness did not give way to immobility. The march through poetry became a march across the world. If poetry cannot change life, as he hoped, then hope too must go. But the insistent drive towards *something* endured. After about 1874 Rimbaud deserted poetry and continued his ascesis by other means. His remaining, adult years were even more punishing (self-punishing, we might suspect) than those that had gone before. He made a living in a variety of ways. Moving from country to country, covering huge distances largely on foot, he found work as a teacher, was employed by a circus company, became a quarry foreman, a mercenary—and deserter—and finally tried to establish himself as an arms-dealer in north Africa—although not, as once wrongly supposed (on the basis of a request he made for 'a mule and two slave boys'), as a slave-trader. The indifference Rimbaud showed towards conventional notions of career and success indicate that to him, since poetry was dead, so was the vision: he did not believe that anything would make the vision happen now. Real life is absent, he wrote in *A Season in Hell*, and it is one of his most conclusive pronouncements. The final phase of Rimbaud's life, the tough years in unforgiving places, show that, in that absence of the real life, he resolved to accommodate

himself to the limitations, as exigent as they are prosaic, of the only world possible. The impulse towards life as ascesis was as strong as in the poetry stage, and it chose poverty as its authentication—for if, in *A Season in Hell*, he claims to loathe poverty, he also says in the same work that sound sleep is impossible for the rich. From now on his life would be lived principally in the fearsome conditions of the Horn of Africa. However, his deprivations, endured with a will of iron, were to prove too much. Rimbaud's body was finally defeated; possibly his spirit too. Shortly before this haunted, cancer-ridden amputee died on a hospital bed in Marseilles, three weeks after his thirty-seventh birthday, his sister Isabelle claimed that he made confession. Whether or not Rimbaud embraced Catholicism on his deathbed, the story is accepted by those who see a religious centre in his make-up.

What Rimbaud's life and poetry certainly do represent is a search for the sense, the truth of *this* life in *this* world. In that he is thoroughly modern—words he uses in the final lines of *A Season in Hell*. Rimbaud's gaze, his intelligence, burn reality's surfaces to find what is beyond. He says, again in *A Season*, that the poet is the one who steals fire, and in his acceptance of that mission, with its Promethean attendant agonies, darknesses, and final failure, Rimbaud is modern, indeed exemplary. Everything about his life seems to have encapsulated modern man's drama, acted out at its most intense pitch.

Rimbaud's most significant artistic influence, arguably, is on Surrealism, the movement which, bent on overthrowing the old icons of art, saw in him one of its few legitimate antecedents. For the Surrealists, Rimbaud was the visionary who taps directly into the unconscious, bringing what is hidden to the surface. Surrealism, the child of Freud and the horrors of the First World War, hates rationality and logic because their inherent mendacity all through history has brought individual unhappiness and general injustice to the world. Surrealism demanded that life should be a permanent revolution in every domain, from the most intimate to the most public. In short, it echoed Rimbaud's call to change life, and his claim that one means of doing so was to produce a poetry which broke the conventional bonds of grammar, syntax, form, and image. However, Surrealism's favouring of automatic writing puts it outside Rimbaud's aesthetic: the material of its poetry is received and transmitted irresponsibly, passively, with eyes closed, as it were. While

this has affinities with Rimbaud's 'I am being thought', his own view of poetry, and the discipline needed to reach the unknown, is that it has to be worked for with a will, with eyes wide open.

Rimbaud has been admired in France by writers and poets as different as Stéphane Mallarmé, Paul Claudel, Paul Valéry, René Char, and Jean Genet. Albert Camus, who evaluated Rimbaud in terms of philosophical *révolte*, while regretting the retreat into silence of the poet he calls the greatest of his time, considered exemplary his wish that 'life must be changed'—a wish that was reiterated with force during the 1968 anti-government uprising in France, the *événements*, when Rimbaud's words became a favoured slogan.

Rimbaud's reputation stands very high today. He has been revered by artists and performers from many different backgrounds, including the Beat generation of poets in America, the singer Bob Dylan, the film-maker Jean-Luc Godard, the actor Gérard Depardieu, the English composers Benjamin Britten and John Tavener, the French footballer Eric Cantona, and the Mexican poet Octavio Paz. The English playwright Christopher Hampton's *Total Eclipse*, about the affair between Rimbaud and Verlaine, reached a wide audience both as a stage-play and as a film.

It is clear, then, that Rimbaud's enduring influence is not exclusively literary and artistic. He lives on as an example, an icon. He has been championed as the great anti-rationalist, not only in France, but also in Germany, Italy, and America, while in the former Soviet Union he was fêted not only as an honorary Communard but also as a Bolshevik. According to requirements, Rimbaud has been claimed variously as prophet, angel, superman, bad boy, God, and Devil.

Legend and influences aside, Rimbaud's writing and life resemble those of no other poet. Verlaine once gave a definition of him that is as accurate as it is evocative: 'l'homme aux semelles de vent'—'the man with the wind in his heels'.

NOTE ON THE TEXT AND TRANSLATION

The editor of Rimbaud faces the considerable headache of establishing the text. It is not always possible to give a date of composition with any certainty, and, as a number of his pieces have more than one version, it can become a matter of personal judgement as to which version to prefer. Over the years editions have often differed one from another, sometimes substantially, and have tended to reflect the state of Rimbaud scholarship at any given time.

The major editions of recent years—by Antoine Adam; by Suzanne Bernard, revised by André Guyaux; by Jean-Luc Steinmetz; and, most recently, by Steve Murphy—present the verse poems each in a more or less different configuration. Murphy's 1999 critical edition of the verse poems, the monumental first volume in a planned series of all Rimbaud's writing, gives every version and variant of every poem (including fragments of poems), and their chronologies. While his research has been exhaustive, Murphy himself recognizes in his preface that no single edition, his own included, can be taken as gospel. If his multi-version edition of Rimbaud is the fullest, the Bernard/Guyaux and the Steinmetz editions are also excellent—well researched and annotated, clearly presented, and informative. The notes in Bernard/Guyaux particularly are very full and valuable. The Steinmetz gives a clear sense of Rimbaud's evolution, from the early verse poems (the so-called 'Douai Notebook') onwards, and, for this reason, I have preferred Steinmetz's order for the present volume. Antoine Adam revised Rolland de Renéville's and Jules Mouquet's original 1946 Gallimard Pléiade edition in 1972, but it remains less informative and up-to-date than Murphy, Bernard/Guyaux, or Steinmetz. Nor does it contain explanatory notes, only textual variants.

All of Rimbaud's poetry, verse and prose poems, is given in the present volume, with the exception of certain fragments and the very early Latin pieces. Some of the prose writing is also included, where I have found its bearing on the poetry especially important. Thus, 'The Deserts of Love' and 'Fragments according to the Gospel'

throw light respectively on Rimbaud's view of love as a desolation, and on Christianity as a pernicious force.

I am all too aware of the considerable debt I owe to the legion of earlier translators of Rimbaud. They are too numerous to list or to comment on in any detail. Not surprisingly, given the difficulties of a lot of Rimbaud's visionary, mysterious writing, the quality of translation has been uneven. Too faithful a rendering, down to exact line length, in the French syllabic tradition, can be pedestrian, especially if accompanied by insistent end-stopping and rhyme. Where Rimbaud flies, the translator will walk, counting steps. The policy of straightforward, no-nonsense prose translation, line by line, is admirable, but to have value, the reading of the original and the resultant translation must be completely accurate—which has not always been the case. At the 'non-faithful' extreme, any number of poets and translators have made 'versions' of Rimbaud, often using him as a launching-pad for their own craft, sometimes with impressive, if startling results. In these cases it is up to the reader to decide if the English constitutes a good poem in its own right. In my own translations I have wanted to keep within fairly tight bounds. That said, I have not opted for rigorous syllabic lines ('Drunken Boat' is one exception), but have tried to vary line length. Sometimes I have taken what I consider justifiable liberties in order to capture essential poetic truth: hence the occasional neologism, for example, or the particularly condensed form of 'Tortured Heart', reduced from eight- to six-line stanzas. Rhyme in English can be tyrannical, and prone to unwanted comic effects; I have almost always eschewed it. Finally, while *Illuminations* is full of traps (which I hope Mark Treharne's excellent renderings have helped me avoid[1]), the enigmatic little poems in *A Season in Hell* are particularly resistant to secure, convincing translation.

Whatever else, I have sought to give English-language readers a feeling of the vigour of Rimbaud's poetic voice, its explosive force, its brilliance, and its poignancy and delicacy too.

Michael Pakenham, Evelyne Hervy, Dave Braund, and Lawrence Sail have each clarified recalcitrant problems. Judith Luna, my editor

[1] *A Season in Hell and Illuminations*, translated by Mark Treharne (London: J. M. Dent, 1998).

at OUP, has steered this book along with her customary tact and skill. In the early 1990s it was a pleasure and an education to have the leading Rimbaud scholar Steve Murphy as a colleague at Exeter. To all, my grateful thanks.

I want particularly to thank Stephen Minta, good friend and most sensitive reader of poetry, for first making me appreciate the greatness of Rimbaud.

Most especially, my thanks go yet again to my wife Claire, patient, encouraging, helpful, and such good company.

SELECT BIBLIOGRAPHY

Given the large quantity of publications concerning Rimbaud, this Bibliography is necessarily most selective. Detailed bibliographies, some including articles about Rimbaud, are to be found in many available publications, including some of those listed here.

Principal Complete Critical Editions, Currently Available

Oeuvres complètes, rev. edn. by Antoine Adam (Paris: Gallimard, Bibliothèque de la Pléiade, 1972).

Oeuvres, rev. edn. by Suzanne Bernard and André Guyaux (Paris: Garnier, 1991).

Oeuvres, 3 vols. ed. Jean-Luc Steinmetz (Paris: Flammarion, 1989).

Oeuvres complètes, vol. 1, ed. Steve Murphy (Paris: Champion, 1999).

Biography

Berrichon, Paterne, *La Vie de Jean-Arthur Rimbaud* (Paris: Mercure de France, 1897). The first, and largely unreliable, biography, by Rimbaud's brother-in-law.

Delahaye, Ernest, *Delahaye témoin de Rimbaud* (Neuchâtel: La Baconnière, 1974). The various writings of Rimbaud's friend brought together.

Izambard, Georges, *Rimbaud tel que je l'ai connu* (Nantes: Le Passeur, 1991). Recollections and reflections of Rimbaud's teacher and friend.

Nicholl, Charles, *Somebody Else: Arthur Rimbaud in Africa 1880–91* (London: Jonathan Cape, 1997). The latest account of Rimbaud's last years. Lively and detailed.

Robb, Graham, *Rimbaud* (London: Picador, 2000). A lively and absorbing critical biography, very substantial.

Starkie, Enid, *Arthur Rimbaud* (London: Faber & Faber, 1938, revised 1947 and 1961). This has been the benchmark critical biography for decades, though some of its findings are now disputed.

Underwood, Vernon, *Rimbaud et l'Angleterre* (Paris: Nizet, 1976). A scholarly work on Rimbaud's time in, and relationship with, England.

Critical Studies

Bonnefoy, Yves, *Rimbaud par lui-même* (Paris: Seuil, 1961, 1994), trans. Paul Schmidt (New York: Harper & Row, 1973). A profound, illuminating study by a major contemporary poet.

Bouillane de Lacoste, Henry de, *Rimbaud et le problème des 'Illuminations'* (Paris: Mercure de France, 1959). A significant contribution to scholarship.

Brunel, Pierre, *Rimbaud: Projets et réalisations* (Paris: Champion, 1983). A shrewd discussion, with an interesting section on 'objective poetry'.

Butor, Michel, *Improvisations sur Rimbaud* (Paris: La Différence, 1989). Twelve essays on aspects of Rimbaud's work by a major French 'new novelist'.

Camus, Albert, *L'Homme révolté* (Paris: Gallimard, 1951). This includes a short appraisal of Rimbaud, in terms of philosophical revolt, seeing his work, but not his life, as exemplary.

Chadwick, Charles, *Études sur Rimbaud* (Paris: Nizet, 1960). Interesting on the dating of some works, and for its classifications of *Illuminations* by theme.

—— *Rimbaud* (London: Athlone Press, 1977). A good, if slightly prejudiced, general introduction.

Étiemble [René], *Le Mythe de Rimbaud*. (Paris: Gallimard, 1952–68). A huge (four-volume), largely bibliographical undertaking; it has done much to dispel more fanciful notions about Rimbaud.

Fowlie, Wallace, *Rimbaud* (Chicago: University of Chicago Press, 1965). A critical survey.

Frohock, W. M., *Rimbaud's Poetic Practice* (Cambridge, Mass.: Harvard University Press, 1963). A sensitive and sensible evaluation.

Gengoux, Jacques, *La Pensée poétique de Rimbaud* (Paris: Nizet, 1950). Rewarding, if often speculative.

Guyaux, André, *Poétique du fragment, essai sur les 'Illuminations' de Rimbaud* (Neuchâtel: La Baconnière, 1985). This reading by an eminent Rimbaud scholar has led to considerable academic debate.

Hackett, Cecil A., *Rimbaud: A Critical Introduction* (Cambridge: Cambridge University Press, 1981). A useful general introduction; one of several studies by this leading Rimbaud scholar.

—— '*Aube*', in P. H. Nurse (ed.), *The Art of Criticism* (Edinburgh: Edinburgh University Press, 1969). A persuasive, detailed analysis of one prose poem from *Illuminations*.

Murphy, Steve, *Le Premier Rimbaud ou l'apprentissage de la subversion* (Paris and Lyon: Editions du CNRS, Presses Universitaires de Lyon, 1990). One of the best studies of Rimbaud's work of 1869–72, by a leading contemporary Rimbaud authority.

—— *Rimbaud et la ménagerie impériale* (Paris and Lyon: Editions du CNRS, Presses Universitaires de Lyon, 1991). A detailed examination of Rimbaud's satirical approach to Napoleon III and the Second Empire.

Noulet, Émilie, *Le Premier visage de Rimbaud* (Brussels: Palais des Académies, 1973). Contains detailed analysis of certain poems.

Osmond, Nick, *Arthur Rimbaud: Illuminations* (London: Athlone Press, 1976). A thorough, well-annotated analysis of all the prose poems in *Illuminations*.

Renéville, Rolland de, *Rimbaud le Voyant* (Paris: Au sans pareil, 1929). Tries, unconvincingly, to show that Rimbaud's work is a unified body of thought.

Richard, Jean-Pierre, *Poésie et profondeur* (Paris: Seuil, 1955). Includes a persuasive chapter on Rimbaud's imaginative world.

Richter, Mario, *La Crise du logos et la quête du mythe* (Neuchâtel: La Baconnière, 1976). Contains a detailed reading of three of Rimbaud's poems.

Ruff, Marcel, *Rimbaud* (Paris: Hatier, 1968). Sound and scholarly.

St Aubyn, F. C., *Arthur Rimbaud* (Boston, Mass: G. K. Hall & Co., Twayne World Authors, 1975). A detailed overview, clearly organized.

Steinmetz, Jean-Luc, *Le Champ d'écoute* (Neuchâtel: La Baconnière, 1985). Contains a chapter in which the concept of Rimbaud's 'charity' is examined.

Reviews, etc. Devoted to Rimbaud Studies

Bulletin des Amis de Rimbaud: 7 numbers, between January 1931 and April 1939.

Le Bateau ivre: 20 numbers, between January 1949 and September 1966.

Études rimbaldiennes: 3 numbers, in 1968, 1970, and 1972.

A. Rimbaud: 4 numbers, in 1972, 1973, 1976, and 1980.

Rimbaud vivant: 27 numbers, between 1973 and 1988.

Circeto: 2 numbers, 1983 and 1984.

Parade sauvage: revue d'études rimbaldiennes (Charleville: Musée-Bibliothèque Arthur Rimbaud). This has appeared regularly since 1984. It also publishes a companion newsletter (*Bulletin*).

Special Review Numbers

La Grive (October 1954).

Europe (May–June 1973).

Littérature (October 1973).

Revue de l'Université de Bruxelles (1982).

Bérénice, 2 (1981); 5 (1982); 32 (1991).

Revue des Sciences humaines, 193 (1984).

Revue d'Histoire littéraire de la France (March–April 1987).

Background

Chadwick, Charles, *Symbolism* (London: Methuen, 1971). Short introductory study, with a chapter on Rimbaud.

Hemmings, F. W. J., *Culture and Society in France, 1848–1898* (London: Batsford, 1971). Describes the France which Rimbaud knew.

Kahn, Gustave, *Symbolistes et décadents* (Paris: Vanier, 1902). Includes some pages on Rimbaud.

Lawler, James, *The Language of French Symbolism* (Princeton: Princeton University Press, 1969). Some pages on Rimbaud, considered in a wider context.

Miller, Christopher L., *Blank Darkness: Africanist Discourse in French* (Chicago: University of Chicago Press, 1985). Includes a good section on Rimbaud's time in the Horn of Africa.

Miller, Henry, *The Time of the Assassins* (Norfolk: New Directions, 1956). One 'outsider' on another; the book says more about Miller than Rimbaud.

Murdoch, Iris, 'The Sickness of the Language', in *Sartre* (London: Bowes & Bowes, 1953). A short, intriguing analysis of why the language of some late-nineteenth-century French poets 'failed'.

Wilson, Edmund, *Axel's Castle: A Study in the Imaginative Literature of 1870–1930* (New York: Scribner's, 1931). A celebrated, influential book, with an important chapter on Rimbaud.

Further Reading in Oxford World's Classics

Baudelaire, Charles, *Prose Poems and La Fanfarlo*, trans. and ed. Rosemary Lloyd.

—— *The Flowers of Evil*, trans. James McGowan, with an introduction by Jonathan Culver.

Huysmans, Joris-Karl, *Against Nature*, trans. Margaret Mauldon, ed. Nicholas White.

Six French Poets of the Nineteenth Century: Lamartine, Hugo, Baudelaire, Verlaine, Rimbaud, Mallarmé, trans. and ed. E. H. and A. M. Blackmore.

Verlaine, Paul, *Selected Poems*, trans. and ed. Martin Sorrell.

A CHRONOLOGY OF ARTHUR RIMBAUD

1853 8 February: marriage of Captain Frédéric Rimbaud and Vitalie Cuif. They set up house in Charleville, north-eastern France, very close to the Belgian border.

1854 20 October: birth of Jean-Nicolas-Arthur (Arthur), their second son, and second of the four children who lived.

1860 Rimbaud's parents separate.

1861 Rimbaud's education begins at Institution Rossat.

1865 Attends Collège de Charleville.

1869 Rimbaud's first poem (in Latin) published. He is aged 14.

1870 Teacher Georges Izambard arrives at Rimbaud's school. January: publication of Rimbaud's first poem in French. May: sends three poems to Théodore Banville in Paris. 19 July: start of the Franco-Prussian War. Late August: first of Rimbaud's flights to Paris. He is arrested for travelling without ticket, and briefly imprisoned. 2 September: France suffers defeat at Sedan. 4 September: the Third Republic proclaimed. A Government of National Defence formed. Rimbaud begins friendship with minor poet Paul Demeny. October: Rimbaud wanders through Belgium, ending up in Brussels. During the autumn and winter Paris is besieged by German forces.

1871 28 January: armistice ends the Franco-Prussian War. 8 February: a new National Assembly elected, with a Royalist majority. 17 February: Adolphe Thiers becomes the government's Head of Executive. 25 February: Rimbaud arrives in Paris, but leaves after two weeks. 18 March: socialist Paris Commune proclaimed, in opposition to the government. Rimbaud is sympathetic to Commune, but it is unclear whether he was in Paris during its existence. 15 May: Rimbaud sends Demeny the so-called 'Visionary letter' (*Lettre du voyant*). 21–8 May: the Commune finally suppressed in the 'Week of Blood' (*la semaine sanglante*). Late September: Rimbaud goes to Paris, at the invitation of Paul Verlaine.

1872 Late January: Rimbaud goes to Arras, north-eastern France. Early May: returns to Paris. 7 July: Verlaine deserts wife and baby to go with Rimbaud to Belgium. 7 September: the two go to live in London. December: Rimbaud returns to Charleville.

1873 January: Rimbaud rejoins Verlaine in London. 11 April: Rimbaud goes to family farm at Roche, near Charleville. 27 May: Rimbaud (and Verlaine) back in London. 7 July: Rimbaud goes to Brussels, summoned by Verlaine. 10 July: when Rimbaud says he intends to leave Verlaine shoots him, wounding him in the left wrist. Verlaine imprisoned. August: Rimbaud writes *A Season in Hell* at Roche. 1 November: Rimbaud is in Paris. He spends the winter in Charleville.

1874 Mid-March: Rimbaud returns to Paris, then goes back to London. 31 July: desperate for money, he leaves for an unknown destination, possibly Scarborough, in Yorkshire. 29 December: returns to Charleville.

1875 13 February: goes to Stuttgart, Germany. 2 March: Rimbaud and Verlaine meet for the final time, in Stuttgart. May: goes to Italy. July: is back in Paris.

1876 Early April: goes to Vienna, then returns to Charleville. May: goes to Brussels, then on to Rotterdam. Enrols in the Dutch Colonial Army. 15 August: having deserted, he travels from Sumatra to Java, and from there to Ireland. 9 December: arrives in Charleville, via Ireland and England.

1877 May: in Germany, going from Cologne to Bremen and on to Hamburg. July: in Stockholm, employed in a circus. Autumn: in Italy. Winter: in Charleville.

1878 In Hamburg, or possibly Switzerland. Summer in Roche. 20 October: travels through Switzerland to Genoa intending to reach Egypt. 16 December: employed as quarry foreman in Larnaca, Cyprus.

1879 Late May: suffering from typhoid, he returns to Roche.

1880 March: returns to Cyprus. July: leaves Cyprus, possibly because he is suspected of the murder of a workman. Finds a position with an import–export company in Aden. December: crosses the Somalian desert and arrives in Harar, central Abyssinia (Ethiopia).

1881 Difficult months in Harar; health deteriorating. 15 December: returns to Aden.

1882 In Aden.

1883 Late March: returns to Harar. October and November: Verlaine's study of Rimbaud published in the Paris review *Lutèce*.

1884 1 March: Rimbaud leaves Harar. 23 April: arrives in Aden.

1885 October: new employment as an arms trader. He sets out with

a cargo of arms destined for King Menelik of Shoa (central Abyssinia), but the cargo is blocked in the port of Tadjoura (Djibouti).

1886 October: his employer having died, Rimbaud tries to go on his own initiative to Shoa.

1887 6 February: reaches Ankober, capital of Shoa, then proceeds to Entotto to clinch the deal with Menelik. 30 July: in Aden. 20 August: in Cairo. 8 October: back in Aden.

1888 3 May: back in Harar, where he sets up a commercial agency.

1891 Increasing pains in his right knee force him to seek medical attention. 7 April: agonizing 300 km. journey, carried on a make-shift litter, to the Red Sea port of Zeila, then to Aden. Cancer of knee diagnosed. 9 May: embarks for France. 20 May: taken directly to a hospital in Marseilles where on 27 May his right leg is amputated. 23 July: travels by train to Roche. His condition worsens. 23 August: with his sister Isabelle he travels back as far as Marseilles, intending to return to Africa, but is immediately hospitalized. Now paralysed by a general cancer. 25 October: Isabelle claims that Rimbaud makes confession and returns to the Catholic faith, but this in not proven. 9 November: dictates letter asking to board next ship for Aden. 10 November: Rimbaud dies, three weeks after his thirty-seventh birthday. On the same day a book of his poetry, entitled *Le Reliquaire*, is published. It is quickly withdrawn. 14 November: Rimbaud buried in Charleville cemetery.

1892 Publication, by Vanier, of *Illuminations* and *Une saison en enfer* in one volume, preface by Verlaine.

1895 Complete poems (*Poésies complètes*), with preface by Verlaine, published by Vanier.

1898 All Rimbaud's known works (*Oeuvres: Poésies, Illuminations, Une saison en enfer*) published by Mercure de France, edited by his brother-in-law, Paterne Berrichon.

COLLECTED POEMS

Poèmes, 1869–1871

Les Étrennes des orphelins

I

La chambre est pleine d'ombre; on entend vaguement
De deux enfants le triste et doux chuchotement.
Leur front se penche, encor, alourdi par le rêve,
Sous le long rideau blanc qui tremble et se soulève...
—Au dehors les oiseaux se rapprochent frileux;
Leur aile s'engourdit sous le ton gris des cieux;
Et la nouvelle Année, à la suite brumeuse,
Laissant traîner les plis de sa robe neigeuse,
Sourit avec des pleurs, et chante en grelottant...

II

Or les petits enfants, sous le rideau flottant,
Parlent bas comme on fait dans une nuit obscure.
Ils écoutent, pensifs, comme un lointain murmure...
Ils tressaillent souvent à la claire voix d'or
Du timbre matinal, qui frappe et frappe encor
Son refrain métallique en son globe de verre...
—Puis, la chambre est glacée... on voit traîner à terre,
Épars autour des lits, des vêtements de deuil:
L'âpre bise d'hiver qui se lamente au seuil
Souffle dans le logis son haleine morose!
On sent, dans tout cela, qu'il manque quelque chose...
—Il n'est donc point de mère à ces petits enfants,
De mère au frais sourire, aux regards triomphants?
Elle a donc oublié, le soir, seule et penchée,
D'exciter une flamme à la cendre arrachée,
D'amonceler sur eux la laine et l'édredon
Avant de les quitter en leur criant: pardon.
Elle n'a point prévu la froideur matinale,
Ni bien fermé le seuil à la bise hivernale?...

Poems, 1869–1871

Orphans' New Year Gifts

I

The room is full of shadow and the sad
Faint whispering of two little ones,
Heads still heavy with dreams
Beneath the long white curtain, stirring slightly...
Outside, birds cluster for warmth,
Wings drooping against the grey sky.
And the New Year, dragging mist,
Trailing its snow-dress on the ground,
Smiles through tears, and shivers a song...

II

Beneath the curtain's movement, the children
Speak low as happens on dark nights.
Thoughtfully they listen to a distant murmur;
Often shudder at the clear gold voice
Of morning, chiming a metal message
In its crystal globe, and chiming again.
—And the room is freezing; round the beds
Mourning clothes lie scattered on the floor.
The fierce winter wind moaning at the door
Blows dismal breath into the house—
There's a sense something's missing...
Where's the mother of these little things,
Sweet-smiling mother with triumphant eyes?
So last night, alone, stooping, she forgot
To stir the fading fire into life,
To pile on blankets, eiderdowns,
Before she left the room, calling out 'Forgive me!'
She hadn't thought it might get cold next morning,
Hadn't closed the door against the winter wind.

—Le rêve maternel, c'est le tiède tapis,
C'est le nid cotonneux où les enfants tapis,
Comme de beaux oiseaux que balancent les branches,
Dorment leur doux sommeil plein de visions blanches!...
—Et là,—c'est comme un nid sans plumes, sans chaleur,
Où les petits ont froid, ne dorment pas, ont peur;
Un nid que doit avoir glacé la bise amère...

III

Votre cœur l'a compris:—ces enfants sont sans mère.
Plus de mère au logis!—et le père est bien loin!...
—Une vieille servante, alors, en a pris soin.
Les petits sont tout seuls en la maison glacée;
Orphelins de quatre ans, voilà qu'en leur pensée
S'éveille, par degrés, un souvenir riant...
C'est comme un chapelet qu'on égrène en priant:
—Ah! quel beau matin, que ce matin des étrennes!
Chacun, pendant la nuit, avait rêvé des siennes
Dans quelque songe étrange où l'on voyait joujoux,
Bonbons habillés d'or, étincelants bijoux,
Tourbillonner, danser une danse sonore,
Puis fuir sous les rideaux, puis reparaître encore!
On s'éveillait matin, on se levait joyeux,
La lèvre affriandée, en se frottant les yeux...
On allait, les cheveux emmêlés sur la tête,
Les yeux tout rayonnants, comme aux grands jours de fête,
Et les petits pieds nus effleurant le plancher,
Aux portes des parents tout doucement toucher...
On entrait!... Puis alors les souhaits,... en chemise,
Les baisers répétés, et la gaîté permise!

IV

Ah! c'était si charmant, ces mots dits tant de fois!
—Mais comme il est changé, le logis d'autrefois:
Un grand feu pétillait, clair, dans la cheminée,
Toute la vieille chambre était illuminée;
Et les reflets vermeils, sortis du grand foyer,
Sur les meubles vernis aimaient à tournoyer...

A mother dreams of wool's warmth,
Of cosy nests where snuggling children
Sleep in peace, dream in white,
Like pretty birds on swaying branches
—But here it's a cold, unfeathered nest
Of shivering children, unsleeping, scared,
A nest frozen by cruel winds.

III

The heart understands these children have no mother.
No mother in the house, and father far away.
An old servant-woman has taken charge.
The little ones are quite alone in the house of ice;
Four-year-old orphans, a smiling memory
Slowly fills their thoughts,
Like a rosary during prayers.
Ah, New Year's Day, what a splendid morning.
Each one has dreamt of gifts to come
Strange dreams of toys,
Gold-wrapped sweets, spangled jewels
An echo of swirling dances,
Vanishing under curtains, back again.
Morning: out of sleep, out of bed,
Eyes rubbed, joyful expectation...
Quick, go, hair uncombed,
Eyes bright, the same as special days,
Bare feet hardly touching the ground,
Off to the parents' room, scarcely daring...
Go in... greetings, good wishes...
Pyjamas, kiss upon kiss, laughter allowed.

IV

Those delicious words said again and again!
But how it's changed, this home from another age.
A great fire used to crackle brightly in the grate,
The old room was lit up,
Crimson reflections leapt from the flames,
Danced over polished furniture—

—L'armoire était sans clefs!... sans clefs, la grande armoire!
On regardait souvent sa porte brune et noire...
Sans clefs!... c'était étrange!... on rêvait bien des fois
Aux mystères dormant entre ses flancs de bois,
Et l'on croyait ouïr, au fond de la serrure
Béante, un bruit lointain, vague et joyeux murmure...
—La chambre des parents est bien vide, aujourd'hui:
Aucun reflet vermeil sous la porte n'a lui;
Il n'est point de parents, de foyer, de clefs prises:
Partant, point de baisers, point de douces surprises!
Oh! que le jour de l'an sera triste pour eux!
—Et, tout pensifs, tandis que de leurs grands yeux bleus,
Silencieusement tombe une larme amère,
Ils murmurent: 'Quand donc reviendra notre mère?'

. . . .

V

Maintenant, les petits sommeillent tristement:
Vous diriez, à les voir, qu'ils pleurent en dormant,
Tant leurs yeux sont gonflés et leur souffle pénible!
Les tout petits enfants ont le cœur si sensible!
—Mais l'ange des berceaux vient essuyer leurs yeux,
Et dans ce lourd sommeil met un rêve joyeux,
Un rêve si joyeux, que leur lèvre mi-close,
Souriante, semblait murmurer quelque chose...
—Ils rêvent que, penchés sur leur petit bras rond,
Doux geste du réveil, ils avancent le front,
Et leur vague regard tout autour d'eux se pose...
Ils se croient endormis dans un paradis rose...
Au foyer plein d'éclairs chante gaîment le feu...
Par la fenêtre on voit là-bas un beau ciel bleu;
La nature s'éveille et de rayons s'enivre...
La terre, demi-nue, heureuse de revivre,
A des frissons de joie aux baisers du soleil...
Et dans le vieux logis tout est tiède et vermeil:
Les sombres vêtements ne jonchent plus la terre,
La bise sous le seuil a fini par se taire...
On dirait qu'une fée a passé dans cela!...
—Les enfants, tout joyeux, ont jeté deux cris... Là,

The cupboard, great cupboard, key missing,
Its brown and ebony door watched...
No key!... Strange... frequent imaginings
Of mysteries hibernating in those wooden walls.
Noise imagined, deep in the gaping lock,
Far-off noise, vague happy murmur...
—Today, the parents' room is quite empty,
No crimson, no hearth, no keys collected,
No farewell kisses, no sweet surprises.
How sad New Year's Day will be for them.
And, lost in thought, silent tears
Stinging from their large blue eyes,
They murmur: 'When will our mother come home?'

. . . .

V

Now, the children sleep in sadness.
To see them, you'd say they were crying behind closed lids,
Their eyes are so puffy, their breathing so strained.
Such sensitive hearts, these tiny children.
But their guardian angel wipes their tears
And puts happy dreams into heavy sleep,
So happy that their half-closed smiling lips
Seem to murmur something...
They dream that, leaning on their small round arms,
In that sweet reflex of waking, they proffer their faces,
And their vague eyes look around...
They think they're asleep in a rosy paradise...
The cheery fire sings and crackles in the hearth...
Through the window, up there, fine blue sky.
Nature wakes up and is heady with light...
The half-starved earth, glad to live again,
Shudders with pleasure at the sun's embrace...
And in the old house all is flushed with warmth.
Dark clothes no longer strew the ground,
The wind's stopped whistling under the door...
As if a fairy had flitted through...
The joyful children have cried out twice... There,

Près du lit maternel, sous un beau rayon rose,
Là, sur le grand tapis, resplendit quelque chose...
Ce sont des médaillons argentés, noirs et blancs,
De la nacre et du jais aux reflets scintillants;
Des petits cadres noirs, des couronnes de verre,
Ayant trois mots gravés en or: 'A NOTRE MÈRE!'

. . . .

Première soirée

—Elle était fort déshabillée
Et de grands arbres indiscrets
Aux vitres jetaient leur feuillée
Malinement, tout près, tout près.

Assise sur ma grande chaise,
Mi-nue, elle joignait les mains.
Sur le plancher frissonnaient d'aise
Ses petits pieds si fins, si fins.

—Je regardai, couleur de cire
Un petit rayon buissonnier
Papillonner dans son sourire
Et sur son sein,—mouche au rosier.

—Je baisai ses fines chevilles.
Elle eut un doux rire brutal
Qui s'égrenait en claires trilles,
Un joli rire de cristal.

Les petits pieds sous la chemise,
Se sauvèrent: 'Veux-tu finir!'
—La premiere audace permise,
Le rire feignait de punir!

—Pauvrets palpitants sous ma lèvre,
Je baisai doucement ses yeux:
—Elle jeta sa tête mièvre
En arrière: 'Oh! c'est encor mieux!...

By the mother's bed, in a lovely rinse of rosy light,
There on the great carpet, something shines splendidly...
Two medallions, silver-plated, black and white,
Jet and mother-of-pearl, darting light;
Little black frames, set round with glass scrolls,
Their three words: 'TO OUR MOTHER' traced in gold.

. . . .

First Night

She was less than scantily dressed,
And large trees blatantly
Pressed leaves against her window,
Curious, close, hard by.

There she sat, half-naked
In my big chair, hands clasped.
On the floor, her dainty little feet
Trembled with pure pleasure.

I watched wax-pale
Fugitive light play
On her breast and in her smile—
A fly on a rose.

I kissed her slender ankles.
She laughed, brutal and low
Little tumbles of brightness,
Laughter like a chandelier.

Small feet vanished
Beneath skirts. 'Now stop it!'
She scolded, her laugh saying
She'd not minded one little bit.

I kissed her eyes so gently,
A helpless tremble under my lips.
She threw her fine head back;
'Ah yes, that's nicer still!

'Monsieur, j'ai deux mots à te dire...'
—Je lui jetai le reste au sein
Dans un baiser, qui la fit rire
D'un bon rire qui voulait bien...

—Elle était fort déshabillée
Et de grands arbres indiscrets
Aux vitres jetaient leur feuillée
Malinement, tout près, tout près.

Sensation

Par les soirs bleus d'été, j'irai dans les sentiers,
Picoté par les blés, fouler l'herbe menue:
Rêveur, j'en sentirai la fraîcheur à mes pieds.
Je laisserai le vent baigner ma tête nue.

Je ne parlerai pas, je ne penserai rien:
Mais l'amour infini me montera dans l'âme,
Et j'irai loin, bien loin, comme un bohémien,
Par la Nature,—heureux comme avec une femme.

Mars 1870.

Le Forgeron

Palais des Tuileries, vers le 10 août 92

Le bras sur un marteau gigantesque, effrayant
D'ivresse et de grandeur, le front vaste, riant
Comme un clairon d'airain, avec toute sa bouche,
Et prenant ce gros-là dans son regard farouche,
Le Forgeron parlait à Louis Seize, un jour
Que le Peuple était là, se tordant tout autour,
Et sur les lambris d'or traînant sa veste sale.
Or le bon roi, debout sur son ventre, était pâle,
Pâle comme un vaincu qu'on prend pour le gibet,
Et, soumis comme un chien, jamais ne regimbait

'Listen. I want to tell you...'
My mouth plunged to her breast; she said
Nothing; but again she laughed,
Frank laughter which said yes.

She was scantily dressed
And large trees blatantly
Pressed leaves against her window,
Curious, close, hard by.

Sensation

On blue evenings in summer, down paths,
Spiked by sharp corn, I'll trample new grass.
Dreaming, I'll feel the cool on my feet,
The wind will bathe my bare head.

I shan't speak, I'll clear out all my thoughts.
But love without end shall fill my soul,
And I'll travel far, very far, Nature's
Vagabond—happy as with a woman.

March 1870

The Blacksmith

Tuileries Palace, around 10 August 1792

Arm on gigantic hammer; drunk,
Huge, frightening; vast forehead; full-bell
Bugle laughter; scything
The fat man with his gaze,
A blacksmith addressed Louis XVI, one day
As the People pressed and thronged,
Its coat of filth against the golden panelling.
Perched above his belly, the king was as white
As a convict marching to his death,
And, like a cowering dog, took without complaint

Car ce maraud de forge aux énormes épaules
Lui disait de vieux mots et des choses si drôles,
Que cela l'empoignait au front, comme cela!

'Or, tu sais bien, Monsieur, nous chantions tra la la
Et nous piquions les bœufs vers les sillons des autres:
Le Chanoine au soleil filait des patenôtres
Sur des chapelets clairs grenés de pièces d'or.
Le Seigneur, à cheval, passait, sonnant du cor
Et l'un avec la hart, l'autre avec la cravache
Nous fouaillaient.—Hébétés comme des yeux de vache,
Nos yeux ne pleuraient plus; nous allions, nous allions,
Et quand nous avions mis le pays en sillons,
Quand nous avions laissé dans cette terre noire
Un peu de notre chair... nous avions un pourboire:
On nous faisait flamber nos taudis dans la nuit;
Nos petits y faisaient un gâteau fort bien cuit.

... 'Oh! je ne me plains pas. Je te dis mes bêtises,
C'est entre nous. J'admets que tu me contredises.
Or, n'est-ce pas joyeux de voir, au mois de juin
Dans les granges entrer des voitures de foin
Énormes? De sentir l'odeur de ce qui pousse,
Des vergers quand il pleut un peu, de l'herbe rousse?
De voir des blés, des blés, des épis pleins de grain,
De penser que cela prépare bien du pain?...
Oh! plus fort, on irait, au fourneau qui s'allume,
Chanter joyeusement en martelant l'enclume,
Si l'on était certain de pouvoir prendre un peu
Étant homme, à la fin! de ce que donne Dieu!
—Mais voilà, c'est toujours la même vieille histoire!

'Mais je sais, maintenant! Moi, je ne peux plus croire,
Quand j'ai deux bonnes mains, mon front et mon marteau,
Qu'un homme vienne là, dague sur le manteau,
Et me dise: Mon gars, ensemence ma terre;
Que l'on arrive encor, quand ce serait la guerre,
Me prendre mon garçon comme cela, chez moi!
—Moi, je serais un homme, et toi, tu serais roi,

What that great wardrobe of a blacksmith
Was telling him—strange things, old-fashioned words
Punched straight into his face.

'Now Sire, you remember how we sang tra la la
As our oxen worked the owners' fields for them.
The Canon paternostered in the sun, fingering
Bright rosaries threaded with gold coins.
Our master rode by rooty-tooting
On his hunting-horn; ropes and riding-crops
Did their worst—Our bewildered
Cow-eyes stopped their tears; we ground on,
And when we'd turned the land neatly into rows,
Put some of our flesh into
The black soil, we got our small reward:
They torched our hovels in the night;
Our children roasted to a crisp.

'...I'm not complaining, just a bit of idle chat
Tell me if I've got it wrong, but
Doesn't it warm the heart to see in June
Great carts of hay enter storage-barns
Or smell things growing;
Soft rain in orchards; sunny grass,
And field after field of wheat bursting with grain,
Soon to fill the shelves with bread?
Oh yes, we'd go off and start the furnace up,
Sing cheery songs to the sound of our hammers,
If we were sure we'd get our share
(We're only human after all) of what God gives.
But always it's the same story.

'Now, I've understood. Since I've got two good hands,
A brain, a hammer, I won't allow
Any man to approach me brandishing
A weapon and say: "You, out into my fields, now!"
Or come and snatch away my boy—
(To hell with your wars).
I'm a man, you're a king, so you think

Tu me dirais: Je veux!... —Tu vois bien, c'est stupide.
Tu crois que j'aime voir ta baraque splendide,
Tes officiers dorés, tes mille chenapans,
Tes palsembleu bâtards tournant comme des paons:
Ils ont rempli ton nid de l'odeur de nos filles
Et de petits billets pour nous mettre aux Bastilles,
Et nous dirons: C'est bien: les pauvres à genoux!
Nous dorerons ton Louvre en donnant nos gros sous!
Et tu te soûleras, tu feras belle fête.
—Et ces Messieurs riront, les reins sur notre tête!

'Non. Ces saletés-là datent de nos papas!
Oh! Le Peuple n'est plus une putain. Trois pas
Et, tous, nous avons mis ta Bastille en poussiètre.
Cette bête suait du sang à chaque pierre
Et c'était dégoûtant, la Bastille debout
Avec ses murs lépreux qui nous racontaient tout
Et, toujours, nous tenaient enfermés dans leur ombre!
—Citoyen! citoyen! c'était le passé sombre
Qui croulait, qui râlait, quand nous prîmes la tour!
Nous avions quelque chose au cœur comme l'amour.
Nous avions embrassé nos fils sur nos poitrines.
Et, comme des chevaux, en soufflant des narines
Nous allions, fiers et forts, et ça nous battait là...
Nous marchions au soleil, front haut,—comme cela—,
Dans Paris! On venait devant nos vestes sales.
Enfin! Nous nous sentions Hommes! Nous étions pâles,
Sire, nous étions soûls de terribles espoirs:
Et quand nous fûmes là, devant les donjons noirs,
Agitant nos clairons et nos feuilles de chêne,
Les piques à la main; nous n'eûmes pas de haine,
—Nous nous sentions si forts, nous voulions être doux!

. . . .

. . . .

'Et depuis ce jour-là, nous sommes comme fous!
Le tas des ouvriers a monté dans la rue,
Et ces maudits s'en vont, foule toujours accrue
De sombres revenants, aux portes des richards.
Moi, je cours avec eux assommer les mouchards:

You can give me orders. You can't.
You think I want to see the sumptuous place
You live in, your powdered minions, your thousand hangers-on,
All the strutting peacock bastards
Who've filled your love-nest with our daughters' smell,
And warrants to throw us in your gaols,
We'd see all that and say: yes, we poor folk know our place,
On our knees. Our pennies will fund your Louvre,
While you and your hell-raisers get blind drunk,
Laugh fit to bust, and shit all over us!

'No. That's our fathers' martyrdom,
The People aren't your whore now. One, two, three,
And down it tumbled, your Bastille.
Those walls oozed blood from every stone,
That putrid carcass standing there
Telling us the whole grim story,
With us still locked in its dungeons.
Citizens! What fell the day we stormed that tower
Was a dark past choked to death.
Something like love filled us.
We picked up our children and kissed them.
Like snorting horses we advanced, proud
And strong, hearts thumping like THAT...
Heads held high, we marched through Paris in the sun,
Like them down there. People fought to touch our filthy coats.
At last, we knew we were Men! We were pale,
Your Majesty, drunk on terrific hope.
And when we arrived outside that hell-hole,
Our bugles and oak-branches held aloft,
Pikes at the ready, we felt no hate.
Knowing we were strong, we wanted to be kind.

. . . .

. . . .

'Since then, we've been like men possessed.
The hordes of workers in the street have grown,
And all those dark figures of the night have gone
To haunt the portals of the rich.
And I go too, hunting down your spies.

Et je vais dans Paris, noir, marteau sur l'épaule,
Farouche, à chaque coin balayant quelque drôle,
Et, si tu me riais au nez, je te tuerais!
—Puis tu peux y compter, tu te feras des frais
Avec tes hommes noirs, qui prennent nos requêtes
Pour se les renvoyer comme sur des raquettes
Et, tout bas, les malins! se disent: "Qu'ils sont sots!"
Pour mitonner des lois, coller de petits pots
Pleins de jolis décrets roses et de droguailles,
S'amuser à couper proprement quelques tailles,
Puis se boucher le nez quand nous marchons près d'eux,
—Nos doux représentants qui nous trouvent crasseux!—
Pour ne rien redouter, rien, que les baïonnettes...,
C'est très-bien. Foin de leur tabatière à sornettes!
Nous en avons assez, là, de ces cerveaux plats
Et de ces ventres-dieux. Ah! ce sont là les plats
Que tu nous sers, bourgeois, quand nous sommes féroces,
Quand nous brisons déjà les sceptres et les crosses!...'

. . . .

II le prend par le bras, arrache le velours
Des rideaux, et lui montre en bas les larges cours
Où fourmille, où fourmille, où se lève la foule,
La foule épouvantable avec des bruits de houle,
Hurlant comme une chienne, hurlant comme une mer,
Avec ses bâtons forts et ses piques de fer,
Ses tambours, ses grands cris de halles et de bouges,
Tas sombre de haillons saignant de bonnets rouges:
L'Homme, par la fenêtre ouverte, montre tout
Au roi pâle et suant qui chancelle debout,
Malade à regarder cela!
'C'est la Crapule,
Sire. Ça bave aux murs, ça monte, ça pullule:
—Puisqu'ils ne mangent pas, Sire, ce sont des gueux!
Je suis un forgeron: ma femme est avec eux,
Folle! Elle croit trouver du pain aux Tuileries!
—On ne veut pas de nous dans les boulangeries.
J'ai trois petits. Je suis crapule.—Je connais
Des vieilles qui s'en vont pleurant sous leurs bonnets
Parce qu'on leur a pris leur garçon ou leur fille:
C'est la crapule.—Un homme était à la bastille,

I move through Paris, hammer slung on shoulder,
Black, wild, flushing human vermin out.
Laugh at me, and I'll kill you.
Make no mistake, the actions of your men in black
Will come home to roost—crumpling up the demands
We wrote, batting them back and forth like
Tennis balls, sneering at our stupidity.
Trumped-up legislation, pink-paper edicts
Plastered everywhere,
People's good name destroyed on a whim,
Noses held when we come too close—
Our kind representatives find that we stink!—
There's nothing to fear except bayonets...
Well no, we've had enough. No more silver-tongued
Inanities, no more bird-brained rhetoricians.
Bourgeois, we've seen what you treat us to,
Once we've acted, smashing sceptres and croziers.'

. . . .

He grabs the royal arm, yanks back the velvet
Curtain, shows him the great courtyards below
Where the mob seethes, seethes, and rises,
The terrifying mob, an ocean-roar,
Wild howl of a dog, great howl of the sea,
Wielding heavy sticks, iron pikes and drums,
The tumult of its markets, its slums,
Dark clutter of rags bloody with liberty caps.
At the open window, the Man shows all this
To the pale, unsteady king,
His insides churning at the sight.
'Scum,
Your Majesty. It slobbers on walls, grows, multiplies.
—They're hungry, sire, that's why they're beggars.
I'm a blacksmith. My wife's with them.
For some reason she thinks there's bread in the Tuileries.
The bakers' shops won't let us in.
I've got three children. I'm scum. I know old women
Wandering around in their bonnets, weeping
Because a son or daughter's disappeared.
Scum, you see. This man was in the Bastille,

Un autre était forçat: et tous deux, citoyens
Honnêtes. Libérés, ils sont comme des chiens:
On les insulte! Alors, ils ont là quelque chose
Qui leur fait mal, allez! C'est terrible, et c'est cause
Que se sentant brisés, que, se sentant damnés,
Ils sont là, maintenant, hurlant sous votre nez!
Crapule.—Là-dedans sont des filles, infâmes
Parce que,—vous saviez que c'est faible, les femmes,—
Messeigneurs de la cour,—que ça veut toujours bien,—
Vous [leur] avez craché sur l'âme, comme rien!
Vos belles, aujourd'hui, sont là. C'est la crapule.

. . . .

'Oh! tous les Malheureux, tous ceux dont le dos brûle
Sous le soleil féroce, et qui vont, et qui vont,
Qui dans ce travail-là sentent crever leur front,
Chapeau bas, mes bourgeois! Oh! ceux-là, sont les Hommes!
Nous sommes Ouvriers, Sire! Ouvriers! Nous sommes
Pour les grands temps nouveaux où l'on voudra savoir,
Où l'Homme forgera du matin jusqu'au soir,
Chasseur des grands effets, chasseur des grandes causes,
Où, lentement vainqueur, il domptera les choses
Et montera sur Tout, comme sur un cheval!
Oh! splendides lueurs des forges! Plus de mal,
Plus!—Ce qu'on ne sait pas, c'est peut-être terrible:
Nous saurons!—Nos marteaux en main, passons au crible
Tout ce que nous savons: puis, Frères, en avant!
Nous faisons quelquefois ce grand rêve émouvant
De vivre simplement, ardemment, sans rien dire
De mauvais, travaillant sous l'auguste sourire
D'une femme qu'on aime avec un noble amour:
Et l'on travaillerait fièrement tout le jour,
Écoutant le devoir comme un clairon qui sonne:
Et l'on se sentirait très heureux: et personne,
Oh! personne, surtout, ne vous ferait ployer!
On aurait un fusil au-dessus du foyer . . .

. . . .

'Oh! mais l'air est tout plein d'une odeur de bataille!
Que te disais-je donc? Je suis de la canaille!
Il reste des mouchards et des accapareurs.

That one in the galleys; both of them
Law-abiding folk. Now they're free, they've become
Like dogs. Insults enrage them—well,
Insults hurt. It's hard to bear, they're broken
Men, they think they're damned forever, that's why
They're down there now, screaming in your face!
Scum, you see. There are dishonoured girls
Down there, because... well, women are weak,
My Lords, aren't they? A smile for everyone...
You've spat on their souls, who cares.
Your pretty girls are down there now. Scum you see.

. . . .

'Oh, all the poor unhappy people, those whose backs
Fry in the fierce sun, who struggle on,
Their heads bursting as they toil,
Hats off to them, you bourgeois. These are what you call
Men. We are Workers, Sire, Workers. Ours is
The Great Day of New Knowledge,
When a man will work his forge from dawn to dusk,
Search out great effects, great causes,
When he'll slowly triumph, conquer everything,
Ride the world like a thoroughbred.
The forges' glowing splendour! The end of evil,
No more evil. What's unknown may yet be terrible.
We shall know. Hammer in hand, let's run everything
We know through the sieve. Then, Brothers, forward!
Sometimes we have that great and moving dream
Of living simply, intensely, saying nothing
Evil, at work beneath the august smile
Of a woman loved with noble love;
And we'd work all day long with pride,
The clarion call of duty in our ears.
We'd feel happy, and no one,
No one would bring us to our knees!
We'd have a rifle ready, hanging near the fire.

. . . .

'Oh, the air's full of the smell of battle.
What did I tell you? I'm one of the rabble.
There are still informers about, racketeers.

Nous sommes libres, nous! Nous avons des terreurs
Où nous nous sentons grands, oh! si grands! Tout à l'heure
Je parlais de devoir calme, d'une demeure...
Regarde donc le ciel!—C'est trop petit pour nous,
Nous crèverions de chaud, nous serions à genoux!
Regarde donc le ciel!—Je rentre dans la foule,
Dans la grande canaille effroyable, qui roule,
Sire, tes vieux canons sur les sales pavés :
—Oh! quand nous serons morts, nous les aurons lavés
—Et si, devant nos cris, devant notre vengeance,
Les pattes des vieux rois mordorés, sur la France
Poussent leurs régiments en habits de gala,
Eh bien, n'est-ce pas, vous tous? Merde à ces chiens-là!'

. . . .

—Il reprit son marteau sur l'épaule.
La foule
Près de cet homme-là se sentait l'âme soûle,
Et, dans la grande cour, dans les appartements,
Où Paris haletait avec des hurlements,
Un frisson secoua l'immense populace.
Alors, de sa main large et superbe de crasse,
Bien que le roi ventru suât, le Forgeron,
Terrible, lui jeta le bonnet rouge au front!

Soleil et chair

I

Le Soleil, le foyer de tendresse et de vie,
Verse l'amour brûlant à la terre ravie,
Et, quand on est couché sur la vallée, on sent
Que la terre est nubile et déborde de sang;
Que son immense sein, soulevé par une âme,
Est d'amour comme dieu, de chair comme la femme,
Et qu'il renferme, gros de sève et de rayons,
Le grand fourmillement de tous les embryons!

Et tout croît, et tout monte!

We are free, we have electrifying moments
When we feel that we are great, so great! Just now
I was talking of calm duty, a home...
Look at the sky! I'm returning to the crowd,
The great frightening rabble rolling
Your ancient cannons over dirty cobbles.
At least our death will wash them clean.
And if, faced by our shrieking vengeance,
The paws of old bronze kings push their regiments
Across France, in their toy-town uniforms,
Why then, my friends, we'll shit on the lot of them.'

. . . .

He shouldered his hammer again.
Beside that man,
The crowd's soul ignited,
And in the great courtyard, in the palace rooms,
Where Paris panted and yelled,
The huge crowd suddenly shivered as one.
Then this awesome Blacksmith, disregarding the fat king's
Cold sweat, raised his huge hand, proud with grime,
And crowned him with the red of Revolution!*

Sun and Skin

I

The Sun, giver of life and tenderness,
Spills burning love onto ravished earth,
And when you're stretched out in the valley, you feel
How nubile the earth is, brimful of blood,
Great bosom, lifting with breath,
Is made of love, like God, of flesh, like woman,
And how it enfolds, plump with sap and sunlight,
The great swarm of embryos.

And everything grows, everything rises!

—Ô Vénus, ô Déesse!
Je regrette les temps de l'antique jeunesse,
Des satyres lascifs, des faunes animaux,
Dieux qui mordaient d'amour l'écorce des rameaux
Et dans les nénufars baisaient la Nymphe blonde!
Je regrette les temps où la sève du monde,
L'eau du fleuve, le sang rose des arbres verts
Dans les veines de Pan mettaient un univers!
Où le sol palpitait, vert, sous ses pieds de chèvre;
Où, baisant mollement le clair syrinx, sa lèvre
Modulait sous le ciel le grand hymne d'amour;
Où, debout sur la plaine, il entendait autour
Répondre à son appel la Nature vivante;
Où les arbres muets, berçant l'oiseau qui chante,
La terre berçant l'homme, et tout l'Océan bleu
Et tous les animaux aimaient, aimaient en Dieu!

Je regrette les temps de la grande Cybèle
Qu'on disait parcourir, gigantesquement belle,
Sur un grand char d'airain, les splendides cités;
Son double sein versait dans les immensités
Le pur ruissellement de la vie infinie.
L'Homme suçait, heureux, sa mamelle bénie,
Comme un petit enfant, jouant sur ses genoux.
—Parce qu'il était fort, l'Homme était chaste et doux.

Misère! Maintenant il dit: Je sais les choses,
Et va, les yeux fermés et les oreilles closes.
—Et pourtant, plus de dieux! plus de dieux! l'Homme est Roi,
L'Homme est Dieu! Mais l'Amour, voilà la grande Foi!
Oh! si l'homme puisait encore à ta mamelle,
Grande mère des dieux et des hommes, Cybèle;
S'il n'avait pas laissé l'immortelle Astarté
Qui jadis, émergeant dans l'immense clarté
Des flots bleus, fleur de chair que la vague parfume,
Montra son nombril rose où vint neiger l'écume,
Et fit chanter, Déesse aux grands yeux noirs vainqueurs,
Le rossignol aux bois et l'amour dans les cœurs!

—Venus, Goddess!
I long for the days when the world was young,
Lecherous satyrs, animal fauns,
The love-bites of gods in the bark of trees,
Their frolics with blond nymphs among lilies.
Oh, for the time when the sap of the world,
River water, rose blood of green trees
Swelled Pan's veins into a universe.
When the green ground shook beneath his goat's hooves,
When, softly kissing the bright syrinx, his lips
Shaped the great hymn of love beneath the sky,
When, standing on the plain, all around he heard
Living Nature answer him,
When silent trees cradling the singing bird,
Earth cradling Man and the blue Ocean,
All the animals knew God's love.

I long for the time of great Cybele,
Gigantically beautiful, said to ride
Through splendid cities in a chariot of bronze.
Her great breasts poured through vastness
The pure stream of unceasing life.
Man sucked her blessed breast in bliss
Like a baby on her knee.
—Because he was strong, Man was pure and gentle.

Look now at the sorry state. Man says: I know,
And goes his way, ears shut, eyes closed.
The gods are dead, long live Man,
Man is King and God. But love, that's true faith!
Oh, if only Man still drank at your breast,
Cybele, great mother of gods and men,
If only he'd not abandoned immortal Astarte,
Who, once, rising from the vast glare
Of blue water, sea-scented flower of flesh,
Revealed her pink navel, white with spray,
And, Goddess of huge eyes, triumphant, dark,
Made nightingales sing in woods, love in human hearts.

II

Je crois en toi! je crois en toi! Divine mère,
Aphrodité marine!—Oh! la route est amère
Depuis que l'autre Dieu nous attelle à sa croix;
Chair, Marbre, Fleur, Vénus, c'est en toi que je crois!
—Oui, l'Homme est triste et laid, triste sous le ciel vaste.
Il a des vêtements, parce qu'il n'est plus chaste,
Parce qu'il a sali son fier buste de dieu,
Et qu'il a rabougri, comme une idole au feu,
Son corps Olympien aux servitudes sales!
Oui, même après la mort, dans les squelettes pâles
Il veut vivre, insultant la première beauté!
—Et l'Idole où tu mis tant de virginité,
Où tu divinisas notre argile, la Femme,
Afin que l'Homme pût éclairer sa pauvre âme
Et monter lentement, dans un immense amour,
De la prison terrestre à la beauté du jour,
La Femme ne sait plus même être Courtisane!
—C'est une bonne farce! et le monde ricane
Au nom doux et sacré de la grande Vénus!

III

Si les temps revenaient, les temps qui sont venus!
—Car l'Homme a fini! l'Homme a joué tous les rôles!
Au grand jour, fatigué de briser des idoles
Il ressuscitera, libre de tous ses Dieux,
Et, comme il est du ciel, il scrutera les cieux!
L'Idéal, la pensée invincible, éternelle,
Tout le dieu qui vit, sous son argile charnelle,
Montera, montera, brûlera sous son front!
Et quand tu le verras sonder tout l'horizon,
Contempteur des vieux jougs, libre de toute crainte,
Tu viendras lui donner la Rédemption sainte!
—Splendide, radieuse, au sein des grandes mers
Tu surgiras, jetant sur le vaste Univers
L'Amour infini dans un infini sourire!
Le Monde vibrera comme une immense lyre

II

I believe in you, yes, divine mother,
Aphrodite of the seas! Oh, the road is pitiless
Now that the other God has strapped us to His cross.
Flesh, Marble, Flower, Venus, it's you I believe in.
Yes, Man is sad and ugly, sad beneath huge skies,
Wearing clothes, now his purity's lost,
Now his splendid godlike body's tainted,
His Olympian splendour reduced
To shabby servitude, an idol in the fire.
Yes, even after death, he wants to survive
In yellow skeletons, and insult first beauty.
And the Idol where you set Virginity up,
Woman, our clay made a divinity
So that Man could lighten his sorry soul
And slowly ascend, in vast love,
From the prison of earth to the beauty of day,
Woman no longer knows how to be a courtesan,
Even. A farce! And the whole world laughs
At the sweet sacred name of great Venus!

III

If only those times came back, times that have been.
For Man's had his day, played all his roles.
In the full light, tired of wrecking idols,
He'll live again, free of all his gods,
And, born in Heaven, he'll scan the great skies.
The Ideal, invincible and eternal thought,
The whole god inside his mortal clay
Will rise, arise, burn on his brow!
And when you see him sound the whole horizon,
Throw off old chains, free of all fear,
You'll come to bring him holy redemption!
—Splendid, radiant, in the belly of great seas
You'll burst free and shower infinite love
Infinitely smiling on the vast Universe.
The World will tremble like a great harp

Dans le frémissement d'un immense baiser!

—Le Monde a soif d'amour: tu viendras l'apaiser.
. . . .

IV

Ô splendeur de la chair! ô splendeur idéale!
Ô renouveau d'amour, aurore triomphale
Où, courbant à leurs pieds les Dieux et les Héros,
Kallipyge la blanche et le petit Éros
Effleureront, couverts de la neige des roses,
Les femmes et les fleurs sous leurs beaux pieds écloses!
Ô grande Ariadné, qui jettes tes sanglots
Sur la rive, en voyant fuir là-bas sur les flots,
Blanche sous le soleil, la voile de Thésée,
Ô douce vierge enfant qu'une nuit a brisée,
Tais-toi! Sur son char d'or brodé de noirs raisins,
Lysios, promené dans les champs Phrygiens
Par les tigres lascifs et les panthères rousses,
Le long des fleuves bleus rougit les sombres mousses.
Zeus, Taureau, sur son cou berce comme une enfant
Le corps nu d'Europé, qui jette son bras blanc
Au cou nerveux du Dieu frissonnant dans la vague,
Il tourne lentement vers elle son œil vague;
Elle, laisse traîner sa pâle joue en fleur
Au front de Zeus; ses yeux sont fermés; elle meurt
Dans un divin baiser, et le flot qui murmure
De son écume d'or fleurit sa chevelure.
—Entre le laurier rose et le lotus jaseur
Glisse amoureusement le grand Cygne rêveur
Embrassant la Léda des blancheurs de son aile;
—Et tandis que Cypris passe, étrangement belle,
Et, cambrant les rondeurs splendides de ses reins,
Étale fièrement l'or de ses larges seins
Et son ventre neigeux brodé de mousse noire,
—Héraclès, le Dompteur, qui, comme d'une gloire
Fort, ceint son vaste corps de la peau du lion,
S'avance, front terrible et doux, à l'horizon!

In the ripple-spread of a great kiss.

—The World thirsts for love; you'll quench that thirst.

. . . .

IV

O splendour of flesh, splendour of the Idea!
Renewal of love, triumphant dawn,
When, as gods and heroes bow slow to them,
Aphrodite of the lovely buttocks and little Eros,
Covered in snow-showers of roses,
Will brush flowers and women spread at their lovely feet.
O great Ariadne,* weeping on the shore
Seeing, there, scudding away on the waves,
Theseus's sail, white against the sun,
Sweet virgin, child, broken in one night,
Quiet! In his golden chariot braided with dark grapes
Lysios, carried through Phrygian* fields
By lascivious tigers and scarlet panthers
Turns sombre mosses red along blue rivers.
—Zeus, the Bull, cradles on his shoulders
Europa's* naked body, like a child, her white arm
Thrown round the God's knotty neck, quivering in the water.
Slowly it turns to her its vacant eye;
She lays her cheek like pale blossom
On Zeus's brow; eyes closed, she dies
In a holy embrace and the murmuring water
Sprays gold into her hair.
—Between the rose-bay and the busy laurel
The great Swan moves past in a dream
Amorously, folding Leda* in his wings's white kiss;
—And while Cypris* goes by, strangely beautiful,
Bending splendid curves, proudly
Offering the gold of her huge breasts,
Her milk-white belly braided with black moss,
Heracles, beast-tamer, strong, covers his vast body
With the lion-skin, golden token of victory,
And—terrible, gentle—strides towards the sky!

Par la lune d'été vaguement éclairée,
Debout, nue, et rêvant dans sa pâleur dorée
Que tache le flot lourd de ses longs cheveux bleus,
Dans la clairière sombre où la mousse s'étoile,
La Dryade regarde au ciel silencieux...
—La blanche Séléné laisse flotter son voile,
Craintive, sur les pieds du bel Endymion,
Et lui jette un baiser dans un pâle rayon...
—La Source pleure au loin dans une longue extase...
C'est la Nymphe qui rêve, un coude sur son vase,
Au beau jeune homme blanc que son onde a pressé.
—Une brise d'amour dans la nuit a passé,
Et, dans les bois sacrés, dans l'horreur des grands arbres,
Majestueusement debout, les sombres Marbres,
Les Dieux, au front desquels le Bouvreuil fait son nid,
—Les Dieux écoutent l'Homme et le Monde infini!

Mai 70.

Ophélie

I

Sur l'onde calme et noire où dorment les étoiles
La blanche Ophélia flotte comme un grand lys,
Flotte très lentement, couchée en ses longs voiles...
—On entend dans les bois lointains des hallalis.

Voici plus de mille ans que la triste Ophélie
Passe, fantôme blanc, sur le long fleuve noir;
Voici plus de mille ans que sa douce folie
Murmure sa romance à la brise du soir.

Le vent baise ses seins et déploie en corolle
Ses grands voiles bercés mollement par les eaux;
Les saules frissonnants pleurent sur son épaule,
Sur son grand front rêveur s'inclinent les roseaux.

In the summer moon's insipid light,
Naked and dreaming, her gold-tinged pallor
Stained by her heavy hair's long blue cascade,
In the dark glade where the mosses spangle,
The Dryad looks up at silent skies...
Nervous, white Selene lets her veil
Settle on the feet of handsome Endymion,*
And, down a pale ray of light, sends him a kiss...
The Spring sobs its long ecstasy, far away...
It's the nymph, one elbow on her vase,
Dreaming of the pale young man, plunged in her waves.
—Love sighed in the night
And was gone, and in sacred woods, in the horror
Of great trees, dark, majestic marble
Forms, the Gods, their brow the bullfinch-nest,
—The Gods listen to Man and the World without end.

May '70

Ophelia

I

In the calm black stream where stars sleep,
White Ophelia floats like a great lily,
Very slowly floats, lying in long veils...
—Up in the woods, dogs bark, men shout.

For a thousand years or more, sad white phantom,
Ophelia has moved down the long black river.
A thousand years or more her sweet song
Of madness has charmed the evening air.

The wind kisses her breasts and like a flower opens
Her long veils gently moving with the water.
On her shoulder willows weep and shiver,
Over her wide dreaming face rushes lean.

Les nénuphars froissés soupirent autour d'elle;
Elle éveille parfois, dans un aune qui dort,
Quelque nid, d'où s'échappe un petit frisson d'aile:
—Un chant mystérieux tombe des astres d'or.

II

Ô pâle Ophélia! belle comme la neige!
Oui tu mourus, enfant, par un fleuve emporté!
—C'est que les vents tombant des grands monts de Norwège
T'avaient parlé tout bas de l'âpre liberté;

C'est qu'un souffle, tordant ta grande chevelure,
À ton esprit rêveur portait d'étranges bruits;
Que ton cœur écoutait le chant de la Nature
Dans les plaintes de l'arbre et les soupirs des nuits;

C'est que la voix des mers folles, immense râle,
Brisait ton sein d'enfant, trop humain et trop doux;
C'est qu'un matin d'avril, un beau cavalier pâle,
Un pauvre fou, s'assit muet à tes genoux!

Ciel! Amour! Liberté! Quel rêve, ô pauvre Folle!
Tu te fondais à lui comme une neige au feu:
Tes grandes visions étranglaient ta parole
—Et l'Infini terrible effara ton œil bleu!

III

—Et le Poète dit qu'aux rayons des étoiles
Tu viens chercher, la nuit, les fleurs que tu cueillis,
Et qu'il a vu sur l'eau, couchée en ses longs voiles,
La blanche Ophélia flotter, comme un grand lys.

Around her, jostling water-lilies sigh;
In a drowsy alder, when sometimes she disturbs
A nest, there's a quick flurry of wings
—Mysterious music tumbles from the golden stars.

II

O pale Ophelia, beautiful as snow!
Yes, poor child, downstream you died.
—Because great Norway mountain winds
Moaned their message of harsh freedom.

A breath that twisted your heavy hair
Brought strange sounds to your absent thoughts,
Your heart heard Nature's song
In the trees' lament and the sigh of night.

The shout of mad seas, huge growl,
Burst your young breast, too soft, too human.
One April morning, a pale, handsome, strange
Demented prince sat with you, saying nothing.

Sky, Love, Freedom! What dreams, poor child!
You melted into him, snow in his fire,
Your great visions* made you speechless
—And terrible Infinity lit your wild blue eyes!

III

—The Poet says that when the stars come out
You come looking for flowers you picked;
He says he's seen, lying in her long veils,
White Ophelia, like some great lily, float by.

Bal des pendus

Au gibet noir, manchot aimable,
Dansent, dansent les paladins
Les maigres paladins du diable,
Les squelettes de Saladins.

Messire Belzebuth tire par la cravate
Ses petits pantins noirs grimaçant sur le ciel,
Et, leur claquant au front un revers de savate,
Les fait danser, danser aux sons d'un vieux Noël!

Et les pantins choqués enlacent leurs bras grêles:
Comme des orgues noirs, les poitrines à jour
Que serraient autrefois les gentes damoiselles,
Se heurtent longuement dans un hideux amour.

Hurrah! Les gais danseurs, qui n'avez plus de panse!
On peut cabrioler, les tréteaux sont si longs!
Hop! qu'on ne sache plus si c'est bataille ou danse!
Belzebuth enragé racle ses violons!

Ô durs talons, jamais on n'use sa sandale!
Presque tous ont quitté la chemise de peau:
Le reste est peu gênant et se voit sans scandale.
Sur les crânes, la neige applique un blanc chapeau:

Le corbeau fait panache à ces têtes fêlées,
Un morceau de chair tremble à leur maigre menton:
On dirait, tournoyant dans les sombres mêlées,
Des preux, raides, heurtant armures de carton.

Hurrah! La bise souffle au grand bal des squelettes!
Le gibet noir mugit comme un orgue de fer!
Les loups vont répondant des forêts violettes:
A l'horizon, le ciel est d'un rouge d'enfer...

Hanged Men Dance

On black gallows, one-armed friend,
First Crusaders dance and dance,
The Devil's wasted Paladins,*
The skeletons of Sultans.

Milord Beelzebub pulls the string that works
His little black puppets leering at the sky.
He beats and kicks them in the head,
Making them dance to carol-tunes.

The bumping puppets mesh their bony arms.
Black organ-pipes, their uncaged ribs,
Which well-bred ladies used to hug,
Clack and clatter in acts of hideous love.

Good for you, cheery dancers, rid of those stomachs!
Swing your hips, this platform can take it.
Turn dance into fight, fight into dance,
As wild Beelzebub fiddles away.

Hard heels, no wear and tear on shoes.
They've nearly all removed their skins—
What they reveal is less than shocking.
On each one, snow settles a skullcap.

Crows on cracked heads, perching plumes.
Stripped flesh dangles from meagre chins.
Swinging back and forth in dark encounters,
They're ramrod knights with cardboard armour.

The wind whistles at the Skeleton's Ball!
The black gibbet moans like an iron organ.
Howling wolves answer from violet forests.
The red sky makes a horizon of hell...

Holà, secouez-moi ces capitans funèbres
Qui défilent, sournois, de leurs gros doigts cassés
Un chapelet d'amour sur leurs pâles vertèbres:
Ce n'est pas un moustier ici, les trépassés!

Oh! voilà qu'au milieu de la danse macabre
Bondit dans le ciel rouge un grand squelette fou
Emporté par l'élan, comme un cheval se cabre:
Et, se sentant encor la corde raide au cou,

Crispe ses petits doigts sur son fémur qui craque
Avec des cris pareils à des ricanements,
Et, comme un baladin rentre dans la baraque,
Rebondit dans le bal au chant des ossements.

Au gibet noir, manchot aimable,
Dansent, dansent les paladins
Les maigres paladins du diable,
Les squelettes de Saladins.

Le Châtiment de Tartufe

Tisonnant, tisonnant son cœur amoureux sous
Sa chaste robe noire, heureux, la main gantée,
Un jour qu'il s'en allait, effroyablement doux,
Jaune, bavant la foi de sa bouche édentée,

Un jour qu'il s'en allait, 'Oremus',—un Méchant
Le prit rudement par son oreille benoîte
Et lui jeta des mots affreux, en arrachant
Sa chaste robe noire autour de sa peau moite!

Châtiment!... Ses habits étaient déboutonnés,
Et le long chapelet des péchés pardonnés
S'égrenant dans son cœur, Saint Tartufe était pâle!...

Shake these macabre villains down,
Their big snapped fingers slyly slipping rosary
Beads of love down their spines, notch by notch.
You dead men, don't mistake this for a church.

Then, right there in this danse macabre,
A great mad skeleton, frenzied, wild,
Leaps at crimson skies like a bucking horse,
And, sensing the lasso still round his neck,

Tightens shrunken fingers on cracking femur
With squeals like sneers,
And like a clown who must go on,
Rejoins the dance, to the music of bones.

On black gallows, one-armed friend,
First Crusaders dance and dance,
The Devil's wasted Paladins,
The skeletons of Sultans.

Tartufe's Punishment

Fanning his amorous eagerness inside
His black robe of chastity, well-pleased, gloved,
Sliding along one day, sickly, saccharine,
Yellow, gobs of faith dripping from his toothless mouth,

Sliding along one day, 'deep in prayer',
An Enemy caught his sainted ear,
Blasted awful words at him, ripped
That chaste black robe off that oleaginy.

Punishment! All his buttons were undone,
The beads of pardoned sins threaded
On his heart; St Tartufe blanched,

Donc, il se confessait, priait, avec un râle!
L'homme se contenta d'emporter ses rabats...
—Peuh! Tartufe était nu du haut jusques en bas!

Vénus Anadyomène

Comme d'un cercueil vert en fer blanc, une tête
De femme à cheveux bruns fortement pommadés
D'une vieille baignoire émerge, lente et bête,
Avec des déficits assez mal ravaudés;

Puis le col gras et gris, les larges omoplates
Qui saillent; le dos court qui rentre et qui ressort;
Puis les rondeurs des reins semblent prendre l'essor;
La graisse sous la peau paraît en feuilles plates;

L'échine est un peu rouge, et le tout sent un goût
Horrible étrangement; on remarque surtout
Des singularités qu'il faut voir à la loupe...

Les reins portent deux mots gravés: *Clara Venus*;
—Et tout ce corps remue et tend sa large croupe
Belle hideusement d'un ulcère à l'anus.

Les Reparties de Nina

. . . .

LUI— Ta poitrine sur ma poitrine,
Hein? nous irions,
Ayant de l'air plein la narine,
Aux frais rayons

Du bon matin bleu, qui vous baigne
Du vin de jour?...
Quand tout le bois frissonnant saigne
Muet d'amour

Made confession, prayed, chattering with fear!
Our man just grabbed his garb and stole away.
Pah! He was naked, our Tartufe, head to toe.

Venus Emerging

It resembles a green tin coffin;
From an ancient bathtub emerges,
Slow and stupid, a woman's head, her thickly
Oiled brown hair ill-concealing bald patches.

Then the fat grey neck, the wide-wing shoulder-blades;
The short back, all dents and bumps;
Then rump roundness rises;
Subcutaneous fat shows like flat leaves;

The spine's a touch red; and the whole thing smells
Strange and strong; and many oddities
To be subjected to the microscope.

Two words are tattooed on the buttocks: CLARA VENUS;*
—And the whole thing stirs, proffering hindquarters
Hideously jewelled with an ulcer on the anus.

Nina Answers Back

. . . .

HE: Your breast against mine,
  Yes? We'd go
Breathing full air
  In crisp light,

One blue morning awash
  With the wine of day.
When the trembling wood bleeds
  Silent with love

De chaque branche, gouttes vertes,
Des bourgeons clairs,
On sent dans les choses ouvertes
Frémir des chairs:

Tu plongerais dans la luzerne
Ton blanc peignoir,
Rosant à l'air ce bleu qui cerne
Ton grand œil noir,

Amoureuse de la campagne,
Semant partout,
Comme une mousse de champagne,
Ton rire fou:

Riant à moi, brutal d'ivresse,
Qui te prendrais
Comme cela,—la belle tresse,
Oh!—qui boirais

Ton goût de framboise et de fraise,
Ô chair de fleur!
Riant au vent vif qui te baise
Comme un voleur,

Au rose églantier qui t'embête
Aimablement:
Riant surtout, ô folle tête,
A ton amant!...

. . . .

[Dix-sept ans! Tu seras heureuse!
Oh! les grands prés,
La grande campagne amoureuse!
—Dis, viens plus près!...]

—Ta poitrine sur ma poitrine,
Mêlant nos voix,
Lents, nous gagnerions la ravine,
Puis les grands bois!...

From every branch, green drops,
    Bright buds.
Feel how things open,
    A quiver of flesh.

Your white gown would plunge
    Into long grass.
The blue around your dark eyes
    Would shade pink.

In love with the country
    Scattering about
Like champagne bubbles,
    Your wild laugh:

You'd laugh, and I'd be drunk, direct,
    And catch you
Thus—fantastic hair!
    —Oh, and I'd savour

Your strawberry and raspberry taste,
    Your flower flesh!
I'd laugh at the keen wind kissing you
    Like a thief,

At the wild rose tangling
    You up in love,
Above all, free, laughing spirit,
    At me, your lover!

. . . .

Seventeen! You, so happy!
    The wide fields,
The open country full of love!
    Closer, come closer...

Your breast against mine,
    Our voices one,
Slowly we'd reach the gully,
    Then the great woods...

Puis, comme une petite morte,
Le cœur pâmé,
Tu me dirais que je te porte,
L'œil mi-fermé...

Je te porterais, palpitante,
Dans le sentier:
L'oiseau filerait son andante:
Au Noisetier...

Je te parlerais dans ta bouche;
J'irais, pressant
Ton corps, comme une enfant qu'on couche,
Ivre du sang

Qui coule, bleu, sous ta peau blanche
Aux tons rosés:
Et te parlant la langue franche...
Tiens!...—que tu sais...

Nos grands bois sentiraient la sève
Et le soleil
Sablerait d'or fin leur grand rêve
Vert et vermeil.

. . . .

Le soir?... Nous reprendrons la route
Blanche qui court
Flânant, comme un troupeau qui broute,
Tout à l'entour.

Les bons vergers à l'herbe bleue
Aux pommiers tors!
Comme on les sent toute une lieue
Leurs parfums forts!

Nous regagnerons le village
Au ciel mi-noir;
Et ça sentira le laitage
Dans l'air du soir;

Then, limp as a corpse,
    Fainting almost,
You'd ask me to carry you,
    Your eyes just slits.

I'd carry your throbbing body
    Down the path.
The bird's song would lead us,
    'By the hazel tree...'

My lips against yours, I'd murmur,
    I'd walk, hugging
Your body, like a bedtime child,
    Drunk on the blood

That flows blue beneath your skin,
    White, hints of pink,
Talking a frank language to you,
    The one you know...

Our forests would smell of sap,
    And the sun
Would thread gold through their green
    And crimson dream.

. . . .

And in the evening? We'll take
    The white road
Meandering where it will
    Like a flock grazing...

The blue grass of good orchards,
    The gnarled apple-trees.
Their fragrance carried on the air
    Mile after mile.

We'll get back to the village
    In circling dark,
The smell of milking will carry
    On the evening air.

Ça sentira l'étable, pleine
De fumiers chauds,
Pleine d'un lent rhythme d'haleine,
Et de grands dos

Blanchissant sous quelque lumière;
Et, tout là-bas,
Une vache fientera, fière,
A chaque pas...

—Les lunettes de la grand'mère
Et son nez long
Dans son missel; le pot de bière
Cerclé de plomb,

Moussant entre les larges pipes
Qui, crânement,
Fument: les effroyables lippes
Qui, tout fumant,

Happent le jambon aux fourchettes
Tant, tant et plus:
Le feu qui claire les couchettes
Et les bahuts.

Les fesses luisantes et grasses
D'un gros enfant
Qui fourre, à genoux, dans les tasses,
Son museau blanc

Frôlé par un mufle qui gronde
D'un ton gentil,
Et pourlèche la face ronde
Du cher petit...

. . . .

[Noire, rogue au bord de sa chaise,
Affreux profil,
Une vieille devant la braise
Qui fait du fil;]

The smell of cowsheds, warm
    With fresh manure,
Filled with slow breathing
    And great backs

Made white by a lantern.
    At the far end
There'll be a stately cow, the soft clap of
    Dung with every step.

Grandma's glasses, and
    Her long nose
In her prayer-book; a pint
    Tankard, pewter-rimmed,

Foaming among big-bowled pipes
    Resolutely
Puffing; fat awful lips,
    Smoking still,

Fork quantities of ham into mouths,
    Then more, then more;
The open fire lighting up bunk beds
    And darkwood chests.

The shiny, chubby bottom of
    A fat baby
Crawling around, sticking its snout
    Into cups,

Sniffed at, tickled by a lowing
    Wet muzzle,
Licking the moon-round face
    Of the little dear...

Dark and distant on the edge of her chair,
    Ghastly profile,
An old woman by the dying fire,
    Spinning.

Que de choses verrons-nous, chère,
Dans ces taudis,
Quand la flamme illumine, claire,
Les carreaux gris!...

—Puis, petite et toute nichée
Dans les lilas
Noirs et frais: la vitre cachée,
Qui rit là-bas...

Tu viendras, tu viendras, je t'aime!
Ce sera beau.
Tu viendras, n'est-ce pas, et même...

Elle—Et mon bureau?

A la musique

Place de la gare, à Charleville.

Sur la place taillée en mesquines pelouses,
Square où tout est correct, les arbres et les fleurs,
Tous les bourgeois poussifs qu'étranglent les chaleurs
Portent, les jeudis soirs, leurs bêtises jalouses.

—L'orchestre militaire, au milieu du jardin,
Balance ses schakos dans la *Valse des fifres*:
—Autour, aux premiers rangs, parade le gandin;
Le notaire pend à ses breloques à chiffres.

Des rentiers à lorgnons soulignent tous les couacs:
Les gros bureaux bouffis traînent leurs grosses dames
Auprès desquelles vont, officieux cornacs,
Celles dont les volants ont des airs de réclames;

Sur les bancs verts, des clubs d'épiciers retraités
Qui tisonnent le sable avec leur canne à pomme,
Fort sérieusement discutent les traités,
Puis prisent en argent, et reprennent: 'En somme!...'

Such things we'll see, my angel,
    In those cottages
When the fire's bright flames light up
    The dusty window-panes.

—Then, tiny and snug among
    Cool, dark
Lilacs; the hidden window
    Smiling there...

I love you! Come! You've never dreamt
    Such beauty. Come,
You will come, please? And even...

SHE: And risk my job?

To Music

Station Square, Charleville

On the square, tailored into meagre lawns,
Where all's as it should be, flowers, trees,
Chesty bourgeois stifling in Thursday-evening
Heat, parade their small-town spite and jealousy.

In the gardens, as they play *The Fife Waltz*,
The bandsmen's peaked caps bob up and down;
The local dandy struts around near the front;
The Notary hangs from the chain of his watch.

Private means in pince-nez underscore bum-notes;
Hefty pen-pushers drag hefty spouses along,
Accompanied—like so many elephant-minders—
By females in flounces flapping like billboards.

On green benches, federations of retired grocers,
Poking at the sand with pommelled walking-sticks,
Talk weightily of Treaties, then out of silver boxes
Take snuff, remarking 'The long and short of it is...'

Épatant sur son banc les rondeurs de ses reins,
Un bourgeois à boutons clairs, bedaine flamande,
Savoure son onnaing d'où le tabac par brins
Déborde—vous savez, c'est de la contrebande;—

Le long des gazons verts ricanent les voyous;
Et, rendus amoureux par le chant des trombones,
Très naïfs, et fumant des roses, les pioupious
Caressent les bébés pour enjôler les bonnes...

—Moi, je suis, débraillé comme un étudiant,
Sous les marronniers verts les alertes fillettes:
Elles le savent bien; et tournent en riant,
Vers moi, leurs yeux tout pleins de choses indiscrètes.

Je ne dis pas un mot: je regarde toujours
La chair de leurs cous blancs brodés de mèches folles:
Je suis, sous le corsage et les frêles atours,
Le dos divin après la courbe des épaules.

J'ai bientôt déniché la bottine, le bas...
—Je reconstruis les corps, brûlé de belles fièvres.
Elles me trouvent drôle et se parlent tout bas...
—Et mes désirs brutaux s'accrochent à leurs lèvres.

Les Effarés

Noirs dans la neige et dans la brume,
Au grand soupirail qui s'allume,
Leurs culs en rond,

A genoux, cinq petits—misère!—
Regardent le boulanger faire
Le lourd pain blond...

Ils voient le fort bras blanc qui tourne
La pâte grise, et qui l'enfourne
Dans un trou clair.

Flattening his balloon-bum on a bench,
A brightly buttoned bourgeois, Flemish gut,
Enjoys a smoke, his filthy pipe spilling
Its tobacco—smuggled in for me, you know.

The local lads loiter on the grass, sneering;
Trombones play, and the thoughts of boy-soldiers,
Smoking standard-issue cigarettes, turn
To love; kiss the baby, that should get the nurse...

—Me, I'm like a scruffy student; I find
Quick little girls under chestnut-trees;
They know my game, and laugh, looking at me,
Eyes wide with indiscretion.

I say not a word; I go on looking
At the whiteness of their necks, the wisps, the curls;
Beneath bodices and flimsy frocks, I trace
Divine backs, starting with shoulders, heading south.

Soon I've laid bare a shoe, a stocking...
—I reconstruct their bodies, flames of fine fever.
They find me odd, and whisper behind hands...
And my brutal desires sink hooks into their lips...

Wide-eyed

Black against the snow and fog,
Beside a friendly heating-duct,
    Rears rounded,

Five children kneeling—sad sight!—
Watch the Baker making
    Thick white bread.

They watch his strong white arm knead
The grey dough, place it
    In the bright hole.

Ils écoutent le bon pain cuire.
Le boulanger au gras sourire
    Chante un vieil air.

Ils sont blottis, pas un ne bouge,
Au souffle du soupirail rouge,
    Chaud comme un sein.

Et quand pendant que minuit sonne,
Façonné, pétillant et jaune,
    On sort le pain,

Quand, sous les poutres enfumées,
Chantent les croûtes parfumées,
    Et les grillons,

Quand ce trou chaud souffle la vie,
Ils ont leur âme si ravie
    Sous leurs haillons,

Ils se ressentent si bien vivre,
Les pauvres petits pleins de givre!
    —Qu'ils sont là, tous,

Collant leurs petits museaux roses
Au grillage, chantant des choses,
    Entre les trous,

Mais bien bas,—comme une prière...
Repliés vers cette lumière
    Du ciel rouvert,

—Si fort, qu'ils crèvent leur culotte,
—Et que leur lange blanc tremblote
    Au vent d'hiver...

20 sept. 70.

They hear the good bread bake,
And the Baker with his jowly smile
    Sing an old tune.

They huddle motionless
In the breath of the glowing duct,
    Warm as a breast.

And when, on the stroke of midnight,
Sculpted, popping, yellow,
    The bread emerges,

When beneath the smoky beams,
The fragrant crusts sing,
    And the crickets,

When this warm hole breathes life,
They're totally transfixed
    Inside their rags,

They feel life pulsing back,
These poor frozen ragbags
    There they all are

Pressing little pink snouts
Against the grating, sing-
    Songing through apertures,

But soft as a prayer...
Bent down towards the lights
    Of this new Heaven,

So earnestly they split their pants,
—And then their shirt-tails wave
    In the winter wind.

20 September '70

Roman

I

On n'est pas sérieux, quand on a dix-sept ans.
—Un beau soir, foin des bocks et de la limonade,
Des cafés tapageurs aux lustres éclatants!
—On va sous les tilleuls verts de la promenade.

Les tilleuls sentent bon dans les bons soirs de juin!
L'air est parfois si doux, qu'on ferme la paupière;
Le vent chargé de bruits,—la ville n'est pas loin,—
A des parfums de vigne et des parfums de bière...

II

—Voilà qu'on aperçoit un tout petit chiffon
D'azur sombre, encadré d'une petite branche,
Piqué d'une mauvaise étoile, qui se fond
Avec de doux frissons, petite et toute blanche...

Nuit de juin! Dix-sept ans!—On se laisse griser.
La sève est du champagne et vous monte à la tête...
On divague; on se sent aux lèvres un baiser
Qui palpite là, comme une petite bête...

III

Le cœur fou Robinsonne à travers les romans,
—Lorsque, dans la clarté d'un pâle réverbère,
Passe une demoiselle aux petits airs charmants,
Sous l'ombre du faux-col effrayant de son père...

Et, comme elle vous trouve immensément naïf,
Tout en faisant trotter ses petites bottines,
Elle se tourne, alerte et d'un mouvement vif...
—Sur vos lèvres alors meurent les cavatines...

Romance

I

No one's serious when they're seventeen.
—One fine night, you turn your back on beer,
Lemonade, rowdy cafés, their glittering lights.
—You walk beneath the green limes on the promenade.

The limes smell good on nice June nights.
Sometimes the air's so soft you shut your eyes.
Noise carries on the wind—the town's not far—
And the fragrance of the vine, the smell of beer.

II

Then, up there, you catch sight of a tiny scrap
Of dark blue, framed by a small branch,
Pinned by some wandering star, perfectly
White and small, trembling light fading...

June nights! Seventeen! It goes to your head.
You get dizzy on sap like champagne...
You drift; you feel on your lips a kiss
Fluttering, a tiny scrap of life...

III

Your crazy heart goes Crusoeing through books
—Then, under thin lamplight, in the cold
Shadow of her father's false collar,
You see a girl go by, all airs and little graces.

Her pixie boots take mincing steps;
And finding you wonderfully naïve,
She turns round, bright as a dart...
The cavatinas you were singing die on your lips...

IV

Vous êtes amoureux. Loué jusqu'au mois d'août.
Vous êtes amoureux.—Vos sonnets La font rire.
Tous vos amis s'en vont, vous êtes *mauvais goût*.
—Puis l'adorée, un soir, a daigné vous écrire...!

—Ce soir-là,... —vous rentrez aux cafés éclatants,
Vous demandez des bocks ou de la limonade...
—On n'est pas sérieux, quand on a dix-sept ans
Et qu'on a des tilleuls verts sur la promenade.

29 sept. 70.

'Morts de Quatre-vingt-douze...'

'... Français de soixante-dix, bonapartistes, républicains, souvenez-vous de vos pères en 92, etc.'

(Paul de Cassagnac, *Le Pays*)

Morts de Quatre-vingt-douze et de Quatre-vingt-treize,
Qui, pâles du baiser fort de la liberté,
Calmes, sous vos sabots, brisiez le joug qui pèse
Sur l'âme et sur le front de toute humanité;

Hommes extasiés et grands dans la tourmente,
Vous dont les cœurs sautaient d'amour sous les haillons,
Ô Soldats que la Mort a semés, noble Amante,
Pour les régénérer, dans tous les vieux sillons;

Vous dont de sang lavait toute grandeur salie,
Morts de Valmy, Morts de Fleurus, Morts d'Italie,
Ô million de Christs aux yeux sombres et doux;

Nous vous laissions dormir avec la République,
Nous, courbés sous les rois comme sous une trique.
—Messieurs de Cassagnac nous reparlent de vous!

fait à Mazas, 3 septembre 1870.

IV

You're in love. Booked till August.
You're in love. Your sonnets make Her laugh.
Friends desert you, you're out of fashion.
—Then, one night, the Beloved deigns to write...!

That night... you return to the bursting cafés,
You order beers, lemonade,
—No one's serious when they're seventeen,
And lime-trees flower on the promenade.

29th September '70

'The dead of '92 and '93...'

'Frenchmen of 1870, Bonapartists, Republicans, remember your forefathers of '92 etc....'

(Paul de Cassagnac, *Le Pays*)

The dead of '92 and '93,
The firm kiss of liberty on your brows,
You, who with your clogs calmly broke the collar
Clamped tight around humanity's soul and neck.

Exalted men, made great by suffering,
You, whose hearts leapt with love beneath your rags,
Soldiers whom Death, noble lover, has sown
In every ancient furrows, to make you live again,

You, whose blood washed clean our soiled greatness,
You, the dead of Valmy, of Fleurus, of Italy,*
You million Christs with soft dark eyes,

We let you slumber with the Republic,
We who cowered under the royal lash
—Cassagnac and Co. have dug you up again!

Mazas Prison, 3 September 1870

Le Mal

Tandis que les crachats rouges de la mitraille
Sifflent tout le jour par l'infini du ciel bleu;
Qu'écarlates ou verts, près du Roi qui les raille,
Croulent les bataillons en masse dans le feu;

Tandis qu'une folie épouvantable, broie
Et fait de cent milliers d'hommes un tas fumant;
—Pauvres morts! dans l'été, dans l'herbe, dans ta joie,
Nature! ô toi qui fis ces hommes saintement!...—

—Il est un Dieu, qui rit aux nappes damassées
Des autels, à l'encens, aux grands calices d'or;
Qui dans le bercement des hosannah s'endort,

Et se réveille, quand des mères, ramassées
Dans l'angoisse, et pleurant sous leur vieux bonnet noir,
Lui donnent un gros sou lié dans leur mouchoir!

Rages de Césars

L'Homme pâle, le long des pelouses fleuries,
Chemine, en habit noir, et le cigare aux dents:
L'Homme pâle repense aux fleurs des Tuileries
—Et parfois son œil terne a des regards ardents...

Car l'Empereur est soûl de ses vingt ans d'orgie!
Il s'était dit: 'Je vais souffler la Liberté
Bien délicatement, ainsi qu'une bougie!'
La Liberté revit! Il se sent éreinté!

Il est pris.—Oh! quel nom sur ses lèvres muettes
Tressaille? Quel regret implacable le mord?
On ne le saura pas. L'Empereur a l'œil mort.

Evil

While the red mouths of machine-guns spit blood
And whistle non-stop in the endless blue,
While—scarlet or green beside their sneering king—*
Massed battalions are blown to bits,

While nightmare madness stacks
A million men on smoking heaps
—You poor beggars, dead in summer's grass,
In your joy, Nature, maker of these saintly men.

There is a God, who laughs at patterned
Altar-cloths, incense, great gold chalices,
Who's lulled to sleep by Hosannas,

And Who wakes when mothers, huddled
In the black of grief, tie a small coin
In their handkerchief, and give it Him.

Caesars' Rage

The pale man walks on flower-dotted lawns,
Dressed in black, cigar jammed between teeth.
The pale man's remembering Tuileries'* flowers
—Sometimes his dead eyes flare with life...

For the Emperor's drunk on two decades of excess!
He'd told himself: 'I'll snuff out Freedom
With one small puff, like a candle.'
Freedom's back, and he's worn out!

He's been caught. And what name trembles
On his silent lips? What regret won't let him go?
We shan't know. The Emperor's eyes are dead.

Il repense peut-être au Compère en lunettes...
—Et regarde filer de son cigare en feu,
Comme aux soirs de Saint-Cloud, un fin nuage bleu.

Rêvé pour l'hiver

A *** Elle

L'hiver, nous irons dans un petit wagon rose
        Avec des coussins bleus.
Nous serons bien. Un nid de baisers fous repose
        Dans chaque coin moelleux.

Tu fermeras l'œil, pour ne point voir, par la glace,
        Grimacer les ombres des soirs,
Ces monstruosités hargneuses, populace
        De démons noirs et de loups noirs.

Puis tu te sentiras la joue égratignée . . .
Un petit baiser, comme une folle araignée,
        Te courra par le cou...

Et tu me diras: 'Cherche!' en inclinant la tête,
—Et nous prendrons du temps à trouver cette bête
        —Qui voyage beaucoup...

En wagon, le 7 octobre 70.

Le Dormeur du val

C'est un trou de verdure où chante une rivière
Accrochant follement aux herbes des haillons
D'argent; où le soleil, de la montagne fière,
Luit: c'est un petit val qui mousse de rayons.

Un soldat jeune, bouche ouverte, tête nue,
Et la nuque baignant dans le frais cresson bleu,
Dort; il est étendu dans l'herbe, sous la nue,
Pâle dans son lit vert où la lumière pleut.

Perhaps he recalls his old bespectacled
Confederate*—and watches, as in the St Cloud*
Days, smoke drift from his cigar in thin blue clouds.

Winter Dream

To *** Her

In Winter, we'll travel in a small pink coach
With blue cushions,
Well installed, mad kisses nesting
In cosy corners.

You'll close your eyes, not to see through the glass
The leer of dark evening,
Snarling monster, droves of black demons,
Packs of black wolves.

Then you'll feel something scratch against your cheek...
A little kiss, brief as a startled spider,
Will run up your neck...

You'll bow your head and say: 'Find it for me!'
—And we'll take the time it takes to find that creature
—Which loves to travel...

Travelling, 7 October '70

Asleep in the Valley

A gully of green, a laughing river
Where silver tatters snag
Madly in grasses; where, from the proud
Mountain the sun shines; foaming trough of light.

A young soldier, mouth open, head bare,
Neck on a pillow of cool cress,
Sleeps, stretched out in the grass, sky above,
Pale on his green bed where light teems down.

Les pieds dans les glaïeuls, il dort. Souriant comme
Sourirait un enfant malade, il fait un somme:
Nature, berce-le chaudement: il a froid.

Les parfums ne font pas frissonner sa narine;
Il dort dans le soleil, la main sur sa poitrine
Tranquille. Il a deux trous rouges au côté droit.

Octobre 1870.

Au Cabaret-Vert, cinq heures du soir

Depuis huit jours, j'avais déchiré mes bottines
Aux cailloux des chemins. J'entrais à Charleroi.
—*Au Cabaret-Vert:* je demandai des tartines
De beurre et du jambon qui fût à moitié froid.

Bienheureux, j'allongeai les jambes sous la table
Verte: je contemplai les sujets très naïfs
De la tapisserie.—Et ce fut adorable,
Quand la fille aux tétons énormes, aux yeux vifs,

—Celle-là, ce n'est pas un baiser qui l'épeure!—
Rieuse, m'apporta des tartines de beurre,
Du jambon tiède, dans un plat colorié,

Du jambon rose et blanc parfumé d'une gousse
D'ail,—et m'emplit la chope immense, avec sa mousse,
Que dorait un rayon de soleil arriéré.

Octobre 70.

La Maline

Dans la salle à manger brune, que parfumait
Une odeur de vernis et de fruits, à mon aise
Je ramassais un plat de je ne sais quel met
Belge, et je m'épatais dans mon immense chaise.

Feet among the flags, he sleeps, smiling how
A sick child might; he takes a nap.
Gather him close, Nature, rock him. He's cold.

No scent makes his nostril quiver.
He sleeps in the sun, one hand on his still
Chest. In his right side, two red holes.

October 1870

At the Green Inn, five p.m.

A full week I'd been on the road, feet
Swollen and blistered. Made it to Charleroi,*
Stopped off at the Green Inn, ordered some
Ham rolls and a tall glass of draught beer.

Nice and relaxed, I stretched out my legs,
Cast my eye over the usual wit...
'You don't have to be mad to work here'
Etc.... And when the barmaid

(Obligatory well-filled blouse and eyes
That say she wouldn't mind one bit)
Brought in my plate of rolls, freshly made,

Chilled butter, soft pink ham, and a slice
Or two of onion, I raised my glass
And saw summer in a splendid head.

October '70

Cunning

Spread carelessly across my massive chair
In that sepia living-room, with its smell
Of fruit and varnish, I settled in and took
A helping of some Belgian dish.

En mangeant, j'écoutais l'horloge,—heureux et coi.
La cuisine s'ouvrit avec une bouffée
—Et la servante vint, je ne sais pas pourquoi,
Fichu moitié défait, malinement coiffée

Et, tout en promenant son petit doigt tremblant
Sur sa joue, un velours de pêche rose et blanc,
En faisant, de sa lèvre enfantine, une moue,

Elle arrangeait les plats, près de moi, pour m'aiser;
—Puis, comme ça,—bien sûr pour avoir un baiser,—
Tout bas: 'Sens donc: j'ai pris *une* froid sur la joue...'

Charleroi, octobre 70.

'Au milieu, l'Empereur...'

—L'éclatante victoire de Sarrebrück,—
remportée aux cris de vive l'Empereur!

(*Gravure belge brillamment coloriée,*
se vend à Charleroi, 35 centimes.)

Au milieu, l'Empereur, dans une apothéose
Bleue et jaune, s'en va, raide, sur son dada
Flamboyant; très heureux,—car il voit tout en rose,
Féroce comme Zeus et doux comme un papa;

En bas, les bons Pioupious qui faisaient la sieste
Près des tambours dorés et des rouges canons,
Se lèvent gentiment. Pitou remet sa veste,
Et, tourné vers le Chef, s'étourdit de grands noms!

A droite, Dumanet, appuyé sur la crosse
De son chassepot, sent frémir sa nuque en brosse,
Et: 'Vive l'Empereur!!'—Son voisin reste coi...

Un schako surgit, comme un soleil noir... Au centre,
Boquillon rouge et bleu, très naïf, sur son ventre
Se dresse, et,—présentant ses derrières—: 'De quoi?...'

Octobre 70.

I ate, listening to the clock, happy, quiet.
Then, a sudden draught, and, from the kitchen
(Why, I don't know), a button undone,
Hair nicely mismanaged, in came the maid.

She ran one dinky finger down the pink
White velvet of a cheek,
Put on a little-girlie pout,

Leant nicely over me to set some plates—
Then, like this, to get a kiss, murmured:
'Feel my cheek, I come over* all cold.'

Charleroi, October '70

'Centre: the Emperor...'

—The Stunning Victory at Sarrebrück,—
Gained to shouts of Long Live the Emperor!

(*Belgian engraving, in dazzling colours*
on sale at Charleroi, 35 centimes)

Centre: the Emperor, apotheosis
Of blue and gold, riding off, stiff as a board
On his dazzling nag; radiant, seeing the world
Through rose-tinted glasses; fierce as Zeus, soppy as papa.

Bottom: poor private soldiers napping
By the gilded drums and red cannons,
Obediently get up. Pitou* buttons his tunic,
Turns to his CO, head swimming with great names.

Right: Dumanet* leans on his rifle-butt,
Feels his close-cropped scalp prickle, and yells:
'Long Live the Emperor!' His neighbour says nothing...

A helmet rises like a black sun... Centre:
Simple Boquillon,* prostrate in red and blue, lifts
Himself up, and, end-first, says: 'Emperor, my arse!'

October '70

Le Buffet

C'est un large buffet sculpté; le chêne sombre,
Très vieux, a pris cet air si bon des vieilles gens;
Le buffet est ouvert, et verse dans son ombre
Comme un flot de vin vieux, des parfums engageants;

Tout plein, c'est un fouillis de vieilles vieilleries,
De linges odorants et jaunes, de chiffons
De femmes ou d'enfants, de dentelles flétries,
De fichus de grand-mère où sont peints des griffons;

—C'est là qu'on trouverait les médaillons, les mèches
De cheveux blancs ou blonds, les portraits, les fleurs sèches
Dont le parfum se mêle à des parfums de fruits.

—Ô buffet du vieux temps, tu sais bien des histoires,
Et tu voudrais conter tes contes, et tu bruis
Quand s'ouvrent lentement tes grandes portes noires.

Octobre 70.

Ma Bohème (Fantaisie)

Je m'en allais, les poings dans mes poches crevées;
Mon paletot aussi devenait idéal;
J'allais sous le ciel, Muse! et j'étais ton féal;
Oh! là là! que d'amours splendides j'ai rêvées!

Mon unique culotte avait un large trou.
—Petit-Poucet rêveur, j'égrenais dans ma course
Des rimes. Mon auberge était à la Grande-Ourse.
Mes étoiles au ciel avaient un doux frou-frou

Et je les écoutais, assis au bord des routes,
Ces bon soirs de septembre où je sentais des gouttes
De rosée à mon front, comme un vin de vigueur;

The Dresser

It's a wide dresser carved in old, dark oak;
Now it's got that lovely look old folk have;
Its doors are open, from its depths
Intriguing fragrances flood like vintage wine.

Stuffed full, it's a ragbag of olden-day old things,
Yellowing scented linens, bits of children's
And women's clothing, tired lace,
Grandma's headscarves printed with griffins;

—This is the place of medals and lockets,
White or blond hair, portraits, the fragrance
Of dried flowers blending with the smell of fruit.

—Dresser of bygone days, you've seen some things,
And could tell a tale or two; which begin
Whenever your great dark doors slowly open.

October '70

My Bohemia (Fantasy)

And so I went, hands thrust in torn pockets.
My coat was more idea than fact.
Beneath the sky—my Muse, my liege—I went;
Oh my! what dreams of splendid loves I had!

My one and only trousers were hugely holed.
—Starry-eyed Tom Thumb, I strewed my path
With verse. I laid my head at Great Bear Inn.
—My stars swished softly in the sky

And, seated on roadsides, I heard them
On lovely evenings in September, feeling dew
Drop on my face, like invigorating wine;

Où, rimant au milieu des ombres fantastiques,
Comme des lyres, je tirais les élastiques
De mes souliers blessés, un pied près de mon cœur!

Les Corbeaux

Seigneur, quand froide est la prairie,
Quand dans les hameaux abattus,
Les longs angelus se sont tus...
Sur la nature défleurie
Faites s'abattre des grands cieux
Les chers corbeaux délicieux.

Armée étrange aux cris sévères,
Les vents froids attaquent vos nids!
Vous, le long des fleuves jaunis,
Sur les routes aux vieux calvaires,
Sur les fossés et sur les trous
Dispersez-vous, ralliez-vous!

Par milliers, sur les champs de France,
Où dorment des morts d'avant-hier,
Tournoyez, n'est-ce pas, l'hiver,
Pour que chaque passant repense!
Sois donc le crieur du devoir,
Ô notre funèbre oiseau noir!

Mais, saints du ciel, en haut du chêne,
Mât perdu dans le soir charmé,
Laissez les fauvettes de mai
Pour ceux qu'au fond du bois enchaîne,
Dans l'herbe d'où l'on ne peut fuir,
La défaite sans avenir.

And rhyming verse among the phantom shadows,
I harped on the laces of my wounded boots,
One foot by my heart.

Crows

When the field is cold, Lord,
When in wasted hamlets
The long angelus has ceased...
Make the dear delicious crows
Swoop down from huge skies
Onto bare Nature.

Strange army of raucous cries,
Cold winds blast your nests!
Disperse, regroup,
Down yellow rivers,
Old Calvary roads,
Above ditches, over holes!

In your thousands, above France's fields
Where the dead of yesterdays* lie sleeping,
Swirl about in winter
Lest passers-by forget.
Be the cry of duty,
Black herald, funeral bird!

But, you saints of heaven, high in the oak,
That mast of evening's enchantment,
Leave the warbling birds of May
For those deep in the wood,
The grass which covers them for good,
Trapped in dead-end defeat.

Les Assis

Noirs de loupes, grêlés, les yeux cerclés de bagues
Vertes, leurs doigts boulus crispés à leurs fémurs
Le sinciput plaqué de hargnosités vagues
Comme les floraisons lépreuses des vieux murs;

Ils ont greffé dans des amours épileptiques
Leur fantasque ossature aux grands squelettes noirs
De leurs chaises; leurs pieds aux barreaux rachitiques
S'entrelacent pour les matins et pour les soirs!

Ces vieillards ont toujours fait tresse avec leurs sièges,
Sentant les soleils vifs percaliser leur peau,
Ou, les yeux à la vitre où se fanent les neiges,
Tremblant du tremblement douloureux du crapaud.

Et les Sièges leur ont des bontés: culottée
De brun, la paille cède aux angles de leurs reins;
L'âme des vieux soleils s'allume emmaillotée
Dans ces tresses d'épis où fermentaient les grains.

Et les Assis, genoux aux dents, verts pianistes
Les dix doigts sous leur siège aux rumeurs de tambour
S'écoutent clapoter des barcarolles tristes,
Et leurs caboches vont dans des roulis d'amour.

—Oh! ne les faites pas lever! C'est le naufrage...
Ils surgissent, grondant comme des chats giflés,
Ouvrant lentement leurs omoplates, ô rage!
Tout leur pantalon bouffe à leurs reins boursouflés.

Et vous les écoutez, cognant leurs têtes chauves
Aux murs sombres, plaquant et plaquant leurs pieds tors.
Et leurs boutons d'habit sont des prunelles fauves
Qui vous accrochent l'œil du fond des corridors!

Seated

Pus-filled growths, cratered skin, green rings under
The eyes, puffy fingers clasping thigh-bones,
Skull splashed with vague liver-spots
Like leprous growths sprouting on old walls;

In epileptic acts of love they've grafted
Ghostly bones onto the black skeletons
Of their chairs; morning noon and night their feet
Wrap themselves round breaking legs and rods.

These old boys have always been like this—bindweed
Round their chairs; feeling bright suns threadbaring
Their skin; or, eyes glued to windows where snows fade,
Trembling the way toads tremble with pain.

And the chairs are good to them; brown-seated
Straw yields to their rears' fixed angles;
The heart of old suns glows, swaddled
In plaited ears of too-ripe corn.

There they sit, knees knocking against teeth, green pianists;
Ten fingers drum the underside of chairs;
They listen to the morse of sad barcaroles,
Heads bobbing on tides of love.

Don't make them rise! Instant shipwreck...
They struggle up, growling like tormented cats;
Shoulder-blades open, so achingly slow!
Round swollen backsides, trousers balloon.

And you listen to them bump their baldness
Against dark walls, stamp and stamp their twisted feet,
And the buttons on their clothes are wild beasts' eyes
Staring at you down long corridors.

Puis ils ont une main invisible qui tue:
Au retour, leur regard filtre ce venin noir
Qui charge l'œil souffrant de la chienne battue
Et vous suez pris dans un atroce entonnoir.

Rassis, les poings noyés dans des manchettes sales
Ils songent à ceux-là qui les ont fait lever
Et, de l'aurore au soir, des grappes d'amygdales
Sour leurs mentons chétifs s'agitent à crever.

Quand l'austère sommeil a baissé leurs visières
Ils rêvent sur leur bras de sièges fécondés,
De vrais petits amours de chaises en lisière
Par lesquelles de fiers bureaux seront bordés;

Des fleurs d'encre crachant des pollens en virgule
Les bercent, le long des calices accroupis
Tels qu'au fil des glaïeuls le vol des libellules
—Et leur membre s'agace à des barbes d'épis.

Les Douaniers

Ceux qui disent: Cré Nom, ceux qui disent macache,
Soldats, marins, débris d'Empire, retraités
Sont nuls, très nuls, devant les Soldats des Traités
Qui tailladent l'azur frontière à grands coups d'hache.

Pipe aux dents, lame en main, profonds, pas embêtés
Quand l'ombre bave aux bois comme un mufle de vache
Ils s'en vont, amenant leurs dogues à l'attache,
Exercer nuitamment leurs terribles gaîtés!

Ils signalent aux lois modernes les faunesses.
Ils empoignent les Fausts et les Diavolos.
'Pas de ça, les anciens! Déposez les ballots!'

Their killing handshake comes from nowhere;
And when you leave, their gaze oozes black poison
Like the wretched eye of a beaten dog,
And you sweat, sucked into an awful vortex.

They sit down again; fists retracted into dirty sleeves;
They think about the helpers who got them up
And from dawn to dusk, ripe goitres
Rise and fall beneath spent chins, about to burst.

When stern sleep pulls their eyeshades down,
Head on arms, they dream of well-shagged seats
Spawning sweet baby chairs, edged with piping,
Destined one day for some noble study.

Ink flowers spurting seed like commas
Lull them in their rows of folded flower-cups
Like dragonflies working their way down the gladioli—
And they stir into life,* pricked by barbs of wheat.

The Customs Men

Those who say: 'For Chrissake', others who say: 'Get lost—'
Soldiers, sailors, scum of Empire, pensioned off—
Are nothings next to the Tariff Soldiers,*
Who hack at azure frontiers with great axes.

Pipes in mouth, knives ready, deeply unconcerned
When darkness dribbles in woods, like a cow;
Off they go, their wolf-hounds on a lead,
To take their awful pleasures, every night.

Citing new laws, they finger Certain Nymphs,
They strong-arm Fausts* and Diavolos,*
With 'You're nicked, my lad. Now, drop that stuff.'

Quand sa sérénité s'approche des jeunesses,
Le Douanier se tient aux appas contrôlés!
Enfer aux Délinquants que sa paume a frôlés!

Le Cœur supplicié

Mon triste cœur bave à la poupe...
Mon cœur est plein de caporal!
Ils y lancent des jets de soupe,
Mon triste cœur bave à la poupe...
Sous les quolibets de la troupe
Qui lance un rire général,
Mon triste cœur bave à la poupe,
Mon cœur est plein de caporal!

Ithyphalliques et pioupiesques
Leurs insultes l'ont dépravé
A la vesprée, ils font des fresques
Ithyphalliques et pioupiesques;
Ô flots abracadabrantesques,
Prenez mon cœur, qu'il soit sauvé!
Ithyphalliques et pioupiesques
Leurs insultes l'ont dépravé!

Quand ils auront tari leurs chiques,
Comment agir, ô cœur volé?
Ce seront des refrains bachiques
Quand ils auront tari leurs chiques!
J'aurai des sursauts stomachiques,
Si mon cœur triste est ravalé!
Quand ils auront tari leurs chiques
Comment agir, ô cœur volé?

When His Majesty the Customs Man decides
To search juveniles, he's after lovely contraband—
God help the Delinquents his hand has frisked.

Tortured Heart

My pooped heart oozes
'Baccy juices
Sad pooped heart.
Yelled abuse
And soupy juices
Smear my sad heart.

Privates parade
Their evening
Painting degrades.
Magical waves
Lift up and save
My tainted heart.

Quid-spitting done
How to go on
Poor swallowed heart
Their booze and smut
My knotted gut
My cheated heart?

Chant de guerre parisien

Le Printemps est évident, car
Du cœur des Propriétés vertes,
Le vol de Thiers et de Picard
Tient ses splendeurs grandes ouvertes!

Ô Mai! quels délirants cul-nus!
Sèvres, Meudon, Bagneux, Asnières,
Écoutez donc les bienvenus
Semer les choses printanières!

Ils ont schako, sabre et tam-tam
Non la vieille boîte à bougies
Et des yoles qui n'ont jam, jam...
Fendent le lac aux eaux rougies!

Plus que jamais nous bambochons
Quand arrivent sur nos tanières
Crouler les jaunes cabochons
Dans des aubes particulières!

Thiers et Picard sont des Éros,
Des enleveurs d'héliotropes,
Au pétrole ils font des Corots:
Voici hannetonner leurs tropes...

Ils sont familiers du Grand Truc!...
Et couché dans les glaïeuls, Favre
Fait son cillement aqueduc,
Et ses reniflements à poivre!

La Grand ville a le pavé chaud,
Malgré vos douches de pétrole,
Et décidément, il nous faut
Vous secouer dans votre rôle...

Paris War-Cry

Spring's in the air; from deep
In the fertile Properties,
Which Thiers and Picard* annexed,
Growing splendours spread.

May! What a Carnival of bare arses!
Sèvres, Meudon, Bagneux, Asnières,*
Just listen to Welcome Spring
Bursting out all over.

Here they come, helmet, sabre, drum;
Not driven by ancient candle-power;
Their skiffs—they've ne... ne... never been to sea—*
Slice through the bloodied waters of the lake.

Our revels now are never-ending
When in the ant-heaps where we live
Yellow hailstorms rain on our heads
Ushering in uncommon dawns.

The Gods of Love: Thiers is one, P(r)ic-
Ard* is too; they dead-head heliotropes,
Paint Corots* with their petrol-bombs:
Here come their troops, picking off whatever moves...

They're on first-name terms with His Nibs!
Stretched out in beds of irises, Favre*
Winks to activate his tear-ducts;
He peppers up his snivels.

The City's cobblestones are hot
Despite your showers of flames;
Only one thing now for you—
You need a rocket up your...

Et les Ruraux qui se prélassent
Dans de longs accroupissements,
Entendront des rameaux qui cassent
Parmi les rouges froissements!

A. Rimbaud.

Mes petites amoureuses

Un hydrolat lacrymal lave
Les cieux vert-chou:
Sous l'arbre tendronnier qui bave,
Vos caoutchoucs

Blancs de lunes particulières
Aux pialats ronds,
Entrechoquez vos genouillères,
Mes laiderons!

Nous nous aimions à cette époque,
Bleu laideron!
On mangeait des œufs à la coque
Et du mouron!

Un soir, tu me sacras poète,
Blond laideron:
Descends ici, que je te fouette
En mon giron;

J'ai dégueulé ta bandoline,
Noir laideron;
Tu couperais ma mandoline
Au fil du front.

Pouah! mes salives desséchées,
Roux laideron
Infectent encor les tranchées
De ton sein rond!

And the fat cats* lying through
Long days of abject sloth
Will hear boughs break among
Disturbances, coloured red.

A. Rimbaud

My Little Lovebirds

Essential tears wash green
  Cabbage skies;
Under the wet tendril tree,
  Your waterproofs,

White with moon rings of
  Tear-drop roundnesses,
Knock your knee-pads together,
  My uglies!

We loved each other then
  My blue ugly!
We used to eat boiled eggs
  And chickweed!

One night you crowned me Poet,
  My blond ugly.
Come here, across my lap
  So I can hit you;

I've puked on your brilliantine,
  My black ugly.
Your sharp forehead would unpick
  My mandolin.

Ugh! My dried-out spit,
  My redhead ugly
Still spreads germs down the trench
  Between your round breasts!

Ô mes petites amoureuses,
Que je vous hais!
Plaquez de fouffes douloureuses
Vos tétons laids!

Piétinez mes vieilles terrines
De sentiment;
—Hop donc! Soyez-moi ballerines
Pour un moment!...

Vos omoplates se déboîtent,
Ô mes amours!
Une étoile à vos reins qui boitent,
Tournez vos tours!

Et c'est pourtant pour ces éclanches
Que j'ai rimé!
Je voudrais vous casser les hanches
D'avoir aimé!

Fade amas d'étoiles ratées,
Comblez les coins!
—Vous crèverez en Dieu, bâtées
D'ignobles soins!

Sous les lunes particulières
Aux pialats ronds,
Entrechoquez vos genouillères,
Mes laiderons!

A. R.

My little lovebirds,
  I loathe you!
Plaster your nasty tits
  With painful smacks!

Trample the old shards
  Of my feelings;
Jump, be my ballerinas
  For today!...

Your shoulder-blades dislocate
  My lovely things!
Star-sewn limping rump,
  Go do your tricks!

Yet it's for these mutton-joints
  I've written verse!
I'd spoil your hips
  For having loved!

You heap of faded stars,
  Weave into corners!
You'll die seeing God, riddled
  With worthy causes!

Under moon rings of
  Teardrop roundnesses,
Knock your knee-pads together,
  My uglies!

A. R.

Accroupissements

Bien tard, quand il se sent l'estomac écœuré,
Le frère Milotus, un œil à la lucarne
D'où le soleil, clair comme un chaudron récuré,
Lui darde une migraine et fait son regard darne,
Déplace dans les draps son ventre de curé.

Il se démène sous sa couverture grise
Et descend, ses genoux à son ventre tremblant,
Effaré comme un vieux qui mangerait sa prise,
Car il lui faut, le poing à l'anse d'un pot blanc,
A ses reins largement retrousser sa chemise!

Or, il s'est accroupi, frileux, les doigts de pied
Repliés, grelottant au clair soleil qui plaque
Des jaunes de brioche aux vitres de papier;
Et le nez du bonhomme où s'allume la laque
Renifle aux rayons, tel qu'un charnel polypier.

. . . .

Le bonhomme mijote au feu, bras tordus, lippe
Au ventre: il sent glisser ses cuisses dans le feu,
Et ses chausses roussir, et s'éteindre sa pipe;
Quelque chose comme un oiseau remue un peu
A son ventre serein comme un monceau de tripe!

Autour, dort un fouillis de meubles abrutis
Dans des haillons de crasse et sur de sales ventres;
Des escabeaux, crapauds étranges, sont blottis
Aux coins noirs: des buffets ont des gueules de chantres
Qu'entrouvre un sommeil plein d'horribles appétits.

L'écœurante chaleur gorge la chambre étroite;
Le cerveau du bonhomme est bourré de chiffons.
Il écoute les poils pousser dans sa peau moite,
Et, parfois, en hoquets fort gravement bouffons
S'échappe, secouant son escabeau qui boite...

. . . .

Squatting Down

It's very late; sick to his stomach,
Brother Milotus,* one eye on the skylight
Through which the saucepan-bright sun
Arrows him a migraine so he can't see straight,
Shifts his sacerdotal guts beneath the covers.

He wriggles under his grey blanket,
Then gets up, knees to trembling belly,
Scared as some veteran choking on snuff—
The problem is, while one hand grabs the potty,
The other's somehow got to hold his night-shirt up!

He's squatting now, feeling the cold, toes
Curled, shivering in the sunlight which slaps yellows
Like choux-pastry onto papery window-panes;
And the old boy's nose, lit up like lacquer,
Sniffs at the sun, a spread of polyps.

. . . .

The old boy's cooking nicely by the fire, arms knotted,
Blubber-lip by belly; he feels his thighs slip firewards,
Breeches scorch, pipe go out;
Something bird-like twitters
In his tummy, peaceable as tripe.

All around, jumbled furniture sleeps stupid
In its dirty rags, bellied out in filth;
Stools like weird toads squat unseen
In dark corners; sideboards open wide as singers' throats,
Mouths agape in the sleep of ghastly greed.

Stomach-turning heat gorges the narrow room;
The old boy's head is stuffed full of rags;
He hears the hairs growing under his damp skin,
And, accompanied by the grave belching of buffoons,
Sometimes takes his leave, upsetting his wobbly stool...

. . . .

Et le soir, aux rayons de lune, qui lui font
Aux contours du cul des bavures de lumière,
Une ombre avec détails s'accroupit, sur un fond
De neige rose ainsi qu'une rose trémière...
Fantasque, un nez poursuit Vénus au ciel profond.

L'Orgie parisienne
ou
Paris se repeuple

Ô lâches, la voilà! dègorgez dans les gares!
Le soleil expia de ses poumons ardents
Les boulevards qu'un soir comblèrent les Barbares.
Voilà la Cité belle, assise à l'occident!

Allez! on préviendra les reflux d'incendie,
Voilà les quais! voilà les boulevards! voilà,
Sur les maisons, l'azur léger qui s'irradie,
Et qu'un soir la rougeur des bombes étoila.

Cachez les palais morts dans des niches de planches!
L'ancien jour effaré rafraîchit vos regards.
Voici le troupeau roux des tordeuses de hanches,
Soyez fous, vous serez drôles, étant hagards!

Tas de chiennes en rut mangeant des cataplasmes.
Le cri des maisons d'or vous réclame. Volez!
Mangez! voici la nuit de joie aux profonds spasmes
Qui descend dans la rue, ô buveurs désolés,

Buvez! Quand la lumière arrive intense et folle,
Fouillant à vos côtés les luxes ruisselants,
Vous n'allez pas baver, sans geste, sans parole,
Dans vos verres, les yeux perdus aux lointains blancs,

Evenings, in saliva circles
Of moonlight dribbling onto his arse,
A shadow squats, detailed against a backdrop
Of pink snow, like a hollyhock...
The weird sight of a nose pursuing planet Venus.

Parisian Orgy
or
Paris Filling Up Again

Here she is, you cowards! Pile out onto station platforms!
The sun's fierce breath has purified
The boulevards which barbarians* raped one night.
Here's the holy city, established in the West.

Go on! We'll stop old fires relighting;
Here's the riverside, the boulevards, here
The houses set against a blue sky's radiance
Which one night was spangled red with bombs.

Board up dead palaces, cosset them in wood!
Old, startled daylight cools your gaze.
Here comes the hip-wriggling red-head gang.
Be wild, you mad and gaunt comedians.

Packs of dogs on heat devouring cataplasms,
The cry from golden houses calls you. Steal!
Eat! The deeply shuddering night of joy
Comes down into the street. Oh, you desolate drinkers,

Drink! When wild, intense light streams down,
Into the rivers of luxury beside you,
You won't slobber into your glass,
With your still, mute eyes fixed on distant nothingness?

Avalez, pour la Reine aux fesses cascadantes!
Écoutez l'action des stupides hoquets
Déchirants. Écoutez sauter aux nuits ardentes
Les idiots râleux, vieillards, pantins, laquais!

Ô cœurs de saleté, bouches épouvantables,
Fonctionnez plus fort, bouches de puanteurs!
Un vin pour ces torpeurs ignobles, sur ces tables...
Vos ventres sont fondus de hontes, ô Vainqueurs!

Ouvrez votre narine aux superbes nausées!
Trempez de poisons forts les cordes de vos cous!
Sur vos nuques d'enfants baissant ses mains croisées
Le Poète vous dit: ô lâches, soyez fous!

Parce que vous fouillez le ventre de la Femme
Vous craignez d'elle encore une convulsion
Qui crie, asphyxiant votre nichée infâme
Sur sa poitrine, en une horrible pression.

Syphilitiques, fous, rois, pantins, ventriloques,
Qu'est-ce que ça peut faire à la putain Paris,
Vos âmes et vos corps, vos poisons et vos loques?
Elle se secouera de vous, hargneux pourris!

Et quand vous serez bas, geignant sur vos entrailles,
Les flancs morts, réclamant votre argent, éperdus,
La rouge courtisane aux seins gros de batailles
Loin de votre stupeur tordra ses poings ardus!

Quand tes pieds ont dansé si fort dans les colères,
Paris! quand tu reçus tant de coups de couteau,
Quand tu gis, retenant dans tes prunelles claires
Un peu de la bonté du fauve renouveau,

Ô cité douloureuse, ô cité quasi morte,
La tête et les deux seins jetés vers l' Avenir
Ouvrant sur ta pâleur ses milliards de portes,
Cité que le Passé sombre pourrait bénir:

Drink it down, for the Queen of the tumbling arse!
Hear the stupid rip of hiccups!
On fervent nights, hear the agitation
Of lunatics, lackeys, empty vessels!

Hearts of filth, god-awful mouths,
Work harder, stinking, hell-hole mouths.
Wine for these foul torpors, at these tables...
Your guts are ripped wide with shame, you Victors!

Open your nostrils to the greatest nauseas!
Soak your neck-cords in violent poisons!
Lowering clasped hands to your young necks
The Poet says: 'Cowards, be as mad as you like!'

As you're delving into Woman's belly,
You fear the wild cry of her convulsion
Which might smother you again, nestling
Squalidly on her breast, and horribly crushed.

Syphilitics, madmen, dummies, kings, ventriloquists,
Do you think that Paris—tart!—cares a rap
For your souls, your bodies, your poisons, your rags?
She'll throw you off, you foul-tempered wrecks.

And when you're laid low, just a gutful of moans,
Dead meat crying out for cash, frantic,
The red courtesan with battle-heavy breasts
Will make hard fists, far from your stupor!

When your feet danced such angry steps,
Paris! when you received such knife-wounds,
And now you lie there, a remnant of wild
Natural goodness still in your eyes,

Oh city of pain, city close to death,
Head and breasts thrust towards the Future
Which opens its million doors to your pallor,
City which a sombre Past might bless,

Corps remagnétisé pour les énormes peines,
Tu rebois donc la vie effroyable! tu sens
Sourdre le flux des vers livides en tes veines,
Et sur ton clair amour rôder les doigts glaçants!

Et ce n'est pas mauvais. Tes vers, tes vers livides
Ne gêneront pas plus ton souffle de Progrès
Que les Stryx n'éteignaient l'œil des Cariatides
Où des pleurs d'or astral tombaient des bleus degrés.

Quoique ce soit affreux de te revoir couverte
Ainsi; quoiqu'on n'ait fait jamais d'une cité
Ulcère plus puant à la Nature verte,
Le Poète te dit: 'Splendide est ta Beauté!'

L'orage t'a sacrée suprême poésie;
L'immense remuement des forces te secourt;
Ton œuvre bout, la mort gronde, Cité choisie!
Amasse les strideurs au cœur du clairon lourd.

Le Poète prendra le sanglot des Infâmes,
La haine des Forçats, la clameur des maudits;
Et ses rayons d'amour flagelleront les Femmes.
Ses strophes bondiront: voilà! voilà! bandits!

—Société, tout est rétabli:—les orgies
Pleurent leur ancien râle aux anciens lupanars:
Et les gaz en délire, aux murailles rougies,
Flambent sinistrement vers les azurs blafards!

Mai 1871.

Les Mains de Jeanne-Marie

Jeanne-Marie a des mains fortes,
Mains sombres que l'été tanna,
Mains pâles comme des mains mortes.
—Sont-ce des mains de Juana?

Body galvanized for colossal pains,
You drink again the horrible life! You feel
White worms swarm through your veins,
And icy fingers crawl across your open love!

Nor is it bad. The worms, the white worms
Won't squeeze the breath of Progress out of you,
As the Vampires of Night couldn't darken
Old splendours, cascading star-gold tears from blue skies.

Though it's grim to find you covered in this way,
Though no city ever became a more putrid
Ulcer in the face of green Nature,
The Poet says to you: 'Your beauty is a splendour.'

The storm has crowned you Poetry Supreme;
The huge stirring of forces rescues you;
City elect, your work comes to the boil, death rumbles!
Gather stridencies into your great trumpet.

The Poet will take on the sob of the Disgusting,
The Convicts' hatred, the shouts of the Damned;
His light-beams of love will lash all womankind.
His stanzas will leap: There, deal with that, you bandits!

—Society, all is restored; orgies weep their hoarse
Ancient tears in the lupanars of old;
On reddened walls, sinister gaslight leaps
In frenzy, up towards the bloodless blue.

May 1871

The Hands of Jeanne-Marie

Jeanne-Marie has strong hands,
Dark hands which summer tanned,
Hands as pale as dead hands
—Are these the hands of Juana?

Ont-elles pris les crèmes brunes
Sur les mares des voluptés?
Ont-elles trempé dans des lunes
Aux étangs de sérénités?

Ont-elles bu des cieux barbares,
Calmes sur les genoux charmants?
Ont-elles roulé des cigares
Ou trafiqué des diamants?

Sur les pieds ardents des Madones
Ont-elles fané des fleurs d'or?
C'est le sang noir des belladones
Qui dans leur paume éclate et dort.

Mains chasseresses des diptères
Dont bombinent les bleuisons
Aurorales, vers les nectaires?
Mains décanteuses de poisons?

Oh! quel Rêve les a saisies
Dans les pandiculations?
Un rêve inouï des Asies,
Des Khenghavars ou des Sions?

—Ces mains n'ont pas vendu d'oranges,
Ni bruni sur les pieds des dieux:
Ces mains n'ont pas lavé les langes
Des lourds petits enfants sans yeux.

Ce ne sont pas mains de cousine
Ni d'ouvrières aux gros fronts
Que brûle, aux bois paunt l'usine,
Un soleil ivre de goudrons.

Ce sont des ployeuses d'échines,
Des mains qui ne font jamais mal,
Plus fatales que des machines,
Plus fortes que tout un cheval!

Did they turn a creamy chocolate
On lakes of sensuality,
Did they swim among moons
In waters of serenity?

Did they drink barbaric skies,
Placed calmly on delicious knees,
Roll cigars
Or trade in diamonds?

Did they winnow golden flowers
On the Madonna's burning feet?
It's black belladonna blood
Which bursts in their palms and sleeps.

Hands which chase two-winged insects,
Whose first-light blueynotes
Rumble round the nectaries?
Hands which measure poison out?

What Dream has caught them, stretched in
Their pandiculation?
Bizarre dream of Asias,
Khenghavars* or Sions?*

—These hands have sold no oranges,
Nor darkened at the feet of gods;
These hands have washed no rags
Of heavy eyeless children.

These aren't the hands of cousins
Or working women whose broad brows
Are scorched by a sun blind-drunk on tar,
Down in the woods that stink of factories.

These are hands that bend backbones,
Hands that never cause harm,
More deadly than machines,
Stronger than a horse.

Remuant comme des fournaises,
Et secouant tous ses frissons,
Leur chair chante des Marseillaises
Et jamais les Eleisons!

Ça serrerait vos cous, ô femmes
Mauvaises, ça broierait vos mains,
Femmes nobles, vos mains infâmes
Pleines de blancs et de carmins.

L'éclat de ces mains amoureuses
Tourne le crâne des brebis!
Dans leurs phalanges savoureuses
Le grand soleil met un rubis!

Une tache de populace
Les brunit comme un sein d'hier;
Le dos de ces Mains est la place
Qu'en baisa tout Révolté fier!

Elles ont pâli, merveilleuses,
Au grand soleil d'amour chargé,
Sur le bronze des mitrailleuses
A travers Paris insurgé!

Ah! quelquefois, ô Mains sacrées,
A vos poings, Mains où tremblent nos
Lèvres jamais désenivrées,
Crie une chaîne aux clairs anneaux!

Et c'est un soubresaut étrange
Dans nos êtres, quand, quelquefois,
On veut vous déhâler, Mains d'ange,
En vous faisant saigner les doigts!

Active as furnaces,
Shaking like tremors, their flesh
Sings out the Marseillaise,
And not one sole Eleison!*

These hands would break your necks, bad
Women, crush your hands,
Noble ladies, your vile hands
Covered in carmine and white.

The radiance of these loving hands
Turns the skulls of tiny lambs!
On each savoury finger-joint
The full sun puts a ruby.

A splash of populace
Stains them brown, like yesterday's breast;
On the back of these Hands every
Proud Revolutionary placed a kiss!

These marvellous hands have paled
In the huge sun filled with love,
On the bronze muzzle of machine-guns,
Everywhere in Paris rising up!

Ah, sometimes, sacred Hands,
Round your wrists, Hands brushed by
Our ever-drunken trembling lips,
A chain of brilliant links cries out.

Then suddenly our whole being gives
A start when some people
Try to whiten your angelic Hands,
By making all your fingers bleed!

Les Sœurs de charité

Le jeune homme dont l'œil est brillant, la peau brune,
Le beau corps de vingt ans qui devrait aller nu,
Et qu'eût, le front cerclé de cuivre, sous la lune
Adoré, dans la Perse un Génie inconnu,

Impétueux avec des douceurs virginales
Et noires, fier de ses premiers entêtements,
Pareils aux jeunes mers, pleurs de nuits estivales
Qui se retournent sur des lits de diamants;

Le jeune homme, devant les laideurs de ce monde
Tressaille dans son cœur largement irrité
Et plein de la blessure éternelle et profonde,
Se prend à désirer sa sœur de charité.

Mais, ô Femme, monceau d'entrailles, pitié douce,
Tu n'es jamais la Sœur de charité, jamais,
Ni regard noir, ni ventre où dort une ombre rousse
Ni doigts légers, ni seins splendidement formés.

Aveugle irréveillée aux immenses prunelles
Tout notre embrassement n'est qu'une question:
C'est toi qui pends à nous, porteuse de mamelles;
Nous te berçons, charmante et grave Passion.

Tes haines, tes torpeurs fixes, tes défaillances
Et les brutalités souffertes autrefois
Tu nous rends tout, ô Nuit pourtant sans malveillances,
Comme un excès de sang épanché tous les mois.

—Quand la femme, portée un instant, l'épouvante,
Amour, appel de vie et chanson d'action
Viennent la Muse verte et la Justice ardente
Le déchirer de leur auguste obsession.

Sisters of Charity

The young man with bright eyes, dark skin,
Copper-laurelled brow, twenty-year old beauty
Meant to go naked, which an unknown Persian
Genie might have adored by moonlight,

Impetuous youth, glowing darkly virginal,
Proud of his first obsessions,
Like young seas, tears on a summer's night,
Rolling on their bed of diamonds.

Facing the world's ugliness,
The young man's irritated heart shudders;
Scored deep by a wound which never heals,
He starts to desire his sister of charity.

But—Women, heap of innards, sweet softness,
You're never the Sister of Charity, never,
Nor dark look, nor belly where an auburn shadow sleeps,
Nor lightest touch, nor splendid breasts.

Sleeping blindness with enormous eyes,
Our whole embrace is just a question;
You bend over us, you, breast-bearer,
And we cradle you, grave and charming Passion.

Your hates, torpors, failings,
Brutalities suffered in the past,
You give us back everything, Night of no ill-will,
Like a monthly overflow of blood.

When Woman, briefly excited, frightens him
With love—that assertion of life, that song of action—
Then the Green Muse and burning Justice come
To tear him apart with lofty obsession.

Ah! sans cesse altéré des splendeurs et des calmes,
Délaissé des deux Sœurs implacables, geignant
Avec tendresse après la science aux bras almes
Il porte à la nature en fleur son front saignant.

Mais la noire alchimie et les saintes études
Répugnent au blessé, sombre savant d'orgueil;
Il sent marcher sur lui d'atroces solitudes.
Alors, et toujours beau, sans dégoût du cercueil,

Qu'il croie aux vastes fins, Rêves ou Promenades
Immenses, à travers les nuits de Vérité
Et t'appelle en son âme et ses membres malades
Ô Mort mystérieuse, ô Sœur de charité.

Juin 1871.

L'Homme juste

[................................]

Le Juste restait droit sur ses hanches solides:
Un rayon lui dorait l'épaule; des sueurs
Me prirent: 'Tu veux voir rutiler les bolides?
Et, debout, écouter bourdonner les flueurs
D'astres lactés, et les essaims d'astéroïdes?

'Par des farces de nuit ton front est épié,
Ô Juste! Il faut gagner un toit. Dis ta prière,
La bouche dans ton drap doucement expié;
Et si quelque égaré choque ton ostiaire,
Dis: Frère, va plus loin, je suis estropié!'

Et le Juste restait debout, dans l'épouvante
Bleuâtre des gazons après le soleil mort:
'Alors, mettrais-tu tes genouillères en vente,
Ô vieillard? Pèlerin sacré! Barde d'Armor!
Pleureur des Oliviers! Main que la pitié gante!

Always thirsting for splendour and calm,
Abandoned by the two unyielding Sisters,
Whimpering softly for knowledge, its embrace of life,
He offers full-blown nature his bloodstained brow.

But dark alchemy, saintly study
Repel the wounded boy, dark expert in pride;
He feels atrocious solitude bear down on him.
Then, beautiful still, untroubled by the grave,

Let him believe in vast purposes, Immense Walks
And Dreams, across Nights of Truth,
And call you into his soul, his ailing limbs—
You, mysterious Death, you sister of charity!

June 1871

The Just Man

[................................]

The Just Man stood upright on firm hips,
One shoulder gold with sun; I started
Sweating: 'You want to see meteors glow,
Stand and hear the flow of milky stars
Hum, the swarms of asteroids?

'Night's shenanigans, Just Man, have marked
Your card! Find a roof. Say your prayer,
Mouth finding sweet atonement in your sheet;
And if some lost soul knocks at your door,
Say: "Brother, try elsewhere, I'm lame!" '

And the Just Man stood there, in the blue
Shock of lawns after the sun died:
'So then, would you sell your knee-pads,
Old man? Holy pilgrim! Breton bard!*
Weeper in the Olive Grove! Hand gloved in pity!

'Barbe de la famille et poing de la cité,
Croyant très doux: ô cœur tombé dans les calices,
Majestés et vertus, amour et cécité,
Juste! plus bête et plus dégoûtant que les lices!
Je suis celui qui souffre et qui s'est révolté!

'Et ça me fait pleurer sur mon ventre, ô stupide,
Et bien rire, l'espoir fameux de ton pardon!
Je suis maudit, tu sais! Je suis soûl, fou, livide,
Ce que tu veux! Mais va te coucher, voyons donc,
Juste! Je ne veux rien à ton cerveau torpide!

'C'est toi le Juste, enfin, le Juste! C'est assez!
C'est vrai que ta tendresse et ta raison sereines
Reniflent dans la nuit comme des cétacés!
Que tu te fais proscrire, et dégoises des thrènes
Sur d'effroyables becs de canne fracassés!

'Et c'est toi l'œil de Dieu! le lâche! Quand les plantes
Froides des pieds divins passeraient sur mon cou,
Tu es lâche! Ô ton front qui fourmille de lentes!
Socrates et Jésus, Saints et Justes, dégoût!
Respectez le Maudit suprême aux nuits sanglantes!'

J'avais crié cela sur la terre, et la nuit
Calme et blanche occupait les Cieux pendant ma fièvre.
Je relevai mon front: le fantôme avait fui,
Emportant l'ironie atroce de ma lèvre...
—Vents nocturnes! venez au Maudit! Parlez-lui!

Cependant que, silencieux sous les pilastres
D'azur, allongeant les comètes et les nœuds
D'univers, remuement énorme sans désastres,
L'ordre, éternel veilleur, rame aux cieux lumineux
Et de sa drague en feu laisse filer des astres!

'Pater famili-ass,* the city's fist,
Gentle believer; heart cupped in chalices,
Majesty, virtues, love, blindness,
Just Man! more stupid and disgusting than a bitch!
I'm the one who suffers, the one who rebelled!

'Stupid, on my stomach, I weep and laugh
At it, the famous hope of your forgiveness!
I'm damned, you know! Drunk, mad, drained white,
What you want! But off to bed with you,
Just Man! I want none of your brain-dead wits.

'The Just Man is you, and that's enough!
It's true your serene tenderness and reason
Void their blow-holes in the night, like whales.
True you get yourself banished, spout threnodies
To ghastly broken door-locks.

'You, you're the eye of God. Coward! Should the cold
Footprints of divinity walk across my neck,
You're a coward! Your brow teems with hatching lice.
Jesuses and all the Socrates,* Saints, Just Men, disgust!
Respect the One who's most damned, on nights of blood!'

I yelled this on earth, and calm, white
Night occupied the sky as my fever raged.
I lifted my head: the ghost had fled,
Taking off my words' awful irony...
—Winds of night, come to the Damned One! Speak to him

As, silent beneath azure portals,
Laying out comets and the universe's
Arcs and curves, enormous heaving, no disasters,
That eternal watchman Order rows down luminous
Skies, and from his burning dragnet lets stars shoot.

Ah qu'il s'en aille, lui, la gorge cravatée
De honte, ruminant toujours mon ennui, doux
Comme le sucre sur la denture gâtée
—Tel que la chienne après l'assaut des fiers toutous,
Léchant son flanc d'où pend une entraille emportée

Qu'il dise charités crasseuses et progrès...
—J'exècre tous ces yeux de Chinois [...] daines,
Mais qui chante: nana, comme un tas d'enfants près
De mourir, idiots doux aux chansons soudaines:
Ô Justes, nous chierons dans vos ventres de grès.

Les Poètes de sept ans

A M. P. Demeny.

Et la Mère, fermant le livre du devoir,
S'en allait satisfaite et très fière, sans voir,
Dans les yeux bleus et sous le front plein d'éminences,
L'âme de son enfant livrée aux répugnances.

Tout le jour il suait d'obéissance; très
Intelligent; pourtant des tics noirs, quelques traits,
Semblaient prouver en lui d'âcres hypocrisies.
Dans l'ombre des couloirs aux tentures moisies,
En passant il tirait la langue, les deux poings
A l'aine, et dans ses yeux fermés voyait des points.
Une porte s'ouvrait sur le soir: à la lampe
On le voyait, là-haut, qui râlait sur la rampe,
Sous un golfe de jour pendant du toit. L'été
Surtout, vaincu, stupide, il était entêté
A se renfermer dans la fraîcheur des latrines:
Il pensait là, tranquille et livrant ses narines.

Quand, lavé des odeurs du jour, le jardinet
Derrière la maison, en hiver, s'illunait,
Gisant au pied d'un mur, enterré dans la marne
Et pour des visions écrasant son œil darne,

Let that one go, wearing round his neck the choker
Of shame, still musing on my disgust, sweet
As sugar lodged in rotting teeth.
—Like a mongrel after the pedigree's assault,
Licking wounds her insides hang from,

Let him hold forth on squalid charity and progress...
—I scorn all those eyes of the fat Chinaman
Singing 'nanana', like a bunch of children soon
To die, simple idiots fluting sudden songs:
O you Just Man, we'll shit in your earthenware guts.

Seven-year-old Poets

To P. Demeny*

And the Mother,* shutting his homework,
Went off proud, well-pleased and oblivious
To the revolted heart of her boy,
In those blue eyes, on that raging brow.

All day he sweated obedience; such
Intelligence; but those give-away
Dark tics showed a sharp hypocrisy.
In the mildew gloom of corridors
He'd run by, sticking out his tongue, fists
In crotch, eyes shut tight, seeing stars.
A door opened onto evening; up
There among the banisters he'd rant
And rave in a pool of ceiling light.
Overwhelmed by summer, he'd stomp off
To the cool latrine, lock himself in,
Bent on quiet, open-nostril thought.

Some nights when the garden-patch behind
The house was washed clean by winter moons
He'd lie by a wall, covered in clay,
Stabbing his cod-eye to see what he

Il écoutait grouiller les galeux espaliers.
Pitié! Ces enfants seuls étaient ses familiers
Qui, chétifs, fronts nus, œil déteignant sur la joue,
Cachant de maigres doigts jaunes et noirs de boue
Sous des habits puant la foire et tout vieillots,
Conversaient avec la douceur des idiots!
Et si, l'ayant surpris à des pitiés immondes,
Sa mère s'effrayait; les tendresses, profondes,
De l'enfant se jetaient sur cet étonnement.
C'était bon. Elle avait le bleu regard,—qui ment!

A sept ans, il faisait des romans, sur la vie
Du grand désert, où luit la Liberté ravie,
Forêts, soleils, rives, savanes!—Il s'aidait
De journaux illustrés où, rouge, il regardait
Des Espagnoles rire et des Italiennes.
Quand venait, l'œil brun, folle, en robes d'indiennes,
—Huit ans,—la fille des ouvriers d'à côté,
La petite brutale, et qu'elle avait sauté,
Dans un coin, sur son dos, en secouant ses tresses,
Et qu'il était sous elle, il lui mordait les fesses,
Car elle ne portait jamais de pantalons;
—Et, par elle meurtri des poings et des talons
Remportait les saveurs de sa peau dans sa chambre.

Il craignait les blafards dimanches de décembre,
Où, pommadé, sur un guéridon d'acajou,
Il lisait une Bible à la tranche vert-chou;
Des rêves l'oppressaient chaque nuit dans l'alcôve.
Il n'aimait pas Dieu; mais les hommes, qu'au soir fauve,
Noirs, en blouse, il voyait rentrer dans le faubourg
Où les crieurs, en trois roulements de tambour,
Font autour des édits rire et gronder les foules.
—Il rêvait la prairie amoureuse, où des houles
Lumineuses, parfums sains, pubescences d'or,
Font leur remuement calme et prennent leur essor!

Might see, hearing the stunted trees growl.
Pity! His only companions were
Sickly, crew-cut kids, bland-eyed, pale-cheeked,
Hiding bone-yellow filth-covered shit-
Stinking fingers inside their old rags,
And talking as sweetly as cretins.
And if, catching him in flagrante,
The mother was frightened, the boy bathed
Her astonishment in tenderness.
Good, she'd received the blue look—which lies!

Seven years old, writing romances
About the Great Desert, rapturous
Light of Freedom, forests, savannahs,
Suns! He'd plunder magazines, looking
At laughing Latin girls, and blushing.
When the sloe-eyed eight-year-old daughter
Of the workers next door came in, wild
And savage in her cotton frock, jumped
On him suddenly, onto his back,
Tossing her hair, he'd bite her buttocks—
She didn't believe in underwear.
Bruised all over by her heels and fists
He took her taste back into his room.

He'd fear December's ghostly Sundays.
Hair smarmed down, at a mahogany
Table, he'd read a green-edged Bible.
Dreams crowded him each night in his bed.
He had no time for God, but rather
Dirt-stained working men in overalls,
Homeward-bound on evenings of huge light
Through the criers' shouts and drums.
He'd dream of fields of love where swelling
Light, wholesome smells, and gold pubescent
Down calmly sway and take to the wing.

Et comme il savourait surtout les sombres choses,
Quand, dans la chambre nue aux persiennes closes,
Haute et bleue, âcrement prise d'humidité,
Il lisait son roman sans cesse médité,
Plein de lourds ciels ocreux et de forêts noyées,
De fleurs de chair aux bois sidérals déployées,
Vertige, écroulements, déroutes et pitié!
—Tandis que se faisait la rumeur du quartier,
En bas,—seul, et couché sur des pièces de toile
Écrue, et pressentant violemment la voile!

26 mai 1871. A. R.

Les Pauvres à l'église

Parqués entre des bancs de chêne, aux coins d'église
Qu'attiédit puamment leur souffle, tous leurs yeux
Vers le chœur ruisselant d'orrie et la maîtrise
Aux vingt gueules gueulant les cantiques pieux;

Comme un parfum de pain humant l'odeur de cire,
Heureux, humiliés comme des chiens battus,
Les Pauvres au bon Dieu, le patron et le sire,
Tendent leurs oremus risibles et têtus.

Aux femmes, c'est bien bon de faire des bancs lisses,
Après les six jours noirs où Dieu les fait souffrir!
Elles bercent, tordus dans d'étranges pelisses,
Des espèces d'enfants qui pleurent à mourir.

Leurs seins crasseux dehors, ces mangeuses de soupe,
Une prière aux yeux et ne priant jamais,
Regardent parader mauvaisement un groupe
De gamines avec leurs chapeaux déformés.

Dehors, le froid, la faim, l'homme en ribote:
C'est bon. Encore une heure; après, les maux sans noms!
—Cependant, alentour, geint, nasille, chuchote
Une collection de vieilles à fanons:

How he relished dark things, above all
When in his tall, bare, blue and empty
Shuttered room, sharp with humidity,
He read his endlessly planned romance
Full of heavy ochre skies and drowned
Forests, flesh-flowers in star-studded woods,
Spiral spins, routs, collapse and pity!
—While down in the street the noise went on,
He lay alone on rough sheets, thinking
Violent thoughts of getting under sail!*

26 May 1871. A. R.

Poor People in Church

Parked among oak pews, in church corners
Warmed by their vile breath, all eyes as one
Turned towards the chancel, dripping gold, and the throats
Of twenty choristers bawling pious hymns,

Soaking up the smell of wax as if it was new bread,
Happy and cowed as whipped dogs,
The Poor raise up to God, our Lord and Master,
Risible prayers which don't let up.

Female buttocks like to wear the benches smooth
After the six dark days God makes them suffer!
In funny coats they try to cradle
What seem like children, howling unto death.

Their dirty dugs exposed, these soup-swallowers,
A prayer in their eyes but never in their souls,
Watch an evil bunch of little girls display
Themselves, in their misshapen hats.

Outside: cold, hunger, rabble-rousing drunks:
That's fine. One more hour, then pain without name!
—Meanwhile, all around, old dears sniff, whine, complain,
Their necks as loose as turkeys'.

Ces effarés y sont et ces épileptiques
Dont on se détournait hier aux carrefours;
Et, fringalant du nez dans des missels antiques,
Ces aveugles qu'un chien introduit dans les cours.

Et tous, bavant la foi mendiante et stupide,
Récitent la complainte infinie à Jésus
Qui rêve en haut, jauni par le vitrail livide,
Loin des maigres mauvais et des méchants pansus,

Loin des senteurs de viande et d'étoffes moisies,
Farce prostrée et sombre aux gestes repoussants;
—Et l'oraison fleurit d'expressions choisies,
Et les mysticités prennent des tons pressants,

Quand, des nefs où périt le soleil, plis de soie
Banals, sourires verts, les Dames des quartiers
Distingués,—ô Jésus!—les malades du foie
Font baiser leurs longs doigts jaunes aux bénitiers.

A. Rimbaud
1871

Ce qu'on dit au Poète à propos de fleurs

A Monsieur Théodore de Banville

I

Ainsi, toujours, vers l'azur noir
Où tremble la mer des topazes,
Fonctionneront dans ton soir
Les Lys, ces clystères d'extases!

A notre époque de sagous,
Quand les Plantes sont travailleuses,
Le Lys boira les bleus dégoûts
Dans tes Proses religieuses!

Crowds of the crazed, those epileptics
Neatly ignored in the street yesterday;
And, noses scavenging old prayer-books,* the blind
Guided into courtyards by a dog.

And all dribble their stupid, pleading faith,
Their non-stop supplication to Jesus
Up on high, stained yellow by the glass, dreaming,
Far from skeletal sinners, pot-bellied rogues,

Far from the smell of meat and mouldy cloths,
The dark, ugly grovellings of this puppet-show;
—And the litany blooms with choice phrases,
Insistent mysticities;

Then, from the nave where sunlight expires, silly
Silks, green smiles, the Ladies from the smart part
Of town—Jesus wept!—liver complainants dip long
Yellow fingers in the stoup of holy water.

A. Rimbaud
1871

What the Poet is Told on the Subject of Flowers

To M. Théodore de Banville

I

On and on like so, in the azure black
Where a topaz ocean trembles,
In your sky there'll be the functioning
Of lilies, those enemas of ecstasy!

In this, our tapioca age
When plants do work,
The Lily will drink blue distaste
From your religious bits of Prose!

—Le lys de monsieur de Kerdrel,
Le Sonnet de mil huit cent trente,
Le Lys qu'on donne au Ménestrel
Avec l'œillet et l'amarante!

Des lys! Des lys! On n'en voit pas!
Et dans ton Vers, tel que les manches
Des Pécheresses aux doux pas,
Toujours frissonnent ces fleurs blanches!

Toujours, Cher, quand tu prends un bain,
Ta Chemise aux aisselles blondes
Se gonfle aux brises du matin
Sur les myosotis immondes!

L'amour ne passe à tes octrois
Que les Lilas,—ô balançoires!
Et les Violettes du Bois,
Crachats sucrés des Nymphes noires!...

II

Ô Poètes, quand vous auriez
Les Roses, les Roses soufflées,
Rouges sur tiges de lauriers,
Et de mille octaves enflées!

Quand BANVILLE en ferait neiger,
Sanguinolentes, tournoyantes,
Pochant l'œil fou de l'étranger
Aux lectures mal bienveillantes!

De vos forêts et de vos prés,
Ô très paisibles photographes!
La Flore est diverse à peu près
Comme des bouchons de carafes!

Royalist Kerdrel's* fleur-de-lis,
The Sonnet of 1830,
The lily that crowns the Bard,
With carnation and amaranth!

Lilies! Lilies! None to be seen!
In your Verse, like the sleeves
Of soft-treading Sinner Women,
These white flowers tremble still!

Respected Sir, always when you take a bath
Your Shirt of the yellow armpits
Swells up in the morning air
Over revolting forget-me-nots.

Love allows only Lilies
Into its tariff-zone—such cant!
And wild woodland violets,
The sugar-spit of black larva-nymphs!...

II

Poets, what if you had
Roses, blown Roses,
Red on laurel stems,
Swelling into endless eight-foot lines!

BANVILLE's roses come down like snow,
In flurries, specked with blood,
Smack in the unversed reader's wild eye,
Generously unforgiving.

In your fields and forests,
Peaceful photographers!—
The Flora's about as diverse
As a row of bottle-corks.

Toujours les végétaux Français,
Hargneux, phtisiques, ridicules,
Où le ventre des chiens bassets
Navigue en paix, aux crépuscules;

Toujours, après d'affreux dessins
De Lotos bleus ou d'Hélianthes,
Estampes roses, sujets saints
Pour de jeunes communiantes!

L'Ode Açoka cadre avec la
Strophe en fenêtre de lorette;
Et de lourds papillons d'éclat
Fientent sur la Pâquerette.

Vieilles verdures, vieux galons!
Ô croquignoles végétales!
Fleurs fantasques des vieux Salons!
—Aux hannetons, pas aux crotales,

Ces poupards végétaux en pleurs
Que Grandville eût mis aux lisières,
Et qu'allaitèrent de couleurs
De méchants astres à visières!

Oui, vos bavures de pipeaux
Font de précieuses glucoses!
—Tas d'œufs frits dans de vieux chapeaux,
Lys, Açokas, Lilas et Roses!...

III

Ô blanc Chasseur, qui cours sans bas
A travers le Pâtis panique,
Ne peux-tu pas, ne dois-tu pas
Connaître un peu ta botanique?

The vegetable-minded French, always
Peevish, chesty, ridiculous;
Their low-slung bassets quietly
Mapping the ground.

Always seeking frightful designs
Of sunflowers or blue Lotuses,
Pink printed cards, holy scenes
For young girls at their First Communion.

The Asoka* Ode squares with
Stanzas like Lorettine glass;
Heavy, brilliant butterflies
Leave droppings on the Daisy.

Old greenery, old bits of rag!
Vegetable nibbles!
Bizarre flowers of old Salons!
—Meant for beetles, not for snakes,

Those blubbing vegetable baby-dolls
Which Grandville* would have crayoned in,
Dolls that gulped the coloured milk
Of vicious vizored stars!

Yes, the panpipes' pulings
Make priceless glucoses!
—Fried eggs piled in old hats,
Lilies, Asokas, Lilacs, Roses!...

III

You, White Hunter, running barefoot
Over Panic Pastures,
You ought to know
Your botany much better.

Tu ferais succéder, je crains,
Aux Grillons roux les Cantharides,
L'or des Rios au bleu des Rhins,
Bref, aux Norwèges les Florides:

Mais, Cher, l'Art n'est plus, maintenant,
—C'est la vérité,—de permettre
A l'Eucalyptus étonnant
Des constrictors d'un hexamètre;

Là!... Comme si les Acajous
Ne servaient, même en nos Guyanes,
Qu'aux cascades des sapajous,
Au lourd délire des lianes!

—En somme, une Fleur, Romarin
Ou Lys, vive ou morte, vaut-elle
Un excrément d'oiseau marin?
Vaut-elle un seul pleur de chandelle?

—Et j'ai dit ce que je voulais!
Toi, même assis là-bas, dans une
Cabane de bambous,—volets
Clos, tentures de perse brune,—

Tu torcherais des floraisons
Dignes d'Oises extravagantes!...
—Poète! ce sont des raisons
Non moins risibles qu'arrogantes!...

IV

Dis, non les pampas printaniers
Noirs d'épouvantables révoltes,
Mais les tabacs, les cotonniers!
Dis les exotiques récoltes!

You'd replace the russet cricket
With the blister-fly, I fear,
The blues of Rhines with Rio gold—
Floridas in place of every Norway.

But, Respected Sir, the truth is
Art's no more a matter of
Hexameter boas constricting
Fantastic Eucalyptuses;

As if Mahoganies
Were only (even in our Guianas)
Good for airborne monkeys,
The heavy delirium of lianas!

—Is a flower, Rosemary,
Lily, live or dead, worth
A single piece of seabird shit?
A single tear dripping from a candle?

—What I said I meant.
You, if you were there, seated
In a bamboo hut—shutters
Closed, brown chintz drapery—

You'd knock out florilegiums
Lush as Oise* pasturelands!...
Poet, this way's not just arrogant,
It's laughable!...

IV

Don't speak of springtime pampas
Dark with dreadful revolt,
Speak of tobaccos, cotton-fields,
Exotic harvest-times!

Dis, front blanc que Phébus tanna,
De combien de dollars se rente
Pedro Velasquez, Habana;
Incague la mer de Sorrente

Où vont les Cygnes par milliers;
Que tes strophes soient des réclames
Pour l'abatis des mangliers
Fouillés des hydres et des lames!

Ton quatrain plonge aux bois sanglants
Et revient proposer aux Hommes
Divers sujets de sucres blancs,
De pectoraires et de gommes!

Sachons par Toi si les blondeurs
Des Pics neigeux, vers les Tropiques,
Sont ou des insectes pondeurs
Ou des lichens microscopiques!

Trouve, ô Chasseur, nous le voulons,
Quelques garances parfumées
Que la Nature en pantalons
Fasse éclore!—pour nos Armées!

Trouve, aux abords du Bois qui dort,
Les fleurs, pareilles à des mufles,
D'où bavent des pommades d'or
Sur les cheveux sombres des Buffles!

Trouve, aux prés fous, où sur le Bleu
Tremble l'argent des pubescences,
Des Calices pleins d'Œufs de feu
Qui cuisent parmi les essences!

Trouve des Chardons cotonneux
Dont dix ânes aux yeux de braises
Travaillent à filer les nœuds!
Trouve des Fleurs qui soient des chaises!

White face tanned by Phoebus,*
Say how many dollars
Pedro Velasquez of Havana's worth;
Fill the Sea of Sorrento*

With the shit of its myriad swans;
Make your stanzas advertise
Mangrove-swamps like offal-piles
Tangled with hydras and sheeted with water!

Your quatrain plunges into bloody woods
And returns to offer Man
A host of subjects: white sugars,
Things for the throat, rubber!

Tell us if the blondnesses
Of snowy peaks near Tropics
Are insects laying eggs,
Or microscopic lichens!

Hunter, we want you to find
Fragrant madder-wort for us,
Which Nature will dye red—
Trousers for our Infantry.

Find, at the Sleeping Wood's edge,
Flowers like slobbering snouts
Dribbling golden pomade
On the murky hair of buffaloes!

In mad fields where the silver
Of pubescence trembles on Blue,
Find Chalices filled with eggs of fire
Cooking among essences!

Find cotton-down Thistles,
Ropes that ten hot-eye
Donkeys try to slip!
Find flowers that could be chairs!

Oui, trouve au cœur des noirs filons
Des fleurs presque pierres,—fameuses!—
Qui vers leurs durs ovaires blonds
Aient des amygdales gemmeuses!

Sers-nous, ô Farceur, tu le peux,
Sur un plat de vermeil splendide
Des ragoûts de Lys sirupeux
Mordant nos cuillers Alfénide!

V

Quelqu'un dira le grand Amour,
Voleur des Sombres Indulgences:
Mais ni Renan, ni le chat Murr
N'ont vu les Bleus Thyrses immenses!

Toi, fais jouer dans nos torpeurs,
Par les parfums les hystéries;
Exalte-nous vers des candeurs
Plus candides que les Maries...

Commerçant! colon! médium!
Ta Rime sourdra, rose ou blanche,
Comme un rayon de sodium,
Comme un caoutchouc qui s'épanche!

De tes noirs Poèmes,—Jongleur!
Blancs, verts, et rouges dioptriques,
Que s'évadent d'étranges fleurs
Et des papillons électriques!

Voilà! c'est le Siècle d'enfer!
Et les poteaux télégraphiques
Vont orner,—lyre aux chants de fer,
Tes omoplates magnifiques!

Yes, deep in dark seams, find
Flowers that could be famous stones
With hard, light-coloured
Goitre-studded ovaries!

Joker, serve us up—your way,
In a splendid purple dish—
Syrupy compotes of Lily fierce enough
To eat the alloy off our spoons!

V

Someone will tell of the Great Love,
Usurper of dark Indulgences:
But neither Renan* nor Tomcat Murr*
Has seen the huge blue Thyrsuses!*

You, set the hysteria of fragrances
To work among our torpitudes;
Exalt us upwards towards candours
Whiter than the Marys...

Tradesmen! Colonial! Medium!
Your rhyme will spurt up, pink or white,
Like a whoosh of sodium,
Or a spread of oozing rubber.

Minstrel, let strange flowers
And electric butterflies—
Refractive reds, whites, greens—
Flutter from your black Poems!

There! It's the Century of hell!
And telegraph-poles, like singing
Steel lyres, will grace
Your splendid shoulder-blades!

Surtout, rime une version
Sur le mal des pommes de terre!
—Et, pour la composition
De Poèmes pleins de mystère

Qu'on doive lire de Tréguier
A Paramaribo, rachète
Des Tomes de Monsieur Figuier,
—Illustrés!—chez Monsieur Hachette!

Alcide Bava.

14 juillet 1871 A. R.

Les Premières Communions

I

Vraiment, c'est bête, ces églises des villages
Où quinze laids marmots encrassant les piliers
Écoutent, grasseyant les divins babillages,
Un noir grotesque dont fermentent les souliers:
Mais le soleil éveille à travers des feuillages
Les vieilles couleurs des vitraux irréguliers.

La pierre sent toujours la terre maternelle.
Vous verrez des monceaux de ces cailloux terreux
Dans la campagne en rut qui frémit solennelle
Portant près des blés lourds, dans les sentiers ocreux,
Ces arbrisseaux brûlés où bleuit la prunelle,
Des nœuds de mûriers noirs et de rosiers fuireux.

Tous les cent ans on rend ces granges respectables
Par un badigeon d'eau bleue et de lait caillé:
Si des mysticités grotesques sont notables
Près de la Notre-Dame ou du Saint empaillé,
Des mouches sentant bon l'auberge et les étables
Se gorgent de cire au plancher ensoleillé.

Especially, give an account
—In rhyme—of potato-blight!
—And, to put together
Poems full of mystery,

To be read from Tréguier*
To Paramaribo,* you should obtain
More of Figuier's* illustrated tomes,
Which may be ordered from Hachette!*

Alcide Bava*

14 July 1871 A. R.

First Communions

I

Really, too stupid, those village churches
Where fifteen ugly brats besmirching the pillars
Listen to the Bible-babble uvulated
By a freak in black, wearing rotted shoes:
But through the leaves the sun wakes up
Old colours in uneven windows.

The stone smells always of mother earth.
You'll see on top of piles of earthy stones,
In the rutting countryside's solemn shiver,
Hard by the heavy corn, in ochre lanes,
Scorched shrubs of blue sloes,
Blackberry tangles and dog-rose.

Every hundred years, these barns are spruced up
With a mix of blue water and sour milk.
While grotesque mysticities command attention
Around a Madonna or a stuffed Saint,
Flies smelling sweetly of stables and inns
Are heady with wax from a sun-drenched floor.

L'enfant se doit surtout à la maison, famille
Des soins naïfs, des bons travaux abrutissants;
Ils sortent, oubliant que la peau leur fourmille
Où le Prêtre du Christ plaqua ses doigts puissants.
On paie au Prêtre un toit ombré d'une charmille
Pour qu'il laisse au soleil tous ces fronts brunissants.

Le premier habit noir, le plus beau jour de tartes,
Sous le Napoléon ou le Petit Tambour
Quelque enluminure où les Josephs et les Marthes
Tirent la langue avec un excessif amour
Et que joindront, au jour de science, deux cartes,
Ces seuls doux souvenirs lui restent du grand Jour.

Les filles vont toujours à l'église, contentes
De s'entendre appeler garces par les garçons
Qui font du genre après messe ou vêpres chantantes.
Eux qui sont destinés au chic des garnisons
Ils narguent au café les maisons importantes
Blousés neuf, et gueulant d'effroyables chansons.

Cependant le Curé choisit pour les enfances
Des dessins; dans son clos, les vêpres dites, quand
L'air s'emplit du lointain nasillement des danses
Il se sent, en dépit des célestes défenses,
Les doigts de pied ravis et le mollet marquant...

—La Nuit vient, noir pirate aux cieux d'or débarquant.

II

Le Prêtre a distingué parmi les catéchistes,
Congrégés des Faubourgs ou des Riches Quartiers,
Cette petite fille inconnue, aux yeux tristes,
Front jaune. Les parents semblent de doux portiers.
'Au grand Jour, le marquant parmi les Catéchistes,
Dieu fera sur ce front neiger ses bénitiers.'

Mostly, the child's duty is to home, to the family
Of simple cares and good mind-numbing work;
They leave, putting out of mind their skin bristling
Where the Priest of Christ placed strong fingers.
The Priest gets gratis his arbour-shaded roof,
So he can let all these faces burn in the sun.

The first black suit; the special pastry day;
Beneath *Napoleon* or *The Little Drummer Boy*
Some picture of Joseph or Martha,
Tongues hanging out in a surfeit of love;
On the Day of Knowledge, two maps will be added,
The sole warm memories they'll have of that great day.

The girls always go to church, happy to hear
Themselves called sluts after Mass or Evensong
By boys who think they have style.
Those who one day will taste the *chic*
Of barrack-rooms now taunt the toffs in cafés,
Sporting new shirts, chanting filthy songs.

Meanwhile the Pastor chooses pictures
For the young; in his fastness, when prayers are done
And the air fills with distant snatches of a dance,
Never mind what Heaven says, he feels
His toes tingle with pleasure, his foot tap the beat—

And Night comes, black pirate on a sky of gold.

II

Among the catechists who've gathered
From Faubourgs and Smart Districts, the Priest's spotted
This little unknown girl with sad eyes under
Sallow brow. Her parents might be quiet janitors.
'On the Great Day, choosing her from all the catechists,
God will shower her with Blessings, like snow.'

III

La veille du grand Jour, l'enfant se fait malade.
Mieux qu'à l'Église haute aux funèbres rumeurs,
D'abord le frisson vient,—le lit n'étant pas fade—
Un frisson surhumain qui retourne: 'Je meurs...'

Et, comme un vol d'amour fait à ses sœurs stupides,
Elle compte, abattue et les mains sur son cœur,
Les Anges, les Jésus et ses Vierges nitides
Et, calmement, son âme a bu tout son vainqueur.

Adonaï!... —Dans les terminaisons latines,
Des cieux moirés de vert baignent les Fronts vermeils
Et tachés du sang pur des célestes poitrines
De grands linges neigeux tombent sur les soleils!

—Pour ses virginités présentes et futures
Elle mord aux fraîcheurs de ta Rémission,
Mais plus que les lys d'eau, plus que les confitures
Tes pardons sont glacés, ô Reine de Sion!

IV

Puis la Vierge n'est plus que la vierge du livre.
Les mystiques élans se cassent quelquefois...
Et vient la pauvreté des images, que cuivre
L'ennui, l'enluminure atroce et les vieux bois;

Des curiosités vaguement impudiques
Épouvantent le rêve aux chastes bleuités
Qui s'est surpris autour des célestes tuniques,
Du linge dont Jésus voile ses nudités.

Elle veut, elle veut, pourtant, l'âme en détresse,
Le front dans l'oreiller creusé par les cris sourds
Prolonger les éclairs suprêmes de tendresse,
Et bave... —L'ombre emplit les maisons et les cours.

III

On the eve of the Great Day, the child makes herself ill.
First comes a shiver: a better one (bed helps)
Than in the tall church with its sombre sounds—
A scarcely human shiver which won't go: 'I'm dying...'

And, like love stolen from her stupid sisters,
Exhausted, her hands crossed over her heart,
She counts Angels, gleaming Virgins, Jesuses—
See, her soul has calmly drunk the Lord.

Adonai! Among Latin endings
Green-mottled skies bathe crimson Brows.
Stained with pure blood from heavenly breasts,
Great snowy whiteness drapes the suns!

—For her virginities, future, present,
She bites the cold of your Remission.
But, more than water-lilies, more than all confections,
Queen of Sion,* your pardon is pure ice!

IV

But now the Virgin's just the virgin of the book.
Mystic élans sometimes come crashing...
Then, the poverty of images, their patina
Of boredom, awful pictures, old woodcuts.

Vaguely indecent curiosities
Horrify pure-blue dreams, startled to find
Themselves among the heavenly robes,
The linen which wraps Christ's nakedness.

Her soul in distress, her face in the pillow
Muffling sobs, she tries to make
The last rays of tenderness endure,
And dribbles... Shadows fill houses and yards.

Et l'enfant ne peut plus. Elle s'agite, cambre
Les reins et d'une main ouvre le rideau bleu
Pour amener un peu la fraîcheur de la chambre
Sous le drap, vers son ventre et sa poitrine en feu...

V

A son réveil,—minuit,—la fenêtre était blanche.
Devant le sommeil bleu des rideaux illunés,
La vision la prit des candeurs du dimanche;
Elle avait rêvé rouge. Elle saigna du nez,

Et se sentant bien chaste et pleine de faiblesse
Pour savourer en Dieu son amour revenant
Elle eut soif de la nuit où s'exalte et s'abaisse
Le cœur, sous l'œil des cieux doux, en les devinant;

De la nuit, Vierge-Mère impalpable, qui baigne
Tous les jeunes émois de ses silences gris;
Elle eut soif de la nuit forte où le cœur qui saigne
Écoule sans témoin sa révolte sans cris.

Et faisant la Victime et la petite épouse,
Son étoile la vit, une chandelle aux doigts
Descendre dans la cour où séchait une blouse,
Spectre blanc, et lever les spectres noirs des toits.

VI

Elle passa sa nuit sainte dans des latrines.
Vers la chandelle, aux trous du toit coulait l'air blanc,
Et quelque vigne folle aux noirceurs purpurines,
En deçà d'une cour voisine s'écroulant.

La lucarne faisait un cœur de lueur vive
Dans la cour où les cieux bas plaquaient d'ors vermeils
Les vitres; les pavés puant l'eau de lessive
Souffraient l'ombre des murs bondés de noirs sommeils.

. . . .

The child can take no more. She rises, reaches,
And her hand opens the blue curtain
To let the room's freshness into her bed,
Down to her belly, on to her rioting breast...

V

When she awoke—midnight—the window was white.
Before the blue sleep of moonlit curtains
She saw visions of Sunday's candour;
She'd been dreaming red. Blood poured

From her nose; and, feeling chaste and full of feebleness,
And to savour in God her love returning,
She hungered for night, when the heart rises
And falls, watched by gentle, guessed-at skies,

For night, impalpable Virgin Mother, bathing every
Young emotion in grey silences;
She thirsted for strong night when the bleeding heart
Oozes mute rebellion, seen by none.

And so, Victim both and little bride,*
Candle in hand, she went down to the courtyard
Where a blouse was drying; like a white ghost,
She raised ghosts from roofs, seen by her star.

VI

She kept her holy vigil in the latrines.
White air streamed through perforated roof;
Some wild purple-black vine straggled
Through cracks in a nearby courtyard wall.

The skylight threw a heart-shaped brightness
On the yard, where low skies plastered purple gold
On windows; paving stones reeked of laundry-water,
Spreading sulphur over dark, dream-crowded walls.

. . . .

VII

Qui dira ces langueurs et ces pitiés immondes,
Et ce qu'il lui viendra de haine, ô sales fous,
Dont le travail divin déforme encor les mondes,
Quand la lèpre à la fin mangera ce corps doux?

. . . .

VIII

Et quand, ayant rentré tous ses nœuds d'hystéries
Elle verra, sous les tristesses du bonheur,
L'amant rêver au blanc million des Maries,
Au matin de la nuit d'amour, avec douleur:

'Sais-tu que je t'ai fait mourir? J'ai pris ta bouche,
Ton cœur, tout ce qu'on a, tout ce que vous avez;
Et moi, je suis malade: Oh! je veux qu'on me couche
Parmi les Morts des eaux nocturnes abreuvés!

'J'étais bien jeune, et Christ a souillé mes haleines.
Il me bonda jusqu'à la gorge de dégoûts!
Tu baisais mes cheveux profonds comme les laines
Et je me laissais faire...ah! va, c'est bon pour vous,

'Hommes! qui songez peu que la plus amoureuse
Est, sous sa conscience aux ignobles terreurs,
La plus prostituée et la plus douloureuse,
Et que tous nos élans vers vous sont des erreurs!

'Car ma Communion première est bien passée.
Tes baisers, je ne puis jamais les avoir sus:
Et mon cœur et ma chair par ta chair embrassée
Fourmillent du baiser putride de Jésus!'

VII

Who'll tell these languors, the piteous miseries,
The hate in store for her, when leprosy at last
Eats up her lovely body, you manic priests
Twisting the world out of shape?

. . . .

VIII

When she's unravelled her hysterias,
In the sadnesses of happiness, she'll find
Her lover musing on a million white Marys,
The morning after love, in pain:

'Do you know I made you die? I took your mouth,
Your heart, all, everything men have;
And now I'm sick. I want to be laid out
Among the dead refreshed by waters of night.

'I was young, Christ soured my breath,
Choked me with loathing.
You kissed my hair as thick as wool,
And I let you... For you men

'It's so easy, with no thought that a woman deeply
In love, in the frightening filth of her conscience,
Is most prostituted, in greatest pain,
With no thought that our love for You is madness.

'For my First Communion was long ago.
It's as if I've never known your touch.
And my heart and flesh which your flesh has known
Crawl with the putrid kiss of Christ.'

IX

Alors l'âme pourrie et l'âme désolée
Sentiront ruisseler tes malédictions.
—Ils auront couché sur ta Haine inviolée,
Échappés, pour la mort, des justes passions.

Christ! ô Christ, éternel voleur des énergies
Dieu qui pour deux mille ans vouas à ta pâleur
Cloués au sol, de honte et de céphalalgies
Ou renversés les fronts des femmes de douleur.

Juillet 1871.

Le Bateau ivre

Comme je descendais des Fleuves impassibles,
Je ne me sentis plus guidé par les haleurs:
Des Peaux-rouges criards les avaient pris pour cibles
Les ayant cloués nus aux poteaux de couleurs.

J'étais insoucieux de tous les équipages,
Porteur de blés flamands ou de cotons anglais.
Quand avec mes haleurs ont fini ces tapages
Les Fleuves m'ont laissé descendre où je voulais.

Dans les clapotements furieux des marées
Moi l'autre hiver plus sourd que les cerveaux d'enfants,
Je courus! Et les Péninsules démarrées
N'ont pas subi tohu-bohus plus triomphants.

La tempête a béni mes éveils maritimes.
Plus léger qu'un bouchon j'ai dansé sur les flots
Qu'on appelle rouleurs éternels de victimes,
Dix nuits, sans regretter l'œil niais des falots!

Plus douce qu'aux enfants la chair des pommes sures
L'eau verte pénétra ma coque de sapin
Et des taches de vins bleus et des vomissures
Me lava, dispersant gouvernail et grappin.

IX

So then the rotted soul and the soul desolated
Will feel Your curses pouring down.
—They'll have lain down with your pure Hate,
Casting aside true passion in favour of death.

Christ, eternal thief of energy
God who for two thousand years made suffering women
Worship your pallor, face to the ground,
Nailed by shame and migraine, or simply knocked down.

July 1871

Drunken Boat

I followed deadpan Rivers down and down,
And knew my haulers had let go the ropes.
Whooping redskins took my men as targets
And nailed them nude to technicolour posts.

I didn't give a damn about the crews,
Or the Flemish wheat and English cotton.
Once the shindig with my haulers finished
I had the current take me where I wished.

In the furious riptides last winter,
With ears as tightly shut as any child's,
I ran, and unanchored Peninsulas
Have never known such carnivals of triumph.

The storm blessed my maritime wakefulness.
Lighter than a cork I danced on the waves
Which some call eternal victim-breakers—
Ten blind nights free of idiot guiding flares.

Sweeter than sour apple-flesh to children
Green water slid inside my pine-clad hull
And washed me clean of vomit and cheap wine,
Sweeping away rudder-post and grapnel.

Et dès lors, je me suis baigné dans le Poème
De la Mer, infusé d'astres, et lactescent,
Dévorant les azurs verts; où, flottaison blême
Et ravie, un noyé pensif parfois descend;

Où, teignant tout à coup les bleuités, délires
Et rhythmes lents sous les rutilements du jour,
Plus fortes que l'alcool, plus vastes que nos lyres
Fermentent les rousseurs amères de l'amour!

Je sais les cieux crevant en éclairs, et les trombes
Et les ressacs et les courants: je sais le soir,
L'Aube exaltée ainsi qu'un peuple de colombes
Et j'ai vu quelquefois ce que l'homme a cru voir!

J'ai vu le soleil bas, taché d'horreurs mystiques,
Illuminant de longs figements violets,
Pareils à des acteurs de drames très-antiques
Les flots roulant au loin leurs frissons de volets!

J'ai rêvé la nuit verte aux neiges éblouies
Baiser montant aux yeux des mers avec lenteurs,
La circulation des sèves inouïes,
Et l'éveil jaune et bleu des phosphores chanteurs!

J'ai suivi, des mois pleins, pareille aux vacheries
Hystériques, la houle à l'assaut des récifs,
Sans songer que les pieds lumineux des Maries
Pussent forcer le mufle aux Océans poussifs!

J'ai heurté, savez-vous, d'incroyables Florides
Mêlant aux fleurs des yeux de panthères à peaux
D'hommes! Des arcs-en-ciel tendus comme des brides
Sous l'horizon des mers, à de glauques troupeaux!

J'ai vu fermenter les marais énormes, nasses
Où pourrit dans les joncs tout un Léviathan!
Des écroulements d'eaux au milieu des bonaces
Et les lointains vers les gouffres cataractant!

From that time on, I bathed in the Poem
Of the Sea, lactescent and steeped in stars,
Devouring green azures; where a drowned man
Like bleached flotsam sometimes sinks in a trance;

Where suddenly tinting the bluities,
Slow deliriums in shimmering light,
Fiercer than alcohol, vaster than lyres,
The bitter rednesses of love ferment.

I know skies splintered by lightning, breakers,
Waterspouts, undertows; I know the dusk,
And dawn, exalted like a host of doves—
And then I've seen what men believe they've seen.

I've seen low suns smeared with mystic horrors
Set fire to monster scars of violet;
Like actors in the very oldest plays
Slatted light shimmered, away on the waves.

Green nights I dreamed bedazzlements of snow,
A kiss rising to the sea's eyes slowly,
Circulation of undiscovered saps,
Blue-yellow wakefulness of phosphorsongs.

For whole months on end I followed the swell
Charging the reefs like hysterical beasts,
Not thinking that luminous Maryfeet
Could force a muzzle onto breathy seas.

I struck, you know, amazing Floridas
Where flowers twine with panther eyes inside
Men's skins! Rainbows flung like bridles under
Sea horizons harnessed the glaucous herds.

I saw great swamps seethe like nets laid in reeds
Where a whole Leviathan lay rotting,
Collapse of water in the midst of calm
And distances tumbling into nothing.

Glaciers, soleil d'argent, flots nacreux, cieux de braises!
Échouages hideux au fond des golfes bruns
Où les serpents géants dévorés des punaises
Choient, des arbres tordus, avec de noirs parfums!

J'aurais voulu montrer aux enfants ces dorades
Du flot bleu, ces poissons d'or, ces poissons chantants.
—Des écumes de fleurs ont bercé mes dérades
Et d'ineffables vents m'ont ailé par instants.

Parfois, martyr lassé des pôles et des zones,
La mer dont le sanglot faisait mon roulis doux
Montait vers moi ses fleurs d'ombre aux ventouses jaunes
Et je restais, ainsi qu'une femme à genoux...

Presque ile, ballottant sur mes bords les querelles
Et les fientes d'oiseaux clabaudeurs aux yeux blonds
Et je voguais, lorsqu'à travers mes liens frêles
Des noyés descendaient dormir, à reculons!

Or moi, bateau perdu sous les cheveux des anses,
Jeté par l'ouragan dans l'éther sans oiseau
Moi dont les Monitors et les voiliers des Hanses
N'auraient pas repêché la carcasse ivre d'eau;

Libre, fumant, monté de brumes violettes,
Moi qui trouais le ciel rougeoyant comme un mur,
Qui porte, confiture exquise aux bons poètes
Des lichens de soleil et des morves d'azur;

Qui courais, taché de lunules électriques,
Planche folle, escorté des hippocampes noirs,
Quand les juillets faisaient crouler à coups de triques
Les cieux ultramarins aux ardents entonnoirs;

Moi qui tremblais, sentant geindre à cinquante lieues
Le rut des Béhémots et les Maelstroms épais
Fileur éternel des immobilités bleues
Je regrette l'Europe aux anciens parapets!

Glaciers, silver suns, pearl seas, firecoal skies!
Hideous wreckages down in brown depths
Where enormous insect-tormented snakes
Crash from twisted trees, reeking with blackness.

I'd have liked to show children blue-water
Dorados, golden fish and fish that sing.
Foam-sprays of flowers cradled my drifting;
At times I flew on ineffable winds.

Sometimes, martyr tired of poles and wastelands,
My pitching was stilled by the sobbing sea
Which raised to me its yellow-sucker
Shadow-flowers—and I, like a woman, knelt.

Floating island where the brawls and guano
Of fierce albino birds bounced off my sides,
I sailed, while down among my fraying ropes
Drowned men descended backwards into sleep.

Now, I, boat tangled in the hair of bights,
Hurled high by hurricanes through birdless space,
Whom no protection-vessel in the world
Would fish up from the drink, half-drowned, half-crazed;

Free, smoking, got up in violet spume,
I, who holed the sky like a wall in flames
Which bears, good poet's exquisite preserve,
Lichen of sun and cerulean snot;

Mad plank streaked with electric crescents, flanked
By dark formations of speeding sea-horse,
When Julys bludgeoned ultramarine skies
And pulverized them into scorching winds;

Trembling as I heard the faraway groans
Of rutting Behemoths and swirling storms;
Eternal spinner of blue stillnesses,
I long for Europe's ancient parapets.

J'ai vu des archipels sidéraux! et des îles
Dont les cieux délirants sont ouverts au vogueur
—Est-ce en ces nuits sans fonds que tu dors et t'exiles,
Million d'oiseaux d'or, ô future Vigueur?—

Mais, vrai, j'ai trop pleuré! Les Aubes sont navrantes,
Toute lune est atroce et tout soleil amer:
L'âcre amour m'a gonflé de torpeurs enivrantes.
Ô que ma quille éclate! O que j'aille à la mer!

Si je désire une eau d'Europe, c'est la flache
Noire et froide où vers le crépuscule embaumé
Un enfant accroupi plein de tristesses, lâche
Un bateau frêle comme un papillon de mai.

Je ne puis plus, baigné de vos langueurs, ô lames,
Enlever leur sillage aux porteurs de cotons,
Ni traverser l'orgueil des drapeaux et des flammes,
Ni nager sous les yeux horribles des pontons.

Les Chercheuses de poux

Quand le front de l'enfant, plein de rouges tourmentes,
Implore l'essaim blanc des rêves indistincts,
Il vient près de son lit deux grandes sœurs charmantes
Avec de frêles doigts aux ongles argentins.

Elles asseoient l'enfant devant une croisée
Grande ouverte où l'air bleu baigne un fouillis de fleurs.
Et dans ses lourds cheveux où tombe la rosée
Promènent leurs doigts fins, terribles et charmeurs.

Il écoute chanter leurs haleines craintives
Qui fleurent de longs miels végétaux et rosés
Et qu'interrompt parfois un sifflement, salives
Reprises sur la lèvre ou désirs de baisers.

I've seen star-sown islands cluster; others
Whose delirious skies summon sailors.
Do you sleep banished in the pit of night,
You myriad golden birds, the Strength to come?

I've wept too much, it's true. Dawn breaks my heart.
All moons are atrocious, all suns bitter.
Acrid love has pumped me with drugged torpor.
Let my keel burst, let me go to the sea!

If I want Europe, it's a dark cold pond
Where a small child plunged in sadness crouches
One fragrant evening at dusk, and launches
A boat, frail as a butterfly in May.

Steeped in your slow wine, waves, no more can I
Cadge rides in the cotton-freighters' slipstream,
Nor brave proud lines of ensigns and streamers,
Nor face the prison-ships' terrible eyes.

Lice-Seekers

When the boy's head, full of red torment,
Pleads for white swarms of cloudy dreams,
Two charming big sisters approach his bed,
—Dainty fingers and silver nails.

They sit the child by an open window
Where blue air bathes a tumult of flowers,
And run enchanting, slender, awful
Fingers through his hair, weighted with dew.

He listens to the edgy music of their breath
Scented with the long rose-honey of plants,
Music broken sometimes by a hiss, saliva
Rescued from lips, longing for more lips;

Il entend leurs cils noirs battant sous les silences
Parfumés; et leurs doigts électriques et doux
Font crépiter parmi ses grises indolences
Sous leurs ongles royaux la mort des petits poux.

Voilà que monte en lui le vin de la Paresse,
Soupir d'harmonica qui pourrait délirer;
L'enfant se sent, selon la lenteur des caresses,
Sourdre et mourir sans cesse un désir de pleurer.

Tête de faune

Dans la feuillée, écrin vert taché d'or,
Dans la feuillée incertaine et fleurie
De fleurs splendides où le baiser dort,
Vif et crevant l'exquise broderie,

Un faune effaré montre ses deux yeux
Et mord les fleurs rouges de ses dents blanches.
Brunie et sanglante ainsi qu'un vin vieux
Sa lèvre éclate en rires sous les branches.

Et quand il a fui—tel qu'un écureuil—
Son rire tremble encore à chaque feuille
Et l'on voit épeuré par un bouvreuil
Le Baiser d'or du Bois, qui se recueille.

Oraison du soir

Je vis assis, tel qu'un ange aux mains d'un barbier,
Empoignant une chope à fortes cannelures,
L'hypogastre et le col cambrés, une Gambier
Aux dents, sous l'air gonflé d'impalpables voilures.

Tels que les excréments chauds d'un vieux colombier,
Mille Rêves en moi font de douces brûlures:
Puis par instants mon cœur triste est comme un aubier
Qu'ensanglante l'or jeune et sombre des coulures.

Hears the dark beat of eyelashes in the scented
Silence; and in his grey, narcotic letting-go,
The royal nails of their electric fingers
Softly make small lice crackle as they die.

The wine of Indolence wells up in him,
Delirium of harmonica sigh; on slow
Caressing tides, the child's need to cry
Ebbs and flows, and flows and ebbs.

Faun's Head

In the foliage, verdant jewel-case splashed with gold,
Among uncertain leaves where splendid
Flowers blossom under drowsy kisses,
Suddenly the exquisite tapestry is pierced—

A startled faun shows two eyes
And bites the red flowers with white teeth.
Stained brown with blood, like old wine,
His mouth cracks with laughter under trees.

And when he's fled—like a squirrel—
His laugh remains, trembling in the leaves,
And then you see, startled by a bullfinch,
The Wood's Golden Kiss settle again.

Evening Prayers

I live life seated, like an angel in a barber's chair,
A fussy deep-ridged beer-mug in my hand,
Neck and hypogastrium bent, my pipe-smoke
Filling out the air like ghostly sails.

Like warm droppings on a dovecote floor,
My thousand Dreams softly incandesce;
Now and then my sad heart's like alburnum wood
Bloodied by the dark, young gold of oozing sap.

Puis, quand j'ai ravalé mes rêves avec soin,
Je me tourne, ayant bu trente ou quarante chopes,
Et me recueille, pour lâcher l'âcre besoin:

Doux comme le Seigneur du cèdre et des hysopes,
Je pisse vers les cieux bruns, très haut et très loin,
Avec l'assentiment des grands héliotropes.

Voyelles

A noir, E blanc, I rouge, U vert, O bleu: voyelles,
Je dirai quelque jour vos naissances latentes:
A, noir corset velu des mouches éclatantes
Qui bombinent autour des puanteurs cruelles,

Golfes d'ombre; E, candeurs des vapeurs et des tentes,
Lances des glaciers fiers, rois blancs, frissons d'ombelles;
I, pourpres, sang craché, rire des lèvres belles
Dans la colère ou les ivresses pénitentes;

U, cycles, vibrements divins des mers virides,
Paix des pâtis semés d'animaux, paix des rides
Que l'alchimie imprime aux grands fronts studieux;

Ô, Suprême Clairon plein des strideurs étranges,
Silences traversés des Mondes et des Anges:
—Ô l'Oméga, rayon violet de Ses Yeux!—

'L'étoile a pleuré...'

L'étoile a pleuré rose au cœur de tes oreilles,
L'infini roulé blanc de ta nuque à tes reins
La mer a perlé rousse à tes mammes vermeilles
Et l'Homme saigné noir à ton flanc souverain.

Then, having downed with care my thousand dreams
With thirty, forty foaming tankards, I prepare
Myself to answer Nature's urgent call:

Sweet as the Lord of Cedar and Hyssop,*
I piss into brown skies, very high, very far,
Complicit with great heliotropes.

Vowels

A black, E white, I red, U green, O blue: vowels.
One day I'll tell your embryonic births:
A, black fur-clad brilliant flies
Clustering round every cruel stench,

Defiles of darkness; E, blank spread of mists and tents,
Proud glacier spears, white kings, sigh of umbel;
I, purples, blood spat, lovely lips laughing
In anger or penitential ecstasies;

U, cycles, divine shudder of viridian seas,
Peace of pastures grazed by cattle, peace of high
Pensive foreheads rucked by alchemy;

O, the last Trumpet, strange crescendo blast,
Navigated silences of Worlds and Angels,
—O Omega, the violet radiance of Those Eyes.*

'The star's wept...'

The star's wept pink deep inside your ears,
Infinity's rolled white from your nape to your hips;
The sea's formed russet beads round your vermilion breasts,
And Man's bled black at your sovereign side.

Poèmes de l'*Album Zutique*

Lys

Ô balançoirs! ô lys! clysopompes d'argent!
Dédaigneux des travaux, dédaigneux des famines!
L'Aurore vous emplit d'un amour détergent!
Une douceur de ciel beurre vos étamines!

Armand Silvestre.
A. R.

Les Lèvres closes
Vu à Rome

Il est, à Rome, à la Sixtine,
Couverte d'emblèmes chrétiens,
Une cassette écarlatine
Où sèchent des nez fort anciens:

Nez d'ascètes de Thébaïde,
Nez de chanoines du Saint Graal
Où se figea la nuit livide,
Et l'ancien plain-chant sépulcral.

Dans leur sécheresse mystique,
Tous les matins, on introduit
De l'immondice schismatique
Qu'en poudre fine on a réduit.

Léon Dierx.
A. R.

Fête galante

Rêveur, Scapin
Gratte un lapin
Sous sa capote.

Poems from Album Zutique

Lilies

Lilies swaying, lillicrap,* silver clyster-pumps!
Scornful of hard work, of famines!
Dawn squirts you full of its detergent love!
A sweetness of skies butters your stamens!

Armand Silvestre
A. R.

Sealed Lips
Seen in Rome

There is, in the Sistine, Rome,
Covered in Christian emblems,
A little scarlet box wherein
A clutch of antique noses lies drying.

Noses of Theban ascetics,
And canons of the Holy Grail
In which white night congealed
And the old tomb-gloom plainsong.

Into their mystic aridity
Every morning schismatic
Filth is funnelled,
Ground to a fine dust.

Léon Dierx
A. R.

Fête galante

Scapin's not with it,
Stroking a rabbit
Inside his jeans.

Colombina,
—Que l'on pina!—
—Do, mi,—tapote

L'œil du lapin
Qui tôt, tapin,
Est en ribote...

Paul Verlaine.
A. R.

'J'occupais un wagon de troisième...'

J'occupais un wagon de troisième: un vieux prêtre
Sortit un brûle-gueule et mit à la fenêtre,
Vers les brises, son front très calme aux poils pâlis.
Puis ce chrétien, bravant les brocarts impolis,
S'étant tourné, me fit la demande énergique
Et triste en même temps d'une petite chique
De caporal,—ayant été l'aumônier chef
D'un rejeton royal condamné derechef;—
Pour malaxer l'ennui d'un tunnel, sombre veine
Qui s'offre aux voyageurs, près Soissons, ville d'Aisne.

'Je préfère sans doute, au printemps...'

Je préfère sans doute, au printemps, la guinguette
Où des marronniers nains bourgeonne la baguette,
Vers la prairie étroite et communale, au mois
De mai. Des jeunes chiens rabroués bien des fois
Viennent près des Buveurs triturer des jacinthes
De plate-bande. Et c'est, jusqu'aux soirs d'hyacinthe,
Sur la table d'ardoise où, l'an dix-sept cent vingt,
Un diacre grava son sobriquet latin
Maigre comme une prose à des vitraux d'église,
La toux des flacons noirs qui jamais ne les grise.

François Coppée.
A. R.

Lady Columbine,
Well-shagged concubine,
Plays notes and beams

In eye of rabbit,
Which—off the planet —
Copiously streams.

Paul Verlaine
A. R.

'I was sitting...'

I was sitting in a Third-Class carriage; an old priest
Took out his pipe and stuck his calm head,
With its pale hair, out of the window, into the wind.
Then this Christian, ignoring gibes and provocations,
Turned and asked me, vigour tinged with sadness,
If I could spare him some tobacco—seems
He'd once been head padre to some Royal or other
Sentenced yet again —
To lessen the boredom of a tunnel, dark vein
Opened to passengers, near Soissons, a town in Aisne.

'In Spring, no doubt...'

In Spring, no doubt I prefer the drinking-place
Where dwarf chestnut-trees stir with new life,
By that little strip of pleasure-ground, in May.
Chastised puppies sniff around The Drinkers,
Trample neatly planted Hyacinths.
And, until purple evening's fragrances,
On the slate-table where, in 1720, a deacon
Carved his Latin nickname, meagre as prose
Read by church-glass light, black bottles splutter,
And fail to get them drunk.

François Coppée
A. R.

L'Humanité chaussait...'

L'Humanité chaussait le vaste enfant Progrès.

Louis-Xavier de Ricard.
A. Rimbaud.

Conneries

I Jeune goinfre

Casquette
De moire,
Quéquette
D'ivoire,

Toilette
Très noire,
Paul guette
L'armoire,

Projette
Languette
Sur poire,

S'apprête
Baguette,
Et foire.

A.R.

II Paris

Al. Godillot, Gambier,
Galopeau, Volf-Pleyel,
—Ô Robinets!—Menier,
—Ô Christs!—Leperdriel!

'Progress, big baby...'

Progress, big baby, wore shoes by Humanity.

Louis-Xavier de Ricard
A. Rimbaud

Stupidities

I Young Glutton

Silky
Cap
Ivory
Chap

In sober
Suit
Paul eyes the
Brute

Tongue
In cheeks'
Abodes

Aims
Full-cock
—Explodes.

A. R.

II Paris

Al. Godillot,* Gambier,
Galopeau, Volf-Pleyel,
—O Taps!—Menier,
You Christs!—Leperdriel!

Kinck, Jacob, Bonbonnel!
Veuillot, Tropmann, Augier!
Gill, Mendès, Manuel,
Guido Gonin!—Panier

Des Grâces! L'Hérissé!
Cirages onctueux!
Pains vieux, spiritueux!

Aveugles!—puis, qui sait?—
Sergents de ville, Enghiens
Chez soi!—Soyons chrétiens!

A. R.

Conneries 2e série

I Cocher ivre

Pouacre
Boit:
Nacre
Voit:

Âcre
Loi,
Fiacre
Choit!

Femme
Tombe:
Lombe

Saigne:
—Clame!
Geigne.

A. R.

Kinck, Jacob, Bonbonnel!
Veuillot, Tropmann, Augier!
Gill, Mendès, Manuel,
Guido Gonin!—Basket

Of Graces! L'Hérissé!
Oily waxes!
Old bread, spirits!

Blind!—but who knows?—
Policemen, Your Own Spa Cure
At home!—Act like Christians!

A. R.

Stupidities—Second Series

1 Drunken Coachman

Drunk
Skunk
Stars
Sees.

Harsh
Law:
Coach →
Trees.

Girl
Hurled,
Much

Blood.
Boo
Hoo!

A. R.

Vieux de la vieille!

Aux paysans de l'empereur!
A l'empereur des paysans!
Au fils de Mars,
Au glorieux 18 Mars!
Où le ciel d'Eugénie a béni les entrailles!

État de siège?

Le pauvre postillon, sous le dais de fer blanc,
Chauffant une engelure énorme sous son gant,
Suit son lourd omnibus parmi la rive gauche,
Et de son aine en flamme écarte la sacoche.
Et tandis que, douce ombre où des gendarmes sont,
L'honnête intérieur regarde au ciel profond
La lune se bercer parmi la verte ouate,
Malgré l'édit et l'heure encore délicate,
Et que l'omnibus rentre à l'Odéon, impur
Le débauché glapit au carrefour obscur!

François Coppée.
A. R.

Le Balai

C'est un humble balai de chiendent, trop dur
Pour une chambre ou pour la peinture d'un mur.
L'usage en est navrant et ne vaut pas qu'on rie.
Racine prise à quelque ancienne prairie
Son crin inerte sèche: et son manche a blanchi,
Tel un bois d'île à la canicule rougi.
La cordelette semble une tresse gelée.
J'aime de cet object la saveur désolée
Et j'en voudrais laver tes larges bords de lait,
Ô Lune où l'esprit de nos Sœurs mortes se plaît.

F. C.

Old Lady's Old Men!

Here's to the emperor's peasants!
Here's to the peasants' emperor!
Here's to the son of Mars,
The glorious 18th March!*
When Heaven blessed the fruit of Eugénie's womb!

State of Siege?

The poor conductor, in his tin shelter,
Warming a huge chilblain inside his glove,
Goes down the Left Bank with his heavy omnibus,
Keeping his moneybag clear of his swollen groin.
And while, in the soft recesses
Of the nark-infested bus, good citizens stare
At the moon nestling in the sky's green cotton-wool,
Despite the curfew, the tricky hour, and as
The bus heads towards the Odéon, a stinking
Debauchee yelps into the darkened square!

François Coppée
A. R.

The Broom

It's just a humble broom, too stiff
To do a room or paint a wall;
Troublesome to use, it's no fun.
Root ripped from some ancient meadow,
Its mane of hair lies drying; its handle has bleached
Like island timber left out in too much sun.
The braided strands seem a frozen plait.
I love this object's devastated flavour,
And I'd like to wash down your milky sides
With it, Moon, where our dead Sisters' spirit thrives.

F. C.

Exils

. . . .

Que l'on s'intéressa souvent, mon cher Conneau!...
Plus qu'à l'Oncle Vainqueur, au Petit Ramponneau!...
Que tout honnête instinct sort du Peuple débile!...
Hélas!! Et qui a fait tourner mal notre bile!...
Et qu'il nous sied déjà de pousser le verrou
Au Vent que les enfants nomment Bari-barou!...

. . . .

Fragment d'une épitre en vers de Napoléon III, 1871.

L'Angelot maudit

Toits bleuâtres et portes blanches
Comme en de nocturnes dimanches,

Au bout de la ville sans bruit
La Rue est blanche, et c'est la nuit.

La Rue a des maisons étranges
Avec des persiennes d'Anges.

Mais, vers une borne, voici
Accourir, mauvais et transi,

Un noir Angelot qui titube,
Ayant trop mangé de jujube.

Il fait caca: puis disparaît:
Mais son caca maudit paraît,

Sous la lune sainte qui vaque,
De sang sale un léger cloaque!

Louis Ratisbonne.
A. Rimbaud.

Exiles

. . . .

That often we were interested, dear Conneau!...
In little Ramponneau more than the triumphant uncle!...
All decent instincts come from the powerless People!...
Which, alas, made our anger turn sour!...
And now, it's right we should bolt the door
To that wind children call Bari-Barou!...

. . . .

Fragment of a verse epistle on Napoleon III, 1871

Damned Cherub

Bluish roofs and whitened doorways
As you'd see on lateish Sundays

In silence, down one end of town;
The street is blank, and night comes down.

Up the road, houses are lined,
Their windows hung with angel-blinds.

But, over by a boundary-stone,
Bad, and frozen to the bone,

A cherub falters, black as pitch;
He's overdosed on liquorice.

He has a dump; and disappears;
His cursèd caca now appears,

Beneath the holey* lunar light,
A pile of bloody dirty shite.

Louis Ratisbonne
A. Rimbaud

'Les soirs d'été...'

Les soirs d'été, sous l'œil ardent des devantures,
Quand la sève frémit sous les grilles obscures
Irradiant au pied des grêles marronniers,
Hors de ces groupes noirs, joyeux ou casaniers,
Suceurs du brûle-gueule ou baiseurs du cigare,
Dans le kiosque mi-pierre étroit où je m'égare,
—Tandis qu'en haut rougoie une annonce d'*Ibled*,—
Je songe que l'hiver figera le Filet
D'eau propre qui bruit, apaisant l'onde humaine,
—Et que l'âpre aquilon n'épargne aucune veine.

François Coppée.
A. Rimbaud.

'Aux livres de chevet...'

Aux livres de chevet, livres de l'art serein,
Obermann et Genlis, Vert-Vert et Le Lutrin,
Blasé de nouveauté grisâtre et saugrenue,
J'espère, la vieillesse étant enfin venue,
Ajouter le Traité du Docteur Venetti.
Je saurai, revenu du public abêti,
Goûter le charme ancien des dessins nécessaires.
Écrivain et graveur ont doré les misères
Sexuelles: et c'est, n'est-ce pas, cordial:
Dr Venetti, Traité de l'Amour conjugal.

F. Coppée.
A. R.

'On summer nights...'

On summer nights, under the shopfront's piercing eyes,
When sap trembles beneath the dark grilles
Glinting round the base of slender chestnut-trees,
I leave those black bunches of people, stay-at-home
Types or full of fun, pipe-suckers, cigar-chewers,
And drift towards the stone-dressed pavilion,
—While up above, there glows an ad for chocolate—
And I think how winter will blanket Tibet
With clean, pure noisy water, stilling the human tide,
—And how the bitter wind snaps every thread of life.

François Coppée
A. Rimbaud

'To my bedside reading...'

To my bedside reading, books of sublime artistry,
Vert-Vert and *Lutrin*, Obermann, Genlis,
Unimpressed by dust-grey vapid novelties,
I hope, in my dotage, when at last it comes,
To add Dr Venetti's* disquisition.
Giving up on the cretinous crowd, I'll be able
To savour the antique charm of explanatory drawings.
Writer's and engraver's ink has gilded sexual miseries,
And THAT, don't you agree? warms the heart:
Dr Venetti's *Treatise on Conjugal Love.*

F. Coppée
A. R.

Hypotyposes saturniennes, ex Belmontet

Quel est donc ce mystère impénétrable et sombre?
Pourquoi, sans projeter leur voile blanche, sombre
Tout jeune esquif royal gréé?

Renversons la douleur de nos lacrymatoires.

. . . .

L'amour veut vivre aux dépens de sa sœur,
L'amitié vit aux dépens de son frère.

. . . .

Le sceptre, qu'à peine on révère,
N'est que la croix d'un grand calvaire
Sur le volcan des nations!

. . . .

Oh! l'honneur ruisselait sur ta mâle moustache.

Belmontet,
archétype Parnassien.

Les Remembrances du vieillard idiot

Pardon, mon père!
Jeune, aux foires de campagne,
Je cherchais, non le tir banal où tout coup gagne,
Mais l'endroit plein de cris où les ânes, le flanc
Fatigué, déployaient ce long tube sanglant
Que je ne comprends pas encore!...
Et puis ma mère,
Dont la chemise avait une senteur amère

Saturnian hypotyposes, ex-Belmontet

So, what's this sombre and opaque mystery?
Why, never thrusting its white jib, does every
    Young rigged-out royal skiff sink?

———

Let's spill our tear-bottles brimming with pain—

. . . .

    Love wants to live off the sister,
    Friendship lives off the brother.

. . . .

The sceptre, scarcely venerated,
Is just a great Calvary cross placed
On the volcano of nations!

. . . .

Oh, honour went streaming down your male moustache.

Belmontet,
Parnassian archetype

Remembrances of Senility

Forgive me, father!
                    At country fairs,
When I was young, I sought out
Not the silly rifle-range where everyone's
A winner, but the place where clapped-out
Braying donkeys showed that long red tube of blood
Which still makes no sense to me!...
                                        And then my mother,
Whose blouse smelled sour, with its frayed hem,

Quoique fripée au bas et jaune comme un fruit,
Ma mère qui montait au lit avec un bruit
—Fils du travail pourtant,—ma mère, avec sa cuisse
De femme mûre, avec ses reins très gros où plisse
Le linge, me donna ces chaleurs que l'on tait!...

Une honte plus crue et plus calme, c'était
Quand ma petite sœur au retour de la classe,
Ayant usé longtemps ses sabots sur la glace,
Pissait, et regardait s'échapper de sa lèvre
D'en bas serrée et rose, un fil d'urine mièvre!...

Ô pardon!
                    Je songeais à mon père parfois:
Le soir, le jeu de carte et les mots plus grivois,
Le voisin, et moi qu'on écartait, choses vues...
—Car un père est troublant!—et les choses conçues!...
Son genou, câlineur parfois; son pantalon
Dont mon doigt désirait ouvrir la fente,... —oh! non!—
Pour avoir le bout, gros, noir et dur, de mon père,
Dont la pileuse main me berçait!...
                                        Je veux taire
Le pot, l'assiette à manche, entrevue au grenier,
Les almanachs couverts en rouge, et le panier
De charpie, et la Bible, et les lieux, et la bonne,
La Sainte-Vierge et le crucifix...
                                        Oh! personne
Ne fut si fréquemment troublé, comme étonné!
Et maintenant, que le pardon me soit donné:
Puisque les sens infects m'ont mis de leurs victimes,
Je me confesse de l'aveu des jeunes crimes!...

. . . .

Puis!—qu'il me soit permis de parler au Seigneur!
Pourquoi la puberté tardive et le malheur
Du gland tenace et trop consulté? Pourquoi l'ombre
Si lente au bas du ventre? et ces terreurs sans nombre
Comblant toujours la joie ainsi qu'un gravier noir?

And yellow as a piece of fruit,
My mother who noisily climbed the stairs to bed
—Child of Labour, note well—my full-thighed
Mother with huge hips making tucks in her clothes,
Caused me fevers one keeps quiet about!...

A calmer, cruder shame was when
My little sister, coming home from school,
Her clogs worn thin by the ice underfoot,
Pissed, and watched the slender thread
Escaping from her tight, pink other lips!...

Oh, please forgive me!
I thought sometimes of my father;
The evening hand of cards, the smutty talk,
The neighbour, me sent packing as I'd seen too much...
—For a father's frightening!—and the things
Imagined!—His knee, sometimes welcoming; his trouser-fly
My fingers wanted to unbutton—no!—
To get to the great, hard, dark nub of him,
The man whose hairy hand rocked me!...
I won't speak
Of the pot, the plate with its handle, glimpsed
In the attic, the red-covered almanacs,
The linen-basket, Bible, corners, maid,
The blessed Virgin and the crucifix...
No, no one
Knew such frequent torments, was so surprised!
Now, may I be forgiven;
Since vile flesh has scored its victory,
I confess my youthful crimes!...

. . . .

And then—allow me to address the Lord!—
Why the slow puberty, the curse
Of the over-consulted stubborn glans? Why
The crotch's shadow, so slowly? and those endless fears,
Black gravel coming after pleasure?

—Moi j'ai toujours été stupéfait! Quoi savoir?
. . . .
Pardonné?...
Reprenez la chancelière bleue,
Mon père.
Ô cette enfance! . . . .
. . . .
. . . . —et tirons-nous la queue!

François Coppée.
A. R.

Ressouvenir

Cette année où naquit le Prince impérial
Me laisse un souvenir largement cordial
D'un Paris limpide où des N d'or et de neige
Aux grilles du palais, aux gradins du manège,
Éclatent, tricolorement enrubannés.
Dans le remous public des grands chapeaux fanés,
Des chauds gilets à fleurs, des vieilles redingotes,
Et des chants d'ouvriers anciens dans les gargotes,
Sur des châles jonchés l'Empereur marche, noir
Et propre, avec la Sainte Espagnole, le soir.

François Coppée.

—I've always been aghast! What can I know?

. . . .

Forgiven?...
Father, have back
The blue footwarmer.
O that childhood! . . . .
. . . .
. . . . —and take ourselves in hand!

François Coppée
A. R.

Recollection

The year the Prince Imperial was born
Leaves me with a largely pleasant memory—
A cleaned-up Paris where gold and snow-white Ns*
Shine from palace railings, carousels,
Ribboned with red, white, and blue.
Among the general bustle, the big faded hats
And warm floral waistcoats, old dress-coats,
Among old workmen's songs coming from canteens,
There in the evening goes the Emperor, clean and dark,
Treading on spread-out shawls, Our Lady of Spain on his arm.

François Coppée

'L'enfant qui ramassa les balles...'

L'enfant qui ramassa les balles, le Pubère
Où circule le sang de l'exil et d'un Père
Illustre, entend germer sa vie avec l'espoir
De sa figure et de sa stature et veut voir
Des rideaux autres que ceux du Trône et des Crèches.
Aussi son buste exquis n'aspire pas aux brèches
De l'Avenir!—Il a laissé l'ancien jouet.—
Ô son doux rêve ô son bel Enghien! Son œil est
Approfondi par quelque immense solitude;
'Pauvre jeune homme, il a sans doute l'Habitude!'

François Coppée.

'The child who picked up bullets...'

The child who picked up bullets, Pubescent Lad
Whose veins course with the blood of exile and Father
Illustrious, hears the new buds of his life
Open, eager to look the part, and wants to see
Different drapes from those you get on Thrones and Cribs.
Besides, his refined features weren't made to go
Once more unto that breach, the Future—he's outgrown
The old plaything—His sweet dream, lovely spa bath
In your home! His eye's a pool of great loneliness;
'Poor young man, he's no doubt got The Habit!'

François Coppée

Les Stupra

L'Idole. Sonnet du Trou du Cul

Obscur et froncé comme un œillet violet
Il respire, humblement tapi parmi la mousse
Humide encor d'amour qui suit la fuite douce
Des Fesses blanches jusqu'au cœur de son ourlet.

Des filaments pareils à des larmes de lait
Ont pleuré sous le vent cruel qui les repousse,
A travers de petits caillots de marne rousse
Pour s'aller perdre où la pente les appelait.

Mon Rêve s'aboucha souvent à sa ventouse;
Mon âme, du coït matériel jalouse,
En fit son larmier fauve et son nid de sanglots.

C'est l'olive pâmée, et la flûte câline,
C'est le tube où descend la céleste praline:
Chanaan féminin dans les moiteurs enclos!

Albert Mérat.
P. V.—A. R.

'Nos fesses ne sont pas les leurs...'

Nos fesses ne sont pas les leurs. Souvent j'ai vu
Des gens déboutonnés derrière quelque haie,
Et, dans ces bains sans gêne où l'enfance s'égaie,
J'observais le plan et l'effet de notre cul.

Plus ferme, blême en bien des cas, il est pourvu
De méplats évidents que tapisse la claie
Des poils; pour elles, c'est seulement dans la raie
Charmante que fleurit le long satin touffu.

The Stupra

The Idol. Arsehole Sonnet

Puckered and obscure, like a violet's eye,
It breathes, humbly bedded down in moss
—Moist with recent love—which lines the buttocks'
White and gentle slopes right to the ridge.

Filaments like streaks of milk
Have wept in cruel winds
That blow them back through little red clots,
To disappear where they're inclined.

Often, it sucked in my murmured dream;
Jealous of coitus that merits the name,
My soul made it a wild, moist eye, its nest of tears.

It's the ecstatic olive, the enchanted flute,
The tube that disgorges the heavenly almond,
The Promised Land of feminine clamminess.

Albert Mérat
P. V.—A. R.

'Our buttocks...'

Our buttocks aren't like theirs. Many times I've seen
Men behind some bush, trousers down,
And, as I watched them splash, happy as sandboys,
I've noted the effect of our arse's geometry.

Firmer, and often pale, our arses have
Planes and elevations underneath the matted
Hair; with women, it's only in the lovely
Parting that the long and tufted satin grows.

Une ingéniosité touchante et merveilleuse
Comme l'on ne voit qu'aux anges des saints tableaux
Imite la joue où le sourire se creuse.

Oh! de même être nus, chercher joie et repos,
Le front tourné vers sa portion glorieuse,
Et libres tous les deux murmurer des sanglots?

'Les anciens animaux saillissaient...'

Les anciens animaux saillissaient, même en course,
Avec des glands bardés de sang et d'excrément.
Nos pères étalaient leur membre fièrement
Par le pli de la gaine et le grain de la bourse.

Au moyen âge pour la femelle, ange ou pource,
Il fallait un gaillard de solide grément;
Même un Kléber, d'après la culotte qui ment
Peut-être un peu, n'a pas dû manquer de ressource.

D'ailleurs l'homme au plus fier mammifère est égal;
L'énormité de leur membre à tort nous étonne;
Mais une heure stérile a sonné: le cheval

Et le bœuf ont bridé leurs ardeurs, et personne
N'osera plus dresser son orgueil génital
Dans les bosquets où grouille une enfance bouffonne.

A touching and wonderful openness, as found
Only on angels' faces in religious art,
Mimics the cheek dimpled by a smile.

Oh, to be naked like that, and find peace and joy,
Face turned towards the loved one's glory,
Able, both of us, to sob what we can't say.

'Once, animals spewed...'

Once, animals spewed sperm as they charged;
Excrement and blood smeared their glans.
Our fathers' members stood out proud—
The lie of the shaft and the swell of the sack.

Medieval woman, sinner or saint,
Needed her man to be properly endowed.
Even a Kléber,* whose pants perhaps flattered
To deceive, must have had what it took.

Anyway, man is like the proudest mammals;
The great size of their glans should not surprise us;
But the sterile hour has struck; the horse

And the ox have reined in their passions; no one
Will dare run a flag up his genital pole
In those thickets where ludicrous children swarm.

Derniers vers

'Qu'est-ce pour nous...'

Qu'est-ce pour nous, mon cœur, que les nappes de sang
Et de braise, et mille meurtres, et les longs cris
De rage, sanglots de tout enfer renversant
Tout ordre; et l'Aquilon encor sur les débris

Et toute vengeance? Rien!... —Mais si, toute encor,
Nous la voulons! Industriels, princes, sénats,
Périssez! puissance, justice, histoire, à bas!
Ça nous est dû. Le sang! le sang! la flamme d'or!

Tout à la guerre, à la vengeance, à la terreur,
Mon Esprit! Tournons dans la Morsure: Ah! passez,
Républiques de ce monde! Des empereurs,
Des régiments, des colons, des peuples, assez!

Qui remuerait les tourbillons de feu furieux,
Que nous et ceux que nous nous imaginons frères?
A nous! Romanesques amis: ça va nous plaire.
Jamais nous ne travaillerons, ô flots de feux!

Europe, Asie, Amérique, disparaissez.
Notre marche vengeresse a tout occupé,
Cités et campagnes!—Nous serons écrasés!
Les volcans sauteront! et l'océan frappé...

Oh! mes amis!—mon cœur, c'est sûr, ils sont des frères:
Noirs inconnus, si nous allions! allons! allons!
Ô malheur! je me sens frémir, la vieille terre,
Sur moi de plus en plus à vous! la terre fond,

Ce n'est rien! j'y suis! j'y suis toujours.

Last Poems

'What do they mean to us...'

What do they mean to us, my heart, the sheets of blood
And fire, the thousand murders, the long cries
Of rage, tears of all the hells upsetting
Every order; and still the north wind across the wreck;

And vengeance? None at all!... But yes,
We still want it! Industrialists, princes, senates,
Die! Down with power, justice, history!
This we are owed. Blood! The golden flame!

All-out war, vengeance, terror,
My soul! We'll writhe among the teeth! Vanish,
Republics of this world! No more emperors,
Regiments, settlers, people!

Who'd stir the furious fires into frenzies,
If not us and those we call our brothers?
Our turn now, Romantic friends; joy now.
We'll never toil, you waves of fire!

Europe, Asia, America, disappear.
Our march of revenge has taken everything
Cities, open land!—We'll be crushed!
Volcanoes will erupt! the ocean whipped...

Oh, my friends! My heart, for sure, they are brothers.
Dark strangers, let's go! Come!
Misery! I feel myself shake, the old earth
On me, more and more yours! earth melts,

It's nothing; I'm here; I'm still here.*

Mémoire

1

L'eau claire; comme le sel des larmes d'enfance,
L'assaut au soleil des blancheurs des corps de femmes;
la soie, en foule et de lys pur, des oriflammes
sous les murs dont quelque pucelle eut la défense;

l'ébat des anges;—Non... le courant d'or en marche
meut ses bras, noirs, et lourds, et frais surtout, d'herbe. Elle
sombre, ayant le Ciel bleu pour ciel-de-lit, appelle
pour rideaux l'ombre de la colline et de l'arche.

2

Eh! l'humide carreau tend ses bouillons limpides!
L'eau meuble d'or pâle et sans fond les couches prêtes.
Les robes vertes et déteintes des fillettes
font les saules, d'où sautent les oiseaux sans brides.

Plus pure qu'un louis, jaune et chaude paupière
le souci d'eau—ta foi conjugale, ô l'Épouse!—
au midi prompt, de son terne miroir, jalouse
au ciel gris de chaleur la Sphère rose et chère.

3

Madame se tient trop debout dans la prairie
prochaine où neigent les fils du travail; l'ombrelle
aux doigts; foulant l'ombelle; trop fière pour elle;
des enfants lisant dans la verdure fleurie

leur livre de maroquin rouge! Hélas, Lui, comme
mille anges blancs qui se séparent sur la route,
s'éloigne par-delà la montagne! Elle, toute
froide, et noire, court! après le départ de l'homme!

Memory

1

Clear water; salty as childhood tears,
The whiteness of women's bodies assaulting the sun;
silk, pure lilies massed, oriflammes
beneath walls which some Maid defended;

angels revelling;—No, the current of flowing gold,
moves its dark, heavy, cool arms of grass. It
sinks; with the blue Sky as canopy, it calls down
the curtain of the hill's and arch's shadow.

2

Look, the humid square offers limpid bubbles!
Water gives the ready beds fathomless pale gold:
little girls' faded green dresses
imitate willows, where birds hop freely.

Purer than a gold coin, warm and yellow eyelid,
the marsh marigold—your conjugal vow, Wife!—
at noon sharp, from its dull mirror, envies
the dear and rosy Orb in a fuddled grey sky.

3

Madame holds herself too stiff in the next field
where sons of toil flurry like snow; clutching
parasol; trampling umbels; too proud for her,
children in the flower-strewn grass, their noses

in books bound in red morocco! Alas, He, like
a thousand angels dispersing down the road,
fades beyond the mountain! She, utterly
cold and dark, runs! after the man has left!

4

Regret des bras épais et jeunes d'herbe pure!
Or des lunes d'avril au cœur du saint lit! Joie
des chantiers riverains à l'abandon, en proie
aux soirs d'août qui faisaient germer ces pourritures!

Qu'elle pleure à présent sous les remparts! l'haleine
des peupliers d'en haut est pour la seule brise.
Puis, c'est la nappe, sans reflets, sans source, grise:
un vieux, dragueur, dans sa barque immobile, peine.

5

Jouet de cet œil d'eau morne, je n'y puis prendre,
ô canot immobile! oh! bras trop courts! ni l'une
ni l'autre fleur: ni la jaune qui m'importune,
là, ni la bleue, amie à l'eau couleur de cendre.

Ah! la poudre des saules qu'une aile secoue!
Les roses des roseaux dès longtemps dévorées!
Mon canot, toujours fixe; et sa chaîne tirée
Au fond de cet œil d'eau sans bords,—à quelle boue?

Larme

Loin des oiseaux, des troupeaux, des villageoises,
Je buvais, accroupi dans quelque bruyère
Entourée de tendres bois de noisetiers,
Par un brouillard d'après-midi tiède et vert.

Que pouvais-je boire dans cette jeune Oise,
Ormeaux sans voix, gazon sans fleurs, ciel couvert.
Que tirais-je à la gourde de colocase?
Quelque liqueur d'or, fade et qui fait suer.

4

Regret for the thick, young arms of pure green growth!
Gold of April moons deep in the sacred bed! Joy
of abandoned riverside yards, prey
to August evenings which bred this decay!

Let her weep now, beneath the ramparts! the breath
of tall poplars is the only breeze.
Then it's the grey, matt sheet of water without source;
an old man in a tranquil boat, dredging.

5

Plaything of this dull eye of water, boat becalmed,
arms too short, I can reach neither one
flower nor the other; not the yellow one bothering me
there, nor the blue, friend to the ash-coloured water.

Ah, the powder shaken by a wing from willows!
The reed-roses long since eaten up!
My boat,* still tied fast; and its chain hauled deep
In this rimless round of water—into what mud?

Tear

Far from birds, flocks, from village girls,
I drank, squatting in heather,
Deep down among soft hazel-trees,
In a warm, green afternoon mist.

What can I have drunk from that young Oise,*
Voiceless elms, flowerless grass, overcast sky.
What did I draw from the colocasia's gourd?
Some pale and golden liquid to make me sweat.

Tel, j'eusse été mauvaise enseigne d'auberge.
Puis l'orage changea le ciel, jusqu'au soir.
Ce furent des pays noirs, des lacs, des perches,
Des colonnades sous la nuit bleue, des gares.

L'eau des bois se perdait sur des sables vierges,
Le vent, du ciel, jetait des glaçons aux mares...
Or! tel qu'un pêcheur d'or ou de coquillages,
Dire que je n'ai pas eu souci de boire!

Mai 1872.

La Rivière de Cassis

La Rivière de Cassis roule ignorée
En des vaux étranges:
La voix de cent corbeaux l'accompagne, vraie
Et bonne voix d'anges:
Avec les grands mouvements des sapinaies
Quand plusieurs vents plongent.

Tout roule avec des mystères révoltants
De campagnes d'anciens temps;
De donjons visités, de parcs importants:
C'est en ces bords qu'on entend
Les passions mortes des chevaliers errants:
Mais que salubre est le vent!

Que le piéton regarde à ces clairevoies:
Il ira plus courageux.
Soldats des forêts que le Seigneur envoie,
Chers corbeaux délicieux!
Faites fuir d'ici le paysan matois
Qui trinque d'un moignon vieux.

Mai 1872.

I'd have been a poor inn-sign, like this.
Then the storm changed the sky until evening.
It was all black lands and lakes and poles,
Colonnades under blue night, railway stations.

Wood-water vanished over virgin sands.
From the sky the wind pelted ponds with ice.
But, like a fisher for gold, a seeker of shells,
To think I didn't trouble to drink!

May 1872

Blackcurrant River

Unsuspected Blackcurrant river rolls
    Through strange valleys.
To the sound of a hundred crows, true
    Good voice of angels,
And sweeping forest pines lean
    When several winds swoop.

Everything rolls with the sickening mysteries
    Of olden-day lands;
Dungeons inspected, substantial parks;
    On these banks you hear
The dead passions of knights-errant—
    But how the wind restores!

Let the walker look through this lattice-work;
    He'll proceed with more courage.
You soldiers of the forest, sent by Heaven,
    Dear delicious crows,
See off the cunning peasant, raising
    A glass in his old stump!

May 1872

Comédie de la Soif

1 Les Parents

Nous sommes tes Grands-Parents,
Les Grands!
Couverts des froides sueurs
De la lune et des verdures.
Nos vins secs avaient du cœur!
Au soleil sans imposture
Que faut-il à l'homme? boire.

MOI— Mourir aux fleuves barbares.

Nous sommes tes Grands-Parents
Des champs.
L'eau est au fond des osiers:
Vois le courant du fossé
Autour du Château mouillé.
Descendons en nos celliers;
Après, le cidre et le lait.

MOI— Aller où boivent les vaches.

Nous sommes tes Grands-Parents;
Tiens, prends
Les liqueurs dans nos armoires;
Le Thé, le Café, si rares,
Frémissent dans les bouilloires.
—Vois les images, les fleurs.
Nous rentrons du cimetière.

MOI— Ah! tarir toutes les urnes!

Comedy of Thirst

I Parents

We're your grandparents,
Your Elders!
Covered in the cold sweat
Of moon and greenery,
Our dry wines had heart!
Beneath the undeceiving sun
What does man need? To Drink.

ME: Die in barbarous waves.

We're your grandparents
Of open fields.
The water lies deep in the reeds:
See it flow in the moat
Round the water-washed castle.
Let's go down into our stores;
Afterwards, cider or milk.

ME: Let's go drink with the cows.

We're your grandparents;
Here, take
Liqueurs from our cupboards;
Teas, Coffees, the rarest,
Tremble in boiling-pans.
—See the portraits, flowers.
We're back from the graveyard.

ME: Ah, empty all the urns!

2 L'Esprit

Éternelles Ondines
    Divisez l'eau fine.
Vénus, sœur de l'azur,
    Émeus le flot pur.

Juifs errants de Norwège
    Dites-moi la neige.
Anciens exilés chers,
    Dites-moi la mer.

MOI— Non, plus ces boissons pures,
    Ces fleurs d'eau pour verres;
Légendes ni figures
    Ne me désaltèrent;

Chansonnier, ta filleule
    C'est ma soif si folle,
Hydre intime sans gueules
    Qui mine et désole.

3 Les Amis

Viens, les Vins vont aux plages,
Et les flots par millions!
Vois le Bitter sauvage
Rouler du haut des monts!

Gagnons, pèlerins sages,
L'absinthe aux verts piliers...

MOI— Plus ces paysages.
Qu'est l'ivresse, Amis?
J'aime autant, mieux, même,
Pourrir dans l'étang,
Sous l'affreuse crème,
Près des bois flottants.

2 Spirit

Eternal Sprites
  Part the gossamer waters.
Venus, sister of the blue,
  Stir the pure wave.

Wandering Norway Jews
  Tell me the snow.
Old and dear exiles,
  Tell me the sea.

ME: No, enough of those pure drinks,
  These water-flowers for vases;
Legends and faces
  Won't quench my thirst;

Songster, your godchild
  Is my mad need to drink
Mouthless Hydra* deep inside
  Spreading desolation.

3 Friends

Come, the Wines are heading for the sea,
And a million waves!
See wild Bitter Beer
Foam down from summits!

Good pilgrims, let's find
The green pillars of Absinthe...

ME: Leave those landscapes.
Friends, what is drunkenness?
I'd as soon—no, rather—
Rot in the pond,
Under frightful scum,
By the floating wood.

4 Le Pauvre Songe

Peut-être un Soir m'attend
Où je boirai tranquille
En quelque vieille Ville,
Et mourrai plus content:
Puisque je suis patient!

Si mon mal se résigne,
Si j'ai jamais quelque or,
Choisirai-je le Nord
Ou le Pays des Vignes?...
—Ah songer est indigne

Puisque c'est pure perte!
Et si je redeviens
Le voyageur ancien
Jamais l'auberge verte
Ne peut bien m'être ouverte.

5 Conclusion

Les pigeons qui tremblent dans la prairie,
Le gibier, qui court et qui voit la nuit,
Les bêtes des eaux, la bête asservie,
Les derniers papillons!... ont soif aussi.

Mais fondre où fond ce nuage sans guide,
—Oh! favorisé de ce qui est frais!
Expirer en ces violettes humides
Dont les aurores chargent ces forêts?

Mai 1872.

Bonne pensée du matin

A quatre heures du matin, l'été,
Le sommeil d'amour dure encore.
Sous les bosquets l'aube évapore
L'odeur du soir fêté.

4 The Poor Man Dreams

Perhaps an Evening awaits me
When I shall quietly drink
In some ancient City
And die more easily:
Since I'm patient!

If I ignore my pain,
If I can ever get gold,
Will I choose the North
Or the Land of Vines?...
—Ah, dreaming is shameful

Since it's utter loss!
And if once more I am
The traveller once I was,
The Green Inn* will never
Welcome me with open doors.

5 Conclusion

The pigeons which tremble in the field,
Game, on the run, seeing night,
Water-creatures, bidden beasts,
The final butterflies... are thirsty too.

But, vanish where the unleashed cloud dissolves
—Smiled on by what is fresh!
Expire among moist violets here
Whose burgeonings fill these forests?

May 1872

Lovely Morning Thought

Four a.m. in summertime,
Love stays fast asleep.
In gardens dawn dispels last
    Evening's headiness.

Mais là-bas dans l'immense chantier
Vers le soleil des Hespérides,
En bras de chemise, les charpentiers
Déjà s'agitent.

Dans leur désert de mousse, tranquilles,
Ils préparent les lambris précieux
Où la richesse de la ville
Rira sous de faux cieux.

Ah! pour ces Ouvriers charmants
Sujets d'un roi de Babylone,
Vénus! laisse un peu les Amants,
Dont l'âme est en couronne.

Ô Reine des Bergers!
Porte aux travailleurs l'eau-de-vie
Pour que leurs forces soient en paix
En attendant le bain dans la mer, à midi.

Mai 1872.

Fêtes de la patience

Bannières de mai

Aux branches claires des tilleuls
Meurt un maladif hallali.
Mais des chansons spirituelles
Voltigent parmi les groseilles.
Que notre sang rie en nos veines,
Voici s'enchevêtrer les vignes.
Le ciel est joli comme un ange.
L'azur et l'onde communient.
Je sors. Si un rayon me blesse
Je succomberai sur la mousse.

But on the vast site stretching up
Towards the golden apple sun*
The shirt-sleeved carpenters
 Already work.

Calm in their deserts of moss
They panel fine ceilings
Where the town's wealth will laugh
 Under false skies.

For these charming Workers,
These Babylon King's men,*
Venus, leave the lovers be
 In aureoles of bliss.

 O Queen of Shepherds!*
Bring the workers eau-de-vie
To calm their strength
Until they can bathe at noon in the sea.

May 1872

Festivals of Patience

Banners of May

Among the lime-trees' bright branches,
A spent hunting-horn;
But lively spring songs
Flit among currant-bushes.
Let our blood laugh in our veins,
See the vines tangle.
The sky's as sweet as angels.
Water and sky become one.
I'm off. Should a ray of light wound me
I'll expire on the moss.

Qu'on patiente et qu'on s'ennuie
C'est trop simple. Fi de mes peines.
Je veux que l'été dramatique
Me lie à son char de fortune.
Que par toi beaucoup, ô Nature,
—Ah moins seul et moins nul!—je meure.
Au lieu que les Bergers, c'est drôle,
Meurent à peu près par le monde.

Je veux bien que les saisons m'usent.
A toi, Nature, je me rends;
Et ma faim et toute ma soif.
Et, s'il te plaît, nourris, abreuve.
Rien de rien ne m'illusionne;
C'est rire aux parents, qu'au soleil,
Mais moi je ne veux rire à rien;
Et libre soit cette infortune.

Mai 1872.

Chanson de la plus haute tour

Oisive jeunesse
À tout asservie,
Par délicatesse
J'ai perdu ma vie.
Ah! Que le temps vienne
Où les cœurs s'éprennent.

Je me suis dit: laisse,
Et qu'on ne te voie:
Et sans la promesse
De plus hautes joies.
Que rien ne t'arrête
Auguste retraite.

Patience, boredom
Are too simple. My pointless pains.
I want dramatic summer
To tie me to its chariot of fortune.
Nature, let me die so much by you,
Less lonely, less useless!
Not like Lovers—strange—who
Die mostly by the world.

I don't mind that the seasons use me.
I give myself up, Nature, to you,
And my hunger, all my thirst.
If it pleases you, nourish and quench.
Nothing at all deceives me;
To laugh at the sun means laughing at parents,
But me, I want nothing, nothing:
And may this misfortune live free.

May 1872

Song from the Highest Tower

Indolent youth
The plaything of all,
Through too much discretion
I've wasted my life.
Ah! roll on the day
When love is for real.

I told myself: leave
And keep out of sight:
Forget any promise
Of loftier joys.
Let nothing impede
Your Olympian retreat.

J'ai tant fait patience
Qu'à jamais j'oublie;
Craintes et souffrances
Aux cieux sont parties.
Et la soif malsaine
Obscurcit mes veines.

Ainsi la Prairie
A l'oubli livrée,
Grandie, et fleurie
D'encens et d'ivraies
Au bourdon farouche
De cent sales mouches.

Ah! Mille veuvages
De la si pauvre âme
Qui n'a que l'image
De la Notre-Dame!
Est-ce que l'on prie
La Vierge Marie?

Oisive jeunesse
À tout asservie
Par délicatesse
J'ai perdu ma vie.
Ah! Que le temps vienne
Où les cœurs s'éprennent!

Mai 1872.

L'Éternité

Elle est retrouvée.
Quoi?—L'Éternité.
C'est la mer allée
Avec le soleil.

Âme sentinelle,
Murmurons l'aveu
De la nuit si nulle
Et du jour en feu.

I've shown such great patience
That now I forget,
All suffering and fear
Are lost in the air.
Unhealthy thirsting
Blackens my veins.

Like the Great Meadow
Left in neglect,
With blossoming darnel
And rosemary, wild
Savage music
Of swarming black flies.

A thousand bereavements
Of this widowed soul
With only the picture
Of the Mother of Christ!
Do we say prayers
To the Virgin on high?

Indolent youth,
The plaything of all,
Through too much discretion
I've wasted my life.
Ah! roll on the day
When love is for real.

May 1872

Eternity

Found again. What?
Eternity.
The sea gone
With the sun.

Sentinel soul,
We'll breathe the truth
Of vacant night
And burning day.

Des humains suffrages,
Des communs élans
Là tu te dégages
Et voles selon.

Puisque de vous seules,
Braises de satin,
Le Devoir s'exhale
Sans qu'on dise: enfin.

Là pas d'espérance,
Nul orietur.
Science avec patience,
Le supplice est sûr.

Elle est retrouvée.
Quoi?—L'Éternité.
C'est la mer allée
Avec le soleil.

Mai 1872.

Âge d'or

Quelqu'une des voix
Toujours angélique
—Il s'agit de moi,—
Vertement s'explique:

Ces mille questions
Qui se ramifient
N'amènent, au fond,
Qu'ivresse et folie;

Reconnais ce tour
Si gai, si facile:
Ce n'est qu'onde, flore,
Et c'est ta famille!

From people's praise,
Vulgar élan,
You free yourself,
Fly where you can.

Since from just you,
Embers of silk,
Rises The Task
With no 'at lasts'.

There, no hope,
No new start.
Truth through patience
Torture for sure.

Found again. What?
Eternity.
The sea gone
With the sun.

May 1872

Golden Age

One of the voices,
Always angelic
—It's about me—
Remonstrates:

These thousand questions
Making more questions
In the end bring only
Madness and intoxication;

Recognize this happy,
Easy round:
It's merely wave, flower,
And it's your family!

Puis elle chante. Ô
Si gai, si facile,
Et visible à l'œil nu...
—Je chante avec elle,—

Reconnais ce tour
Si gai, si facile,
Ce n'est qu'onde, flore,
Et c'est ta famille!...etc....

Et puis une voix
—Est-elle angélique!—
Il s'agit de moi,
Vertement s'explique;

Et chante à l'instant
En sœur des haleines:
D'un ton Allemand,
Mais ardente et pleine:

Le monde est vicieux;
Si cela t'étonne!
Vis et laisse au feu
L'obscure infortune.

Ô! joli château!
Que ta vie est claire!
De quel Âge es-tu,
Nature princière
De notre grand frère! etc....,

Je chante aussi, moi:
Multiples sœurs! voix
Pas du tout publiques!
Environnez-moi
De gloire pudique...etc....,

Juin 1872.

Then it sings. O
So happy, so easy,
Visible to the naked eye...
—I sing too—

Recognize this happy,
Easy round,
It's merely wave, flower,
And it's your family!... etc....

And then a voice
—So angelic!—
It's about me,
Remonstrates;

And suddenly sings
Like a sister of air:
Sounding Germanic
But ardent, full:

The world's vicious;
You're scarcely surprised!
Live and bequeath to the fire
Dark misfortune.

O, beautiful chateau!
How full of light your life!
Which Age is yours,
Princely nature
Of our older brother! etc....

Me too, I sing:
Several sisters! Voices
Not to be broadcast!
Ring me round
With modest glory... etc....

June 1872

Jeune ménage

La chambre est ouverte au ciel bleu-turquin;
Pas de place: des coffrets et des huches!
Dehors le mur est plain d'aristoloches
Où vibrent les gencives des lutins.

Que ce sont bien intrigues de génies,
Cette dépense et ces désordres vains!
C'est la fée africaine qui fournit
La mûre, et les résilles dans les coins.

Plusieurs entrent, marraines mécontentes,
En pans de lumière dans les buffets,
Puis y restent! le ménage s'absente
Peu sérieusement, et rien ne se fait.

Le marié a le vent qui le floue
Pendant son absence, ici, tout le temps.
Même des esprits des eaux, malfaisants
Entrent vaguer aux sphères de l'alcôve.

La nuit, l'amie oh! la lune de miel
Cueillera leur sourire et remplira
De mille bandeaux de cuivre le ciel.
Puis ils auront affaire au malin rat.

—S'il n'arrive pas un feu follet blême,
Comme un coup de fusil, après des vêpres.
—Ô Spectres saints et blancs de Bethléem,
Charmez plutôt le bleu de leur fenêtre!

A. Rimbaud,
27 juin 72.

Young Couple

The room opens onto a slate-blue sky;
Lack of space; boxes, bins!
Outside the birthwort-covered walls
Vibrate with gummy goblins.

So much the intrigues of genies.
This expense, this vain disorder!
An African fairy puts mulberry
And nets of cobwebs in corners.

Several displeased godmothers,
Spangled with light, go into cupboards
And stay! Without much thought
The household leaves, and nothing's done.

The husband's cheated by a buffeting wind
While he's away, here, all the time.
Even malicious water-sprites
Investigate the bed.

In smiling night the honeymoon
Will gather their smiles and fill the sky
With a thousand copper crowns;
And then they'll confront the wily rat.

—If no pale will-o'-the-wisp happens by,
Like gunshot, after Evensong,
—Holy, white spectres of Bethlehem,
Cast spells instead on the blue of their window!

A. Rimbaud
27 June '72

Michel et Christine

Zut alors si le soleil quitte ces bords!
Fuis, clair déluge! Voici l'ombre des routes.
Dans les saules, dans la vieille cour d'honneur
L'orage d'abord jette ses larges gouttes.

Ô cent agneaux, de l'idylle soldats blonds,
Des aqueducs, des bruyères amaigries,
Fuyez! plaine, déserts, prairie, horizons
Sont à la toilette rouge de l'orage!

Chien noir, brun pasteur dont le manteau s'engouffre,
Fuyez l'heure des éclairs supérieurs;
Blond troupeau, quand voici nager ombre et soufre,
Tâchez de descendre à des retraits meilleurs.

Mais moi, Seigneur! voici que mon Esprit vole,
Après les cieux glacés de rouge, sous les
Nuages célestes qui courent et volent
Sur cent Solognes longues comme un railway.

Voilà mille loups, mille graines sauvages
Qu'emporte, non sans aimer les liserons,
Cette religieuse après-midi d'orage
Sur l'Europe ancienne où cent hordes iront!

Après, le clair de lune! partout la lande,
Rougissant leurs fronts aux cieux noirs, les guerriers
Chevauchent lentement leurs pâles coursiers!
Les cailloux sonnent sous cette fière bande!

—Et verrai-je le bois jaune et le val clair,
L'Épouse aux yeux bleus, l'homme au front rouge,—ô Gaule,
Et le blanc agneau Pascal, à leurs pieds chers,
—Michel et Christine,—et Christ!—fin de l'Idylle.

Michael and Christine

I'd curse if the sun left these shores!
Flee, bright flood! Here's the shadow of the roads.
In the willows, in the old courtyard,
The storm first rains down great drops.

Hundred lambs, the idyll's blond soldiers,
Run from the aqueducts, the meagre bracken!
Plain, deserts, meadow, horizons
Are rinsed red by the storm.

Black dog, brown shepherd in smothering cloak,
Flee from the vault of lightning;
Blond flock, when the sulphur darkness billows in,
Try to huddle down in better shelters.

But me, Lord! now my spirit flies,
Once the skies have frozen red, beneath
Celestial clouds scudding and racing
Across so many Solognes,* long as a railway.

Here are a thousand wolves, a thousand wild seeds
This religious afternoon of storms bears away—
With some love for the bindweed—over
Old Europe where a hundred hordes are on the move.

Afterwards, moonlight! Across the open plain
Reddened warriors face black skies,
Astride their slow, pale horses!
Stones ring beneath this proud procession!

—And shall I see the yellow wood, the lit-up valley,
The Blue-eyed Bride, the red-faced man, Gaul,
And the white Paschal Lamb, at their worshipped feet,
—Michael and Christine—and Christ!—the idyll's end.

'Plates-bandes d'amarantes...'

Juillet. Bruxelles, Boulevart du Régent.

Plates-bandes d'amarantes jusqu'à
L'agréable palais de Jupiter.
—Je sais que c'est Toi, qui, dans ces lieux,
Mêles ton Bleu presque de Sahara!

Puis, comme rose et sapin du soleil
Et liane ont ici leurs jeux enclos,
Cage de la petite veuve!...
Quelles
Troupes d'oiseaux! o iaio, iaio!...

—Calmes maisons, anciennes passions!
Kiosque de la Folle par affection.
Après les fesses des rosiers, balcon
Ombreux et très-bas de la Juliette.

—La Juliette, ça rappelle l'Henriette,
Charmante station du chemin de fer
Au cœur d'un mont comme au fond d'un verger
Où mille diables bleus dansent dans l'air!

Banc vert où chante au paradis d'orage,
Sur la guitare, la blanche Irlandaise.
Puis de la salle à manger guyanaise
Bavardage des enfants et des cages.

Fenêtre du duc qui fais que je pense
Au poison des escargots et du buis
Qui dort ici-bas au soleil. Et puis
C'est trop beau! trop! Gardons notre silence.

—Boulevard sans mouvement ni commerce,
Muet, tout drame et toute comédie,
Réunion des scènes infinie,
Je te connais et t'admire en silence.

'Flowerbeds of amaranth...'

July. Brussels, Boulevard du Regent

Flowerbeds of amaranth as far as
The pleasant palace of Jupiter.*
—You I know it is who's mixing
A Blue that could be Saharan!

Then, as rose and pine of the sun
And liana play in this enclosure,
The little widow's cage!...
                              What
Flocks of birds, o iaio, iaio!...

—Calm houses, old passions!
Kiosk for the Woman crazed with love.
After the bending rosebush branches,
Juliet's balcony, very low and cast in shade.

Juliet calls Henriette to mind,
Delightful railway station,
High on a hill, like an orchard's end
Where a thousand blue devils dance in the air!

Green bench where, to a guitar, the white Irish girl
Sings to the paradise of storms.
Then, from the Guiana dining-room,
The chatter of children and cages.

The duke's window which makes me think
Of the poison of snails, and of the boxwood
Sleeping down here in the sun.
                              And then
It's too beautiful! We must stay silent.

—Boulevard without movement or commerce,
Soundless, all drama, all comedy,
Endless collection of scenes,
I know you, admire you in silence.

'Est-elle almée?...'

Est-elle almée?... aux premières heures bleues
Se détruira-t-elle comme les fleurs feues...
Devant la splendide étendue où l'on sente
Souffler la ville énormément florissante!

C'est trop beau! c'est trop beau! mais c'est nécessaire
—Pour la Pêcheuse et la chanson du Corsaire,
Et aussi puisque les derniers masques crurent
Encore aux fêtes de nuit sur la mer pure!

Juillet 1872.

Fêtes de la faim

Ma faim, Anne, Anne,
Fuis sur ton âne.

Si j'ai du *goût*, ce n'est guères
Que pour la terre et les pierres
Dinn! dinn! dinn! dinn! je pais l'air,
Le roc, les terres, le fer.

Tournez, les faims! paissez, faims,
Le pré des sons!
Puis l'humble et vibrant venin
Des liserons;

Les cailloux qu'un pauvre brise;
Les vieilles pierres d'élises,
Les galets, fils des déluges,
Pains couchés aux vallées grises!

Mes faims, c'est les bouts d'air noir;
L'azur sonneur;
—C'est l'estomac qui me tire.
C'est le malheur.

'Does she dance?...'

Does she dance?... in the first blue hours
Will she perish like dead flowers...
Before this stretch of splendour where we should feel
The breath of the city in bloom!

Too beautiful! Too beautiful! but needed
—For the Fishermaid and the Corsair's song,
And because since the last masks still wanted
Midnight carnivals on pure seas!

July 1872

Festivals of Hunger

Anne, Anne, my hunger,
Flee on your donkey.

If I have a *taste*, it's for scarcely more
Than earth and stones.
Dinn! dinn! dinn! dinn! I eat air,
Rock, earth, iron.

Turn, my hungers! Hungers, feed,
    Field of bran!
Then the vibrant humble poison
    Of bindweed;

Stones a poor man breaks,
Old stones of churches,
Pebbles, children of floods,
Loaves lying in grey valleys!

My hungers, scraps of black air;
    Ringing blue;
—Pullings of my stomach.
    Misery.

Sur terre ont paru les feuilles!
Je vais aux chairs de fruit blettes.
Au sein du sillon je cueille
La doucette et la violette.

Ma faim, Anne, Anne!
Fuis sur ton âne.

'Ô saisons, ô châteaux'

Ô saisons, ô châteaux
Quelle âme est sans défauts?

Ô saisons, ô châteaux,

J'ai fait la magique étude
Du Bonheur, que nul n'élude.

Ô vive lui, chaque fois
Que chante son coq Gaulois.

Mais! je n'aurai plus d'envie,
Il s'est chargé de ma vie.

Ce Charme! il prit âme et corps
Et dispersa tous efforts.

Que comprendre à ma parole?
Il fait qu'elle fuie et vole!

Ô saisons, ô châteaux!

[Et, si le malheur m'entraîne,
Sa disgrâce m'est certaine.

Il faut que son dédain, las!
Me livre au plus prompt trépas!

On earth leaves have appeared!
I'm for the soft mush of fruit.
In the furrow's heart I pluck
Lamb's lettuce and violets.

Anne, Anne, my hunger!
Flee on your donkey.

'O seasons, o chateaux...'

O seasons, o chateaux...
Which soul has no flaw?

O seasons, o chateaux...

I've made the magic study
Of Happiness, no one evades.

Long live happiness, each time
The Gallic cockerel crows.

But! I've finished with wanting,
It's taken my life over.

That Spell! took soul and body,
And wasted all effort.

What to make of my words?
It would have them take flight.

O seasons, o chateaux!

[And, if I'm unlucky,
I'll surely know ruin.

Its disregard, alas!
Must bring me instant death!

—Ô Saisons, ô Châteaux!
Quelle âme est sans défauts?]

'Entends comme brame'

Entends comme brame
près des acacias
en avril la rame
viride du pois!

Dans sa vapeur nette,
vers Phœbé! tu vois
s'agiter la tête
de saints d'autrefois...

Loin des claires meules
des caps, des beaux toits,
ces chers Anciens veulent
ce philtre sournois...

Or ni fériale
ni astrale! n'est
la brume qu'exhale
ce nocturne effet.

Néanmoins ils restent,
—Sicile, Allemagne,
dans ce brouillard triste
et blêmi, justement!

—O Seasons, o Chateaux!
Which soul has no flaw?]

'Hear the bellow'

Hear the bellow
Of vivid stakes
for peas, in April,
by the acacias.

In its neat haze
by Phoebe! You can see
Early saints'
heads moving...

Far from bright headland
stacks, fine rooftops,
these dear Ancients desire
this cunning philtre...

Now, the mist-breath
of this nocturne
is neither of stars
nor festive days.

But still they stay
—Sicily, Germany,
in this sad, bland
fog, just so!

Honte

Tant que la lame n'aura
Pas coupé cette cervelle,
Ce paquet blanc vert et gras
À vapeur jamais nouvelle,

(Ah! Lui, devrait couper son
Nez, sa lèvre, ses oreilles,
Son ventre! et faire abandon
De ses jambes! ô merveille!)

Mais, non, vrai, je crois que tant
Que pour sa tête la lame
Que les cailloux pour son flanc
Que pour ses boyaux la flamme

N'auront pas agi, l'enfant
Gêneur, la si sotte bête,
Ne doit cesser un instant
De ruser et d'être traître

Comme un chat des Monts-Rocheux;
D'empuantir toutes sphères!
Qu'à sa mort pourtant, ô mon Dieu!
S'élève quelque prière!

Shame

So long as the blade has
Not sliced that brain,
That white and green parcel of grease,
Full of stale steam,

(Ah, it is He* who should cut off
His nose, lip, ears,
Cut out his stomach, abandon
His legs! Marvel!)

But no: I believe that so long
As the blade hasn't done its work
On his head, the stones
On his body, the flame

On his guts, the troublesome
Child, that so stupid creature
Must not stop for one moment
His cheating, his lies, his betrayal,

And like a Rocky Mountain cat,*
Must make every place stink!
But when he dies, dear God,
Let at least some prayers be said!

La Chambrée de nuit

Rêve

On a faim dans la chambrée—
        C'est vrai...
Émanations, explosions. Un génie:
        'Je suis le gruère!'—
Lefêbvre: 'Keller!'
Le génie: 'Je suis le Brie!'—
Les soldats coupent sur leur pain:
        'C'est la vie!'
Le génie.—'Je suis le Roquefort!'
          —'Ça s'ra not' mort!...'
          Je suis le gruère
          Et le Brie!... etc.

Valse

On nous a joints, Lefêbvre et moi, etc.

Mess-room by Night

Dream

Hunger stalks the mess—
    Oh, yes...
Emanations, explosions. A genie:
    'I'm gruyère'—
Lefêbvre: 'Keller!'
Genie: 'I'm Brie!'—
Soldiers grab bread, wield knife:
    'That's life!'
Genie—'I'm Roquefort!'
    —'We're done for!...'
    I'm Gruyère
    And I'm Brie!... etc.

Waltz

We're as one, Lefêbvre and me, etc.

Les Déserts de l'amour

AVERTISSEMENT

Ces écritures-ci sont d'un jeune, tout jeune *homme*, dont la vie s'est développée n'importe où; sans mère, sans pays, insoucieux de tout ce qu'on connaît, fuyant toute force morale, comme furent déjà plusieurs pitoyables jeunes hommes. Mais, lui, si ennuyé et si troublé, qu'il ne fit que s'amener à la mort comme à une pudeur terrible et fatale. N'ayant pas aimé de femmes,—quoique plein de sang!—il eut son âme et son cœur, toute sa force, élevés en des erreurs étranges et tristes. Des rêves suivants,—ses amours!—qui lui vinrent dans ses lits ou dans les rues, et de leur suite et de leur fin, de douces considérations religieuses se dégagent. Peut-être se rappellera-t-on le sommeil continu des Mahométans légendaires,— braves pourtant et circoncis! Mais, cette bizarre souffrance possédant une autorité inquiétante, il faut sincèrement désirer que cette Ame, égarée parmi nous tous, et qui veut la mort, ce semble, rencontre en cet instant-là des consolations sérieuses et soit digne!

A. Rimbaud.

[I]

C'est certes la même campagne. La même maison rustique de mes parents: la salle même où les dessus de porte sont des bergeries roussies, avec des armes et des lions. Au dîner, il y a un salon avec des bougies et des vins et des boiseries rustiques. La table à manger est très grande. Les servantes! Elles étaient plusieurs, autant que je m'en suis souvenu.—Il y avait là un de mes jeunes amis anciens, prêtre et vêtu en prêtre, maintenant: c'était pour être plus libre. Je me souviens de sa chambre de pourpre, à vitres de papier jaune; et ses livres, cachés, qui avaient trempé dans l'océan!

Moi j'étais abandonné, dans cette maison de campagne sans fin: lisant dans la cuisine, séchant la boue de mes habits devant les hôtes, aux conversations du salon: ému jusqu'à la mort par le murmure du lait du matin et de la nuit du siècle dernier.

J'étais dans une chambre très sombre: que faisais-je? Une servante vint près de moi: je puis dire que c'était un petit chien: quoiqu'elle

The Deserts of Love

FOREWORD

These writings are those of a young man, a very young *man*, whose life has evolved here, there, and everywhere; no mother, no country, indifferent to things that matter, avoiding all moral imperatives, the way so many wretched young men already were. He, though, was bored and vexed to such a degree that he simply marched on towards death as if towards a terrible and fatal grace. Not having loved women—yet full-blooded!—his heart, his soul, all his strength grew up in strange and sad mistakes. Successive dreams—his loves!—came to him in his beds or in the streets, and from their twists and endings issued soft religious thoughts. Think, perhaps, of the unbroken sleep of legendary Mahomedans—good men, and circumcised! But since this strange suffering has a troubling authority, we must fervently hope that this Soul, which has strayed into our midst, this Soul which seems to yearn to die, will find true consolation when death comes, and be worthy of it!

I

This, no doubt, is the same countryside. The same cottage as my parents'; the same living-room with rustic scenes above the doors, scorched paintings of lions and coats-of-arms. At dinner, a room of candles and wines and rustic carvings. The dining-table is huge. Maidservants, lots of them, as many as I've remembered. One of my old young friends was there, a priest dressed as a priest, now, in the interests of greater freedom. I recall his purple bedroom, its yellow paper window-panes; and his hidden books which had known the waters of the sea!

Me, I was abandoned in this endless country cottage; reading in the kitchen, drying my muddy clothes in front of the guests conversing in the drawing-room; moved to death by the murmur of the morning milk and of the night of the last century.

I was in a darkened room; doing what? A serving-girl came near; she was, I'd say, a puppy dog, though beautiful, and with a maternal

fût belle, et d'une noblesse maternelle inexprimable pour moi: pure, connue, toute charmante! Elle me pinça le bras.

Je ne me rappelle même plus bien sa figure: ce n'est pas pour me rappeler son bras, dont je roulai la peau dans mes deux doigts; ni sa bouche, que la mienne saisit comme une petite vague désespérée, minant sans fin quelque chose. Je la renversai dans une corbeille de coussins et de toiles de navire, en un coin noir. Je ne me rappelle plus que son pantalon à dentelles blanches.—Puis, ô désespoir, la cloison devint vaguement l'ombre des arbres; et je me suis abîmé sous la tristesse amoureuse de la nuit.

[II]

Cette fois, c'est la Femme que j'ai vue dans la Ville, et à qui j'ai parlé et qui me parle.

J'étais dans une chambre sans lumière. On vint me dire qu'elle était chez moi: et je la vis dans mon lit, toute à moi, sans lumière. Je fus très ému, et beaucoup parce que c'était la maison de famille: aussi une détresse me prit: j'étais en haillons, moi, et elle, mondaine, qui se donnait, il lui fallait s'en aller! Une détresse sans nom: je la pris, et la laissai tomber hors du lit, presque nue; et, dans ma faiblesse indicible, je tombai sur elle et me traînai avec elle parmi les tapis sans lumière. La lampe de la famille rougissait l'une après l'autre les chambres voisines. Alors la femme disparut. Je versai plus de larmes que Dieu n'en a pu jamais demander.

Je sortis dans la ville sans fin. Ô Fatigue! Noyé dans la nuit sourde et dans la fuite du bonheur. C'était comme une nuit d'hiver, avec une neige pour étouffer le monde décidément. Les amis auxquels je criais: où reste-t-elle, répondaient faussement. Je fus devant les vitrages de là où elle va tous les soirs: je courais dans un jardin enseveli. On m'a repoussé. Je pleurais énormément, à tout cela. Enfin je suis descendu dans un lieu plein de poussieère, et assis sur des charpentes, j'ai laissé finir toutes les larmes de mon corps avec cette nuit.—Et mon épuisement me revenait pourtant toujours.

J'ai compris qu'elle était à sa vie de tous les jours, et que le tour de bonté serait plus long à se reproduire qu'une étoile. Elle n'est pas revenue, et ne reviendra jamais, l'Adorable qui s'était rendue chez moi,—ce que je n'aurais jamais présumé.—Vrai, cette fois j'ai pleuré plus que tous les enfants du monde.

nobility I can't explain; pure, familiar, utterly charming! She pinched my arm.

I don't even remember her face properly, nor can I see her arm, whose skin I rolled between my fingers; nor her mouth, onto which I poured my lips like a despairing little wave, no doubt eroding something. I wrestled her into a basket of cushions and paintings of ships, in some dark corner. All I remember now are her white frilly knickers.

Then, despair! The walls became vague tree-shadows, and I foundered in night's loving sadness.

II

This time, it's Woman whom I've seen in the City; I've spoken to her, and she to me.

I was in an unlit room. Her arrival was announced; and I saw her in my bed, completely mine, no light! I was very moved, the more so as it was the family home; and then I became agonized! I was dressed in rags, and she, the woman of the world, was offering herself. She had to go! Distress beyond words; I took her, and let her fall from the bed, half-naked; and in my indescribable weakness, I fell on her, and we rolled around the carpets in the dark. The family light reddened the adjoining rooms, one by one. Then the woman disappeared. I shed more tears than God has ever asked for.

I went into the endless city. Fatigue! Immersed in muffled night and in the flight of happiness. It was like a winter's night, and with a fall of snow enough to bury the world. Friends, to whom I shouted my question: where is she? answered me with lies. I was in front of the windows of where she goes every evening; I ran through a sunken garden. I was rebuffed. All this made me cry and cry and cry. In the end, I went down into a place full of dust, and, sitting on timbers, I wept every tear in my body in time with the night—And yet exhaustion still would not release its hold.

I've understood that she was at her daily tasks; and that goodness would take longer than a star to come round again. She hasn't returned, nor will she again, ever, the Adored Woman who'd entered my room—something I'd never have dared to hope. But, true, this time, I've wept more than all the children of the world.

Proses évangéliques

[I]

A Samarie, plusieurs ont manifesté leur foi en lui. Il ne les a pas vus. Samarie [s'enorgueillissait] la parvenue, [la perfide], l'égoïste, plus rigide observatrice de sa loi protestante que Juda des tables antiques. Là la richesse universelle permettait bien peu de discussion éclairée. Le sophisme, esclave et soldat de la routine, y avait déjà après les avoir flattés, égorgé plusieurs prophètes.

C'était un mot sinistre, celui de la femme à la fontaine: 'Vous êtes prophète, vous savez ce que j'ai fait.'

Les femmes et les hommes croyaient aux prophètes. Maintenant on croit à l'homme d'état.

A deux pas de la ville étrangère, incapable de la menacer matériellement, s'il était pris comme prophète, puisqu'il s'était montré là si bizarre, qu'aurait-il fait?

Jésus n'a rien pu dire à Samarie.

[II]

L'air léger et charmant de la Galilée: les habitants le reçurent avec une joie curieuse: ils l'avaient vu, secoué par la sainte colère, fouetter les changeurs et les marchands de gibier du temple. Miracle de la jeunesse pâle et furieuse, croyaient-ils.

Il sentit sa main aux mains chargées de bagues et à la bouche d'un officier. L'officier était à genoux dans la poudre: et sa tête était assez plaisante, quoique à demi chauve.

Les voitures filaient dans les étroites rues [de la ville]; un mouvement, assez fort pour ce bourg; tout semblait devoir être trop content ce soir-là.

Jésus retira sa main: il eut un mouvement d'orgueil enfantin et féminin. 'Vous autres, si vous ne voyez [point] des miracles, vous ne croyez point.'

Jésus n'avait point encor fait de miracles. Il avait, dans une noce, dans une salle à manger verte et rose, parlé un peu hautement à la Sainte Vierge. Et personne n'avait parlé du vin de Cana à Capharnaum, ni sur le marché, ni sur les quais. Les bourgeois peut-être.

Fragments According to the Gospel

I

In Samaria, many people have shown their faith in him. He has not seen them. Samaria, the perfidious egotistical parvenu puffed up with pride, more inflexible in its protestant law than Judea with its ancient tables. Widespread wealth was conducive to virtually no enlightened discussion. Sophistry, the slave and soldier of routine, first flattered, then butchered several prophets there.

Sinister words, those he heard from the woman at the well: 'You are a prophet, you know what I have done.'

Once, men and women believed in prophets. Today, they believe in statesmen.

Just outside the foreign town, unable to threaten it significantly, were he taken for a prophet, having appeared there in such a strange light, what would he have done?

Jesus was incapable of saying anything in Samaria.

II

The light and enchanting air of Galilee; its inhabitants received him with curious joy; they had seen him, shaking with saintly rage, thrash the moneylenders and the animal-sellers in the temple. A miracle performed by youth, pale with rage, they thought.

He felt his hands between hands weighted with rings, on the mouth of an officer. The officer was kneeling in the dirt; and his head was pleasing, though half-bald.

Carriages trundled through the narrow streets; movement, significant enough for this town; everything, that evening, seemed just too content.

Jesus withdrew his hand; then a sudden gesture of childish, feminine pride. 'Those of you who see no wonder, you will not believe.'

Jesus had performed no miracle thus far. At a wedding, in a green and pink dining-hall, he had raised his voice a little to the Blessed Virgin Mary. And no one in Capernaum had spoken of the Cana wine, not in the marketplace, not on the quays. The town-dwellers, perhaps.

Jésus dit: 'Allez, votre fils se porte bien.' L'officier s'en alla, comme on porte quelque pharmacie légère, et Jésus continua par les rues moins fréquentées. Des liserons [oranges], des bourraches montraient leur lueur magique entre les pavés. Enfin il vit au loin la prairie poussiéreuse, et les boutons d'or et les marguerites demandant grâce au jour.

[III]

Bethsaïda, la piscine des cinq galeries, était un point d'ennui. Il semblait que ce fût un sinistre lavoir, toujours accablé de la pluie et noir; et les mendiants s'agitant sur les marches intérieures;—blêmies par ces lueurs d'orages précurseurs des éclairs d'enfer, en plaisantant sur leurs yeux bleus aveugles, sur les linges blancs ou bleus dont s'entouraient leurs moignons. Ô buanderie militaire, ô bain populaire. L'eau était toujours noire, et nul infirme n'y tombait même en songe.

C'est là que Jésus fit la première action grave; avec les infâmes infirmes. Il y avait un jour, de février, mars ou avril, où le soleil de deux heures après midi, laissait s'étaler une grande faux de lumière sur l'eau ensevelie, et comme, là-bas, loin derrière les infirmes, j'aurais pu voir tout ce que ce rayon seul éveillait de bourgeons et de cristaux et de vers, dans le reflet, pareil à un ange blanc couché sur le côté, tous les reflets infiniment pâles remuaient.

Alors tous les péchés, fils légers et tenaces du démon, qui pour les cœurs un peu sensibles, rendaient ces hommes plus effrayants que les monstres, voulaient se jeter à cette eau. Les infirmes descendaient, ne raillant plus; mais avec envie.

Les premiers entrés sortaient guéris, disait-on. Non. Les péchés les rejetaient sur les marches, et les forçaient de chercher d'autres postes: car leur Démon ne peut rester qu'aux lieux où l'aumône est sûre.

Jésus entra aussitôt après l'heure de midi. Personne ne lavait ni ne descendait de bêtes. La lumière dans la piscine était jaune comme les dernières feuilles des vignes. Le divin maître se tenait contre une colonne: il regardait les fils du Péché; le démon tirait sa langue en leur langue; et riait ou [ma...].

Le Paralytique se leva, qui était resté couché sur le flanc, franchit la galerie et ce fut d'un pas singulièrement assuré qu'ils le virent franchir la galerie et disparaître dans la ville, les Damnés.

Jesus said: 'Go your way, your son lives.' The officer left as if bearing some small remedy, and Jesus continued on his way, down the side streets. Bindweed and borage lit their magic lights among the paving-stones. At last, in the distance, he saw the dusty meadow, and daisies and buttercups beneath the sun, bent in supplication.

III

Bethesda, the five porches of its pool, was a place of troubles. It was like a sinister wash-house, rotting and forever rain-rinsed; and the beggars stirred on the inner steps bleached by those storm-flashes which announced the lightning of Hell, and made jokes about their blind, blue eyes and the white or blue bindings round their stumps. O military laundry, o bath-house of the people. The water was always filthy, and no invalid fell in, even in their dreams.

It is there that Jesus performed his first serious action, with the dreadful invalids. A day in February or March or April, when the sun of early afternoon scythed a swathe of light across the dark water; over there, far behind the sick, I could have seen everything that this single ray awoke of buds and crystal and verse in that reflection; like a white angel lying on its side, every infinitely pale reflection shimmered.

Then all sins, the Devil's easy and tenacious children, making these men more frightening than monsters to sensitive souls, wanted to hurl themselves into that water. The sick descended, not jeering now, but eager.

The first to enter the water emerged healed, so it was said. No. Their sins threw them back onto the steps, and forced them to position themselves elsewhere; for their Demon allows them to settle only where they are sure to receive alms.

Jesus entered shortly after noon. No one was washing nor bringing cattle to drink. The light in the pool was yellow, like the last leaves on the vine. The divine master stood against a pillar, watching the sons of sin; the Devil stuck out his tongue in their tongue; and laughed or...

The Paralytic, who had been lying on his side, rose; watching him cross the gallery with a firm step, and disappear into the city, were the Damned.

Une saison en enfer

Jadis, si je me souviens bien, ma vie était un festin où s'ouvraient tous les cœurs, où tous les vins coulaient.

Un soir, j'ai assis la Beauté sur mes genoux.—Et je l'ai trouvée amère.—Et je l'ai injuriée.

Je me suis armé contre la justice.

Je me suis enfui. Ô sorcières, ô misère, ô haine, c'est à vous que mon trésor a été confié!

Je parvins à faire s'évanouir dans mon esprit toute l'espérance humaine. Sur toute joie pour l'étrangler j'ai fait le bond sourd de la bête féroce.

J'ai appelé les bourreaux pour, en périssant, mordre la crosse de leurs fusils. J'ai appelé les fléaux, pour m'étouffer avec le sable, le sang. Le malheur a été mon dieu. Je me suis allongé dans la boue. Je me suis séché à l'air du crime. Et j'ai joué de bons tours à la folie.

Et le printemps m'a apporté l'affreux rire de l'idiot.

Or, tout dernièrement m'étant trouvé sur le point de faire le dernier *couac!* j'ai songé à rechercher la clef du festin ancien, où je reprendrais peut-être appétit.

La charité est cette clef.—Cette inspiration prouve que j'ai rêvé!

'Tu resteras hyène, etc...,' se récrie le démon qui me couronna de si aimables pavots. 'Gagne la mort avec tous tes appétits, et ton égoïsme et tous les péchés capitaux.'

Ah! j'en ai trop pris:—Mais, cher Satan, je vous en conjure, une prunelle moins irritée! et en attendant les quelques petites lâchetés en retard, vous qui aimez dans l'écrivain l'absence des facultés descriptives ou instructives, je vous détache ces quelques hideux feuillets de mon carnet de damné.

Mauvais sang

J'ai de mes ancêtres gaulois l'œil bleu blanc, la cervelle étroite, et la maladresse dans la lutte. Je trouve mon habillement aussi barbare que le leur. Mais je ne beurre pas ma chevelure.

A Season in Hell

Once, if I remember well, my life was a banquet where all hearts opened, all wines flowed.

One evening, I sat Beauty on my knees.—And I found her sour.—And I insulted her.

I armed myself against justice.

I fled. O witches, poverty, hatred, it was to you my treasure was entrusted!

I succeeded in making all human hope disappear from my mind. Silent as the predator, I pounced on every joy, to strangle it.

I summoned the executioners so that I could bite their rifle-butts as I died. I have summoned up plagues, to suffocate myself with sand, with blood. Misfortune has been my god. I have stretched out in the mud. I have dried off in the air heavy with crime. And I have played fine tricks on madness.

And Spring has brought me the idiot's hideous laugh.

Now, recently, finding myself on the point of my final *croak*, I had the idea that I would look for the key of the former banquet, where perhaps my appetite would return.

This key is charity.—A flash of inspiration which proves I have been dreaming!

'You'll go on being a hyena, etc...', yells the demon who had placed on my head a crown of the most lovely poppies. 'Meet death with all your appetites, your selfishness and all the deadly sins.'

Ah, too much and too many:—But, dear Satan, I beg you, look less annoyed! and while we are waiting for the final few shabby deeds, as you like in writers a total lack of descriptive or instructive ability, let me offer you this handful of hideous pages torn from my diary of damnation.

Bad Blood

From my ancestors the Gauls I have inherited pale blue eyes, a narrow skull, and clumsiness in fighting. I consider my apparel as barbaric as theirs. But I don't rub butter into my hair.

Les Gaulois étaient les écorcheurs de bêtes, les brûleurs d'herbes les plus ineptes de leur temps.

D'eux, j'ai: l'idolâtrie et l'amour de sacrilège;— oh! tous les vices, colère, luxure,—magnifique, la luxure;—surtout mensonge et paresse.

J'ai horreur de tous les métiers. Maîtres et ouvriers, tous paysans, ignobles. La main à plume vaut la main à charrue.—Quel siècle à mains!—Je n'aurai jamais ma main. Après, la domesticité mène trop loin. L'honnêteté de la mendicité me navre. Les criminels dégoûtent comme des châtrés: moi, je suis intact, et ça m'est égal.

Mais! qui a fait ma langue perfide tellement, qu'elle ait guidé et sauvegardé jusqu'ici ma paresse? Sans me servir pour vivre même de mon corps, et plus oisif que le crapaud, j'ai vécu partout. Pas une famille d'Europe que je ne connaisse.—J'entends des familles comme la mienne, qui tiennent tout de la déclaration des Droits de l'Homme.—J'ai connu chaque fils de famille!

Si j'avais des antécédents à un point quelconque de l'histoire de France!

Mais non, rien.

Il m'est bien évident que j'ai toujours été race inférieure. Je ne puis comprendre la révolte. Ma race ne se souleva jamais que pour piller: tels les loups à la bête qu'ils n'ont pas tuée.

Je me rappelle l'histoire de la France fille aînée de l'Eglise. J'aurais fait, manant, le voyage de terre sainte; j'ai dans la tête des routes dans les plaines souabes, des vues de Byzance, des remparts de Solyme; le culte de Marie, l'attendrissement sur le crucifié s'éveillent en moi parmi mille féeries profanes.—Je suis assis, lépreux, sur les pots cassés et les orties, au pied d'un mur rongé par le soleil.—Plus tard, reître, j'aurais bivaqué sous les nuits d'Allemagne.

Ah! encore: je danse le sabbat dans une rouge clairière, avec des vieilles et des enfants.

Je ne me souviens pas plus loin que cette terre-ci et le christianisme. Je n'en finirais pas de me revoir dans ce passé. Mais toujours seul; sans famille; même, quelle langue parlais-je? Je ne me vois jamais dans les conseils du Christ; ni dans les conseils des Seigneurs,—représentants du Christ.

The Gauls were the most inept flayers of beasts and burners of grass of their age.

From them I have inherited: idolatry and love of sacrilege;—oh! all the vices, anger, lust,—splendid, magnificent lust;—above all lying and indolence.

I abhor every trade. Owners and workers, peasants, the lot of them, mean and petty. The hand which writes is as good as the hand which ploughs.—What a century of hands! —I shall never get my hand in. Then, servitude takes you too far. The honesty of begging is too much for me. Criminals revolt me as much as men without balls: I have mine, and that is fine by me.

But! who, what has made my tongue so treacherous that it has been able, up to now, to guide and guard my indolence? Without using even my body to make a living, lazier than a toad, I have lived everywhere. Not a single family in Europe I don't know.—By that I mean families like mine, who owe everything to the Declaration of the Rights of Man.*—I have known each young man of good family!

If only I had antecedents at some point or other in the history of France!

But no, nothing.

It is quite obvious to me that I have always belonged to an inferior race. I cannot understand rebellion. My race never rose up except to pillage: like wolves tearing at the animal they have not killed.

I remember the history of France, eldest of the Church. I, serf, would have made the journey to the Holy Land; I have in my head the routes across the Swabian plain,* views of Constantinople, ramparts of Solyma;* the cult of the Virgin Mary, compassion for the man on the cross stir in me among a thousand profane enchantments.—I sit, stricken with leprosy, on the broken pots and the nettles, at the foot of a wall eaten by the sun.—Later on, become a mercenary, I would have bivouacked under the stars in Germany.

Ah! there is more: I am dancing at a witches' sabbath in a red clearing, with ancient women and children.

I cannot remember anything beyond this land and Christianity. I could never stop seeing myself in this past. But always alone; without family: I even have to ask what language I spoke. I never see myself as a disciple of Christ; nor of the Great Lords, Christ's representatives.

Qu'étais-je au siècle dernier: je ne me retrouve qu'aujourd'hui. Plus de vagabonds, plus de guerres vagues. La race inférieure a tout couvert—le peuple, comme on dit, la raison; la nation et la science.

Oh! la science! On a tout repris. Pour le corps et pour l'âme,—le viatique,—on a la médecine et la philosophie,—les remèdes de bonnes femmes et les chansons populaires arrangés. Et les divertissements des princes et les jeux qu'ils interdisaient! Géographie, cosmographie, mécanique, chimie!...

La science, la nouvelle noblesse! Le progrès. Le monde marche! Pourquoi ne tournerait-il pas?

C'est la vision des nombres. Nous allons à l'*Esprit*. C'est très-certain, c'est oracle, ce que je dis. Je comprends, et ne sachant m'expliquer sans paroles païennes, je voudrais me taire.

Le sang païen revient! L'Esprit est proche, pourquoi Christ ne m'aide-t-il pas, en donnant à mon âme noblesse et liberté. Hélas! l'Évangile a passé! l'Évangile! l'Évangile.

J'attends Dieu avec gourmandise. Je suis de race inférieure de toute éternité.

Me voici sur la plage armoricaine. Que les villes s'allument dans le soir. Ma journée est faite; je quitte l'Europe. L'air marin brûlera mes poumons; les climats perdus me tanneront. Nager, broyer l'herbe, chasser, fumer surtout; boire des liqueurs fortes comme du métal bouillant,—comme faisaient ces chers ancêtres autour des feux.

Je reviendrai, avec des membres de fer, la peau sombre, l'œil furieux: sur mon masque, on me jugera d'une race forte. J'aurai de l'or: je serai oisif et brutal. Les femmes soignent ces féroces infirmes retour des pays chauds. Je serai mêlé aux affaires politiques. Sauvé.

Maintenant je suis maudit, j'ai horreur de la patrie. Le meilleur, c'est un sommeil bien ivre, sur la grève.

On ne part pas.—Reprenons les chemins d'ici, chargé de mon vice, le vice qui a poussé ses racines de souffrance à mon côté, dès l'âge de raison—qui monte au ciel, me bat, me renverse, me traîne.

What was I in the last century? I can recognize myself only today. No more vagabonds, no more vague wars. The inferior race spread everywhere—the people, as they say, reason; the nation, science.

Oh! Science! Everything has been appropriated. For the body and the soul,—the viaticum—We have medicine and philosophy,—old wives' remedies and popular songs arranged. And princes' entertainments and the games which they forbade! Geography, cosmography, mechanics, chemistry!...

Science, the new nobility! Progress. The world strides on! Why might it not also spin?

It is the vision of numbers. We are moving towards the *Spirit*. What I am saying is absolutely true, the voice of the oracle. I understand, and, incapable of expressing myself without pagan words, I would rather say nothing.

Pagan blood returns! The Spirit is nearby, why does Christ not help me by giving my soul nobility and freedom. Alas! The Gospel has come and gone! The Gospel! The Gospel.

Hungrily, I await God. I have belonged to an inferior race since time itself began.

Now I am here, on the Brittany shore. Let the cities light up in the evening. My day is done; I am leaving Europe. Sea air will burn into my lungs; the furthest climates will tan my skin. To swim, trample the grass, hunt, most of all smoke; drink alcohol as strong as molten metal,—as did my dear ancestors around their fires.

I shall return, with limbs of iron, dark skin, furious eyes; from my mask, it will be thought I belong to a mighty race. I shall have gold; I shall be idle and brutal. Women nurse ferocious invalids like these on their return from hot countries. I shall be involved in politics. Saved.

In the meantime I am damned, I abhor my country. The best thing to do is to fall into a really drunken sleep, on the shore.

No one leaves. Let us take again to the roads round here, weighed down by my vice, the vice which has forced its roots of suffering into my side, when I attained the age of reason—and which rises to the sky, beats me, knocks me to the ground, drags me along.

La dernière innocence et la dernière timidité. C'est dit. Ne pas porter au monde mes dégoûts et mes trahisons.

Allons! La marche, le fardeau, le désert, l'ennui et la colère.

A qui me louer? Quelle bête faut-il adorer? Quelle sainte image attaque-t-on? Quels cœurs briserai-je? Quel mensonge dois-je tenir?—Dans quel sang marcher?

Plutôt, se garder de la justice.—La vie dure, l'abrutissement simple,—soulever, le poing desséché, le couvercle du cercueil, s'asseoir, s'étouffer. Ainsi point de vieillesse, ni de dangers: la terreur n'est pas française.

—Ah! je suis tellement délaissé que j'offre à n'importe quelle divine image des élans vers la perfection.

Ô mon abnégation, ô ma charité merveilleuse! ici-bas, pourtant!

De profondis Domine, suis-je bête!

Encore tout enfant, j'admirais le forçat intraitable sur qui se referme toujours le bagne; je visitais les auberges et les garnis qu'il aurait sacrés par son séjour; je voyais *avec son idée* le ciel bleu et le travail fleuri de la campagne; je flairais sa fatalité dans les villes. Il avait plus de force qu'un saint, plus de bon sens qu'un voyageur—et lui, lui seul! pour témoin de sa gloire et de sa raison.

Sur les routes, par des nuits d'hiver, sans gîte, sans habits, sans pain, une voix étreignait mon cœur gelé: 'Faiblesse ou force: te voilà, c'est la force. Tu ne sais ni où tu vas ni pourquoi tu vas, entre partout, réponds à tout. On ne te tuera pas plus que si tu étais cadavre.' Au matin j'avais le regard si perdu et la contenance si morte, que ceux que j'ai rencontrés *ne m'ont peut-être pas vu*.

Dans les villes la boue m'apparaissait soudainement rouge et noire, comme une glace quand la lampe circule dans la chambre voisine, comme un trésor dans la forêt! Bonne chance, criais-je, et je voyais une mer de flammes et de fumée au ciel; et, à gauche, à droite, toutes les richesses flambant comme un milliard de tonnerres.

Mais l'orgie et la camaraderie des femmes m'étaient interdites. Pas même un compagnon. Je me voyais devant une foule exaspérée, en face du peloton d'exécution, pleurant du malheur qu'ils n'aient pu

The last remainder of innocence, the last timidity. It is said and done. Not to take into the world my loathings and betrayals.

Oh, then! Walk, road, desert, boredom, anger.

Hire myself out to whom? Worship which beast? Savage which holy image? Break which hearts? Which lie maintain? Walk in which blood?

Better to guard against the law.—The hard life, moronic with exhaustion,—to lift the coffin-lid with a scrawny hand, sit down inside, and suffocate. In this way, no old age, nor dangers run: terror is not known to the French.

— Ah! I am so abandoned that I will offer to any divine image my impulse to perfection.

O my abnegation! My marvellous charity! and yet, I am down here, still!

De profundis Domine,* can I be so stupid?

When I was still a little child, I used to admire the hardened criminal on whom the prison gates must always close; I frequented the inns and rented rooms which his presence might have consecrated; it was *through his eyes* I saw the blue sky and the flower-covered work of the countryside; through cities I followed the scent of his fate. He had more strength than a saint, more good sense than any traveller—and he, he alone! witness to his glory and his rightness.

On the roads, on winter nights, no shelter, no clothes, no bread, a voice would clutch at my frozen heart: 'Weakness or strength; you are here, that is strength. You don't know where you're going, or why; go in everywhere, respond to everything. You won't be killed, any more than if you were a corpse.' In the morning, my eyes were so vacant, my expression so lifeless, that the people I met *perhaps did not even see me*.

In the cities, the mud suddenly seemed red and black to me, like a mirror when a lamp moves around in the next room, like treasure in the forest! Good luck, I would shout, and I saw an ocean of flames and smoke in the sky; and to left and right every kind of wealth blazing like a billion thunderbolts.

But orgies and the company of women were forbidden me. Not even a companion. I saw myself before an ugly mob, facing a firing squad, weeping miserably because they had not understood, and

comprendre, et pardonnant!—Comme Jeanne d'Arc!—'Prêtres, professeurs, maîtres, vous vous trompez en me livrant à la justice. Je n'ai jamais été de ce peuple-ci; je n'ai jamais été chrétien; je suis de la race qui chantait dans le supplice; je ne comprends pas les lois; je n'ai pas le sens moral, je suis une brute: vous vous trompez...'

Oui, j'ai les yeux fermés à votre lumière. Je suis une bête, un nègre. Mais je puis être sauvé. Vous êtes de faux nègres, vous maniaques, féroces, avares. Marchand, tu es nègre; magistrat, tu es nègre; général, tu es nègre; empereur, vieille démangeaison, tu es nègre: tu as bu d'une liqueur non taxée, de la fabrique de Satan.—Ce peuple est inspiré par la fièvre et le cancer. Infirmes et vieillards sont tellement respectables qu'ils demandent à être bouillis.—Le plus malin est de quitter ce continent, où la folie rôde pour pourvoir d'otages ces misérables. J'entre au vrai royaume des enfants de Cham.

Connais-je encore la nature? me connais-je?—*Plus de mots*. J'ensevelis les morts dans mon ventre. Cris, tambour, danse, danse, danse, danse! Je ne vois même pas l'heure où, les blancs débarquant, je tomberai au néant.

Faim, soif, cris, danse, danse, danse, danse!

Les blancs débarquent. Le canon! Il faut se soumettre au baptême, s'habiller, travailler.

J'ai reçu au cœur le coup de la grâce. Ah! je ne l'avais pas prévu!

Je n'ai point fait le mal. Les jours vont m'être légers, le repentir me sera épargné. Je n'aurai pas eu les tourments de l'âme presque morte au bien, où remonte la lumière sévère comme les cierges funéraires. Le sort du fils de famille, cercueil prématuré couvert de limpides larmes. Sans doute la débauche est bête, le vice est bête; il faut jeter la pourriture à l'écart. Mais l'horloge ne sera pas arrivée à ne plus sonner que l'heure de la pure douleur! Vais-je être enlevé comme un enfant, pour jouer au paradis dans l'oubli de tout le malheur!

Vite! est-il d'autres vies?—Le sommeil dans la richesse est impossible. La richesse a toujours été bien public. L'amour divin seul octroie les clefs de la science. Je vois que la nature n'est qu'un spectacle de bonté. Adieu chimères, idéals, erreurs.

Le chant raisonnable des anges s'élève du navire sauveur: c'est l'amour divin.—Deux amours! je puis mourir de l'amour terrestre, mourir de dévouement. J'ai laissé des âmes dont la peine s'accroîtra

forgiving them!—Like Joan of Arc!—'Priests, teachers, masters, you are making a mistake in delivering me up to justice. I have never been one of you; I have never been a Christian; I belong to the race which sang on the scaffold; I understand nothing of laws; I have no moral sense, I am an animal; you are making a mistake...'

Yes, I close my eyes against your light. I am an animal, a nigger. But I can be saved. You people are phoney niggers, maniacs, savages, misers. Tradesman, you're a nigger; courtroom judge, nigger; general, nigger; emperor, you piece of pus, nigger; you've drunk untaxed liquor from Satan's distillery.—Fever and cancer are the inspiration of this people. The sick and the old are so respectful that they demand to be boiled. The cleverest thing to do is to leave this continent, where madness roams, searching out hostages for this dismal bunch. I am entering the true kingdom of the children of Ham.*

Do I understand nature yet? do I know myself?—*No more words.* I bury the dead in my stomach. Shouts, drums, dance, dance, dance, dance! I cannot even envisage the time when, as the white men disembark, I shall plummet into nothingness.

Hunger, thirst, shouts, dance, dance, dance, dance!

The white men are landing. Cannon fire! Now we will have to accept baptism, clothes, work.

Saving grace has stabbed my heart. Ah! this I had not foreseen!

I have done nothing evil. My days will be easy, I shall be spared repentance. I shall not have endured the torments of the soul half-dead to goodness, light rising bleak as funeral candles. The fate of the son of good family, a premature coffin covered with limpid tears. Debauchery is stupid no doubt, vice is stupid; rottenness must be cast out. But the clock cannot yet have reached the point when it will strike only the hour of pure pain! Will I now be carried off like a child, to play in paradise, all unhappiness forgotten!

Quick! are there other lives?—Sound sleep is impossible for the rich. Wealth has always been a public asset. Only Divine Love can bestow the keys to knowledge. I see that nature is merely a show of goodness. Farewell chimeras, ideals, mistakes.

The sensible song of angels rises from the rescue ship; it is divine love.—Two loves! I could die of earthly love, die of devotion. I have left behind souls whose grief can only grow because I have gone! You

de mon départ! Vous me choisissez parmi les naufragés; ceux qui restent sont-ils pas mes amis?

Sauvez-les!

La raison m'est née. Le monde est bon. Je bénirai la vie. J'aimerai mes frères. Ce ne sont plus des promesses d'enfance. Ni l'espoir d'échapper à la vieillesse et à la mort. Dieu fait ma force, et je loue Dieu.

L'ennui n'est plus mon amour. Les rages, les débauches, la folie, dont je sais tous les élans et les désastres,—tout mon fardeau est déposé. Apprécions sans vertige l'étendue de mon innocence.

Je ne serais plus capable de demander le réconfort d'une bastonnade. Je ne me crois pas embarqué pour une noce avec Jésus-Christ pour beau-père.

Je ne suis pas prisonnier de ma raison. J'ai dit: Dieu. Je veux la liberté dans le salut: comment la poursuivre? Les goûts frivoles m'ont quitté. Plus besoin de dévouement ni d'amour divin. Je ne regrette pas le siècle des cœurs sensibles. Chacun a sa raison, mépris et charité: je retiens ma place au sommet de cette angélique échelle de bon sens.

Quant au bonheur établi, domestique ou non... non, je ne peux pas. Je suis trop dissipé, trop faible. La vie fleurit par le travail, vieille vérité: moi, ma vie n'est pas assez pesante, elle s'envole et flotte loin au-dessus de l'action, ce cher point du monde.

Comme je deviens vieille fille, à manquer du courage d'aimer la mort!

Si Dieu m'accordait le calme céleste, aérien, la prière,—comme les anciens saints.—Les saints! des forts! les anachorètes, des artistes comme il n'en faut plus!

Farce continuelle! Mon innocence me ferait pleurer. La vie est la farce à mener par tous.

Assez! Voici la punition.—*En marche!*

Ah! les poumons brûlent, les tempes grondent! la nuit roule dans mes yeux, par ce soleil! le cœur... les membres...

Où va-t-on? au combat? Je suis faible! les autres avancent. Les outils, les armes... le temps!...

are choosing me from among the castaways; aren't those who remain my friends?

Save them!

Reason is born in me. The world is good. I shall bless life. I shall love my brothers. These are not childhood promises any more. Nor the hope of escaping old age and death. God is my strength, and I praise God.

I am no longer in love with listlessness. Anger, debauchery, madness, whose surges and crashes I know full well,—all my burden is laid down. Let us assess with composure the extent of my innocence.

I would no longer be capable of asking for the consolation of a beating. I do not imagine myself off to celebrate a wedding with Jesus Christ for father-in-law.

I am not a prisoner of my own reason. I have said: God. I want freedom in salvation: how to set about the search? My taste for frivolity has left me. No further need for devotion or divine love. I would not want back the century of emotion and fine feelings. Contempt and charity, each has reason on its side; I keep my place at the top of this angelic ladder of good sense.

As for settled happiness, domestic or otherwise... no, I simply cannot. I am too dissipated, too weak. Work makes life blossom, an old truth: me though, my life lacks solidity, it flits and floats way up above action, that focus the world holds so dear.

What an old maid I'm becoming, with this lack of courage to welcome death!

If only God would grant me celestial calm, ethereal calm, prayer,—like the old saints.—The saints! strong men! anchorites, artists such as we no longer need!

Farce without end! My innocence is enough to make me cry. Life is the farce we all of us must act out.

Enough! This is the punishment.—*Forward march!*

Ah! My lungs burn, my head throbs! night rolls in my eyes beneath this sunlight! My heart... my limbs...

Where are we going? into battle? I am weak! the others are advancing. Tools, weapons... time!...

Feu! feu sur moi! Là! ou je me rends.—Lâches!—Je me tue! Je me jette aux pieds des chevaux!

Ah!...

—Je m'y habituerai.

Ce serait la vie française, le sentier de l'honneur!

Nuit de l'enfer

J'ai avalé une fameuse gorgée de poison.—Trois fois béni soit le conseil qui m'est arrivé!—Les entrailles me brûlent. La violence du venin tord mes membres, me rend difforme, me terrasse. Je meurs de soif, j'étouffe, je ne puis crier. C'est l'enfer, l'éternelle peine! Voyez comme le feu se relève! Je brûle comme il faut. Va, démon!

J'avais entrevu la conversion au bien et au bonheur, le salut. Puis-je décrire la vision, l'air de l'enfer ne souffre pas les hymnes! C'était des millions de créatures charmantes, un suave concert spirituel, la force et la paix, les nobles ambitions, que sais-je?

Les nobles ambitions!

Et c'est encore la vie!—Si la damnation est éternelle! Un homme qui veut se mutiler est bien damné, n'est-ce pas? Je me crois en enfer, donc j'y suis. C'est l'exécution du catéchisme. Je suis esclave de mon baptême. Parents, vous avez fait mon malheur et vous avez fait le vôtre. Pauvre innocent!—L'enfer ne peut attaquer les païens.—C'est la vie encore! Plus tard, les délices de la damnation seront plus profondes. Un crime, vite, que je tombe au néant, de par la loi humaine.

Tais-toi, mais tais-toi!... C'est la honte, le reproche, ici: Satan qui dit que le feu est ignoble, que ma colère est affreusement sotte.—Assez!... Des erreurs qu'on me souffle, magies, parfums faux, musiques puériles.—Et dire que je tiens la vérité, que je vois la justice: j'ai un jugement sain et arrêté, je suis prêt pour la perfection... Orgueil.—La peau de ma tête se dessèche. Pitié! Seigneur, j'ai peur. J'ai soif, si soif! Ah! l'enfance, l'herbe, la pluie, le lac sur les pierres, *le clair de lune quand la clocher sonnait douze*... le diable est au clocher, à cette heure. Marie! Sainte-Vierge!... —Horreur de ma bêtise.

Fire! fire at me! Go on, or I'll surrender.—Cowards!—I shall kill myself! I shall throw myself under the horses' hooves!

Ah!...

—I'll get used to it.

That would be the French way of life, the path of honour!

Night in Hell

I have swallowed a mighty gulp of poison.—Thrice blessed be the counsel I was given!—My insides burn. The violence of the poison racks my limbs, renders me deformed, lays me out. I die of thirst, I choke, I cannot cry out. This is hell, the eternal torment! See how the fire burns more fiercely! I am roasting nicely. So there, demon!

I had glimpsed, once, the conversion to goodness and happiness, salvation. I might want to describe the vision, but the air of hell does not suffer hymns! There were a myriad charming creatures, a mellifluous spiritual concert, strength and peace, noble ambitions, and more, no doubt.

Noble ambitions!

And still I am here, alive! Could damnation be eternal? A man who wants to mutilate himself is truly damned, no? I think I am in hell, therefore I am. That is the catechism in action. I am the slave of my baptism. Parents, you have caused my unhappiness and your own. Poor innocent!—Hell cannot touch the heathen.—Still I am alive! Later, the delights of damnation will get deeper. Quick, a crime, so that I may plunge into nothingness, according to human law.

Shut up, shut up!... Here, everything is shame and reproach: Satan who says that hellfire lacks nobility, that my anger is impossibly stupid.—Enough!... Untruths whispered to me, magic, false scents, puerile music.—And to think I have the truth, and see justice: my judgement is sane and sound, I am ready for perfection... Pride. The skin on my head is drying up. Mercy, Lord, I am afraid! I am thirsty, so thirsty! Ah, childhood, the grass, the rain, the lake on the stones, *the moonlight as the church clock struck twelve*... the devil is in the belfry, at this very moment.—Mary! Holy Virgin!...—The horror of my stupidity.

Là-bas, ne sont-ce pas des âmes honnêtes, qui me veulent du bien... Venez... J'ai un oreiller sur la bouche, elles ne m'entendent pas, ce sont des fantômes. Puis, jamais personne ne pense à autrui. Qu'on n'approche pas. Je sens le roussi, c'est certain.

Les hallucinations sont innombrables. C'est bien ce que j'ai toujours eu: plus de foi en l'histoire, l'oubli des principes. Je m'en tairai: poëtes et visionnaires seraient jaloux. Je suis mille fois le plus riche, soyons avare comme la mer.

Ah ça! l'horloge de la vie s'est arrêtée tout à l'heure. Je ne suis plus au monde.—La théologie est sérieuse, l'enfer est certainement *en bas*—et le ciel en haut.— Extase, cauchemar, sommeil dans un nid de flammes.

Que de malices dans l'attention dans la campagne... Satan, Ferdinand, court avec les graines sauvages... Jésus marche sur les ronces purpurines, sans les courber... Jésus marchait sur les eaux irritées. La lanterne nous le montra debout, blanc et des tresses brunes, au flanc d'une vague d'émeraude...

Je vais dévoiler tous les mystères: mystères religieux ou naturels, mort, naissance, avenir, passé, cosmogonie, néant. Je suis maître en fantasmagories.

Écoutez!...

J'ai tous les talents!—Il n'y a personne ici et il y a quelqu'un: je ne voudrais pas répandre mon trésor.—Veut-on des chants nègres, des danses de houris? Veut-on que je disparaisse, que je plonge à la recherche de l'*anneau*? Veut-on? Je ferai de l'or, des remèdes.

Fiez-vous donc à moi, la foi soulage, guide, guérit. Tous, venez,—même les petits enfants,—que je vous console, qu'on répande pour vous son cœur,—le cœur merveilleux!—Pauvres hommes, travailleurs! Je ne demande pas de prières; avec votre confiance seulement, je serai heureux.

—Et pensons à moi. Ceci me fait peu regretter le monde. J'ai de la chance de ne pas souffrir plus. Ma vie ne fut que folies douces, c'est regrettable.

Bah! faisons toutes les grimaces imaginables.

Décidément, nous sommes hors du monde. Plus aucun son. Mon tact a disparu. Ah! mon château, ma Saxe, mon bois de saules. Les soirs, les matins, les nuits, les jours... Suis-je las!

Je devrais avoir mon enfer pour la colère, mon enfer pour l'orgueil,—et l'enfer de la caresse; un concert d'enfers.

Over there, are they not honest souls, who wish me well?... Come... A pillow stops my mouth, they cannot hear me, they are ghosts. And then, no one ever thinks of others. Do not come near. I stink of burnt flesh, for sure.

The hallucinations cannot be counted. That is how it has always been for me: no more faith in history, principles forgotten. I shall be silent on this matter: poets and visionaries would be jealous. I am a thousand times richer than they, like the sea I shall store it up.

And see this, the clock of life stopped a while ago. I am no longer of the world.—Theology means it, hell is certainly *down below*—and heaven is above.—Ecstasy, nightmare, sleep in a nest of flames.

How the mind plays up in the country... Satan, Old Nick, runs with the wild seed... Jesus walks on crimson tangles of thorn and does not bend them... Jesus walked on troubled waters once. In the lantern-light we saw him, robed in white, his hair brown and lank, standing on an emerald wave...

I shall unveil every mystery: religious or natural mysteries, death, birth, future, past, cosmogony, the void. I am the master of phantasmagoria.

Listen!...

I have all the talents!—There is no one here and there is someone: I do not want to spill my treasure.—What would you like, negro songs, Eastern dancing-girls? Or shall I disappear, or dive in search of the *ring*? Ask, and I shall make gold, cures.

Trust me, then, faith relieves, guides, heals. Come, everyone,—even the little children—let me console you, let someone give his heart for you—the marvellous heart!—Poor men, workers! I do not ask for prayers; with your trust alone I shall be happy.

—And let us think of me. All this scarcely makes me regret the world. I am lucky not to suffer more. My life was only sweet madness, and that is a shame.

Bah! why not pull every conceivable face.

There can be no doubt, we have left the world. Not a sound anywhere. My sense of touch has gone. Ah, my chateau, my Saxony, my willow wood. Evenings, mornings, nights, days... Such fatigue!

I should have a hell for my anger, a hell for my pride—there should be a hell for sex; a symphony of hells.

I am dying of fatigue. This is the grave, I am headed for the

Je meurs de lassitude. C'est le tombeau, je m'en vais aux vers, horreur de l'horreur! Satan, farceur, tu veux me dissoudre, avec tes charmes. Je réclame. Je réclame! un coup de fourche, une goutte de feu.

Ah! remonter à la vie! Jeter les yeux sur nos difformités. Et ce poison, ce baiser mille fois maudit! Ma faiblesse, la cruauté du monde! Mon Dieu, pitié, cachez-moi, je me tiens trop mal!—Je suis caché et je ne le suis pas.

C'est le feu qui se relève avec son damné.

Délires I

Vierge folle
L'Époux infernal

Écoutons la confession d'un compagnon d'enfer:

'Ô divin Époux, mon Seigneur, ne refusez pas la confession de la plus triste de vos servantes. Je suis perdue. Je suis soûle. Je suis impure. Quelle vie!

'Pardon; divin Seigneur, pardon! Ah! pardon! Que de larmes! Et que de larmes encore plus tard, j'espère!

'Plus tard, je connaîtrai le divin Époux! Je suis née soumise à Lui.—L'autre peut me battre maintenant!

'A présent, je suis au fond du monde! Ô mes amies!... non, pas mes amies... Jamais délires ni tortures semblables... Est-ce bête!

'Ah! je souffre, je crie. Je souffre vraiment. Tout pourtant m'est permis, chargée du mépris des plus méprisables cœurs.

'Enfin, faisons cette confidence, quitte à la répéter vingt autres fois,—aussi morne, aussi insignifiante!

'Je suis esclave de l'Époux infernal, celui qui a perdu les vierges folles. C'est bien ce démon-là. Ce n'est pas un spectre, ce n'est pas un fantôme. Mais moi qui ai perdu la sagesse, qui suis damnée et morte au monde,—on ne me tuera pas!—Comment vous le décrire! Je ne sais même plus parler. Je suis en deuil, je pleure, j'ai peur. Un peu de fraîcheur, Seigneur, si vous voulez, si vous voulez bien!

worms, horror of horrors! Satan, you joker, you want to undo me with your spells. I beg, I demand you spike me with your pitchfork, drop fire on me.

Ah, to return to life! Cast eyes on our deformities. And that poison, that kiss damned a thousand times! My weakness, the cruelty of the world! Mercy, my God, hide me, I cannot look out for myself!—I am hidden and not hidden.

And there, the flames rise up again with the damned soul.

First Delirium

The Foolish Virgin
The Infernal Bridegroom

Let us listen to the confession of a companion in hell:

'O heavenly Bridegroom, my Lord, do not refuse the confession of one of the most unhappy of your handmaidens. I am undone. I am unclean. What a life!

'Forgive me, Lord of heaven, forgive me! Ah! forgive me! So much weeping! So much more weeping to come, I hope!

'In time I shall come to know the heavenly Bridegroom! I was born His servant.—For the present, the other one can beat me!

'Now, I am in the very depths of the world! O you women, my friends!... no, not my friends... Never have there been ravings and torment like this... Too ridiculous!

'Ah, I am in pain, I yell. Such real pain. Yet I am allowed everything, encumbered as I am with the contempt of the most contemptible hearts.

'So then, let me confide this, even if I have to repeat it twenty times,—such dreariness, such insignificance!

'I am a slave of the infernal Bridegroom, the one who has been the ruin of the foolish virgins. That is the devil I mean. No spectre, no ghost. But how can I, a woman no longer reasonable, damned and dead to the world,—I can scarcely be killed!—How can I possibly describe him to you! I cannot even speak any more. I am in mourning, I weep, I am scared. Please, Lord, a little fresh air, if you would be so very good.

'Je suis veuve... —J'étais veuve... —mais oui, j'ai été bien sérieuse jadis, et je ne suis pas née pour devenir squelette!... —Lui était presque un enfant... Ses délicatesses mystérieuses m'avaient séduite. J'ai oublié tout mon devoir humain pour le suivre. Quelle vie! La vraie vie est absente. Nous ne sommes pas au monde. Je vais où il va, il le faut. Et souvent il s'emporte contre moi, *moi, la pauvre âme*. Le Démon!—C'est un Démon, vous savez, *ce n'est pas un homme*.

'Il dit: "Je n'aime pas les femmes. L'amour est à réinventer, on le sait. Elles ne peuvent plus que vouloir une position assurée. La position gagnée, cœur et beauté sont mis de côté: il ne reste que froid dédain, l'aliment du mariage, aujourd' hui. Ou bien je vois des femmes, avec les signes du bonheur, dont, moi, j'aurai pu faire de bonnes camarades, dévorées tout d'abord par des brutes sensibles comme des bûchers..."

'Je l'écoute faisant de l'infamie une gloire, de la cruauté un charme. "Je suis de race lointaine: mes pères étaient Scandinaves: ils se perçaient les côtes, buvaient leur sang.—Je me ferai des entailles partout le corps, je me tatouerai, je veux devenir hideux comme un Mongol: tu verras, je hurlerai dans les rues. Je veux devenir bien fou de rage. Ne me montre jamais de bijoux, je ramperais et me tordrais sur le tapis. Ma richesse, je la voudrais tachée de sang partout. Jamais je ne travaillerai..." Plusieurs nuits, son démon me saisissant, nous nous roulions, je luttais avec lui!—Les nuits, souvent, ivre, il se poste dans des rues ou dans des maisons, pour m'épouvanter mortellement.—"On me coupera vraiment le cou; ce sera dégoûtant." Oh! ces jours où il veut marcher avec l'air du crime!

'Parfois il parle, en une façon de patois attendri, de la mort qui fait repentir, des malheureux qui existent certainement, des travaux pénibles, des départs qui déchirent les cœurs. Dans les bouges où nous nous enivrions, il pleurait en considérant ceux qui nous entouraient, bétail de la misère. Il relevait les ivrognes dans les rues noires. Il avait la pitié d'une mère méchante pour les petits enfants.—Il s'en allait avec des gentillesses de petite fille au catéchisme.—Il feignait d'être éclairé sur tout, commerce, art, médecine.— Je le suivais, il le faut!

'Je voyais tout le décor dont, en esprit, il s'entourait; vêtements, draps, meubles : je lui prêtais des armes, une autre figure. Je voyais tout ce qui le touchait, comme il aurait voulu le créer pour lui.

'I am a widow... I was a widow... no, I assure you that I was a serious woman once, and was not born to become a skeleton!... As for him, he was scarcely more than a child... His mysterious care and attention had quite charmed me. I forgot all my human responsibilities to follow him. What a life! True life is somewhere else. We are not in the real world. I follow him wherever he goes, I must. And often he rants and raves at me—me, *poor soul that I am*. Devil!—Yes, he is a Devil, you know, *he is not a human being*.

'He says: "I do not love women. Love must be reinvented, that is clear. All they can do now is to seek security. Once that is achieved, beauty and heart are abandoned: all that remains is cold disdain, the sustenance of marriage today. Or else I see women who bear the marks of happiness, and whom I could have made into real companions; but too late, they have been devoured by brutes as sensitive as stakes..."

'I listen to him glorifying infamy, turning cruelty into a magic charm. "My origins go a long way back: my forebears were Scandinavian: they pierced their sides, drank their own blood.—I shall cut my body all over, tattoo myself, I want to become as hideous as a Mongol: you'll see, I'll go screaming down the streets. I want to go quite mad with rage. Never show me jewels, I'd writhe in convulsions around the carpet. I would wish my wealth to be stained with blood all over. I shall never do a jot of work"... Many nights, when the devil which possessed him possessed me, we rolled together on the ground, I fought with him!—At night, often, drunk, somewhere in the street or in a house, he jumps out on me and frightens me to death—"Someone is really going to slit my throat; it will be quite sickening." Oh! those days when he decides he wants to walk around looking like a criminal!

'Sometimes, in a kind of soft patois, he speaks of death which brings repentance, of the all-too-real existence of the wretched, the harshness of certain work, the heartbreak of departure. In the dives where we got drunk, he wept with sympathy for those around us, the lowest cattle of humanity. In dark streets, he would help drunkards to their feet. His was the pity a severe mother has for small children.—He went, full of the benevolence of a little girl learning her catechism.—He pretended to know about everything, commerce, art, medicine.—I followed him, what else?

'I could see the whole decor in the midst of which he placed

Quand il me semblait avoir l'esprit inerte, je le suivais, moi, dans des actions étranges et compliquées, loin, bonnes ou mauvaises: j'étais sûre de ne jamais entrer dans son monde. A côté de son cher corps endormi, que d'heures des nuits j'ai veillé, cherchant pourquoi il voulait tant s'évader de la réalité. Jamais homme n'eût pareil vœu. Je reconnaissais,—sans craindre pour lui,—qu'il pouvait être un sérieux danger dans la société.—Il a peut-être des secrets pour *changer la vie?* Non, il ne fait qu'en chercher, me répliquais-je. Enfin sa charité est ensorcelée, et j'en suis la prisonnière. Aucune autre âme n'aurait assez de force,—force de désespoir!—pour la supporter,—pour être protégée et aimée par lui. D'ailleurs, je ne me le figurais pas avec une autre âme: on voit son Ange, jamais l'Ange d'un autre,—je crois. J'étais dans son âme comme dans un palais qu'on a vidé pour ne pas voir une personne si peu noble que vous: voilà tout. Hélas! je dépendais bien de lui. Mais que voulait-il avec mon existence terne et lâche? Il ne me rendait pas meilleure, s'il ne me faisait pas mourir! Tristement dépitée, je lui dis quelquefois: "Je te comprends." Il haussait les épaules.

'Ainsi, mon chagrin se renouvelant sans cesse, et me trouvant plus égarée à mes yeux,—comme à tous les yeux qui auraient voulu me fixer, si je n'eusse été condamnée pour jamais à l'oubli de tous!—j'avais de plus en plus faim de sa bonté. Avec ses baisers et ses étreintes amies, c'était bien un ciel, un sombre ciel, où j'entrais, et où j'aurais voulu être laissée, pauvre, sourde, muette, aveugle. Déjà j'en prenais l'habitude. Je nous voyais comme deux bons enfants, libres de se promener dans le Paradis de tristesse. Nous nous accordions. Bien émus, nous travaillions ensemble. Mais, après une pénétrante caresse, il disait: "Comme ça te paraîtra drôle, quand je n'y serai plus, ce par quoi tu as passé. Quand tu n'auras plus mes bras sous ton cou, ni mon cœur pour t'y reposer, ni cette bouche sur tes yeux. Parce qu'il faudra que je m'en aille, très-loin, un jour. Puis il faut que j'en aide d'autres: c'est mon devoir. Quoique ce ne soit guère ragoûtant..., chère âme..." Tout de suite je me pressentais, lui parti, en proie au vertige, précipitée dans l'ombre la plus affreuse: la mort. Je lui faisais promettre qu'il ne me lâcherait pas. Il l'a faite vingt fois, cette promesse d'amant. C'était aussi frivole que moi lui disant: "Je te comprends."

'Ah! je n'ai jamais été jalouse de lui. Il ne me quittera pas, je crois. Que devenir? Il n'a pas une connaissance; il ne travaillera jamais. Il

himself in his imagination: clothes, drapery, furniture; I lent him weapons, a different countenance. I could see everything which affected him, the way he would have wanted to make it. Whenever he seemed to me at his most lethargic, I would follow him far into strange and complicated ventures, for better or for worse; I could be certain I would never enter his world. Next to his dear sleeping body, how many hours of how many nights have I stayed awake, trying to work out why he wanted so much to escape reality. No man ever had such a wish. I realized,—without being afraid for him—that he could become a serious threat to society.—Perhaps he has secrets which would *change life itself*? No, he is just trying to uncover them, I told myself. The fact is that his charity is a thing bewitched, and I am its prisoner. No other being would have the strength,—the strength of despair!—to bear it,—to be cherished and loved by him. And besides, I could not imagine him with someone else: we see our own Angel, never other people's,—I think. I existed in his soul as if in a palace which has been emptied so that no one as inferior as oneself might be seen: that is all. But alas, I was so dependent on him. But what did he want with my gutless, drab existence? He did not make me a better person, though neither did he finish me off! Sad, vexed, I said to him sometimes: "I understand you." He would shrug his shoulders.

'And so, with my pain endlessly renewed, finding myself yet more distraught,—as would anyone who cared to look at me closely enough, had I not been condemned for ever to be forgotten by all!—I became more and more hungry for his goodness. His kisses and warm embraces made it a heaven, a dark heaven, which I entered and where I would happily have stayed, poor, deaf, dumb, blind. Already I was getting used to it. I saw us as a pair of nice children, free to wander in the Paradise of sorrow. We were as one. With deep emotion, we set to work together. But after a profoundly moving caress, he would say: "How strange it will seem to you when I have gone, all that you've been through. When you won't have my arms around your neck, nor my heart to rest on, nor these lips on your eyes. For I will have to go some day, go very far away. There are others who also need my help: that is my task. Though hardly to my taste..., my dearest..." And straight away I saw myself, with him gone, sick with dizziness, plunged into the most terrible darkness: death. I made him promise not to leave me. Twenty times over he made me that

veut vivre somnambule. Seules, sa bonté et sa charité lui donneraient-elles droit dans le monde réel? Par instants, j'oublie la pitié où je suis tombée: lui me rendra forte, nous voyagerons, nous chasserons dans les déserts, nous dormirons sur les pavés des villes inconnues, sans soins, sans peines. Ou je me réveillerai, et les lois et les mœurs auront changé,—grâce à son pouvoir magique,—le monde, en restant le même, me laissera à mes désirs, joies, nonchalances. Oh! la vie d'aventures qui existe dans les livres des enfants, pour me récompenser, j'ai tant souffert, me la donneras-tu? Il ne peut pas. J'ignore son idéal. Il m'a dit avoir des regrets, des espoirs: cela ne doit pas me regarder. Parle-t-il à Dieu? Peut-être devrais-je m'adresser à Dieu. Je suis au plus profond de l'abîme, et je ne sais plus prier.

'S'il m'expliquait ses tristesses, les comprendrais-je plus que ses railleries? Il m'attaque, il passe des heures à me faire honte de tout ce qui m'a pu toucher au monde, et s'indigne si je pleure.

"—Tu vois cet élégant jeune homme, entrant dans la belle et calme maison: il s'appelle Duval, Dufour, Armand, Maurice, que sais-je? Une femme s'est dévouée à aimer ce méchant idiot: elle est morte, c'est certes une sainte au ciel, à présent. Tu me feras mourir comme il a fait mourir cette femme. C'est notre sort, à nous, cœurs charitables..." Hélas! il avait des jours où tous les hommes agissant lui paraissaient les jouets de délires grotesques: il riait affreusement, longtemps.—Puis, il reprenait ses manières de jeune mère, de sœur aimée. S'il était moins sauvage, nous serions sauvés! Mais sa douceur aussi est mortelle. Je lui suis soumise.—Ah! je suis folle!

'Un jour peut-être il disparaîtra merveilleusement; mais il faut que je sache, s'il doit remonter à un ciel, que je voie un peu l'assomption de mon petit ami!'

Drôle de ménage!

lover's promise. It was as empty as my telling him "I understand you."

'Ah, I have never been jealous of him. I believe he will never leave me. What could he do? He knows nobody at all; he will never do a stroke of work. He wants to go through life like a sleepwalker. Would his kindness and charity be enough to grant him any favours in the real world? At odd moments, I forget the lamentable state I have got into: he will make me strong, we will travel, go hunting in virgin lands, sleep on the paving in unknown cities, carefree and light-hearted. Or else I shall wake up and find that laws and customs have been changed by his magic power,—the world, though still the same, will leave me to my desires, my joys, my easy mind. Oh! that life of adventure in the books of childhood, will you give it me as recompense for all my suffering? He cannot. I do not have the first idea of his ideal world. He has told me that he has regrets, hopes: but that can be no concern of mine. Does he speak to God! I am at the very bottom of the abyss, and no longer know how to pray.

'If he explained why he is so sad, would I understand that any more than his mockery? He attacks me, he spends hours making me feel ashamed of everything which has ever affected me, and then it riles him if I cry.

"—You see that stylish young man going into that beautiful calm house: his name is Duval, Dufour, Armand, Maurice, or some such. Some woman has dedicated herself to loving that nasty buffoon: She is now dead, without doubt a saint in heaven. You will be the death of me, as he was of her. That is the destiny of us generous hearts..." Alas, he had days when their antics made all men seem to him like puppets of grotesque deliriums: he would laugh long and horribly.—Then he would start acting again like a young mother, an adored sister. If he were less wild, we would be saved! But even his sweetness is deadly. I am in his power.—Ah, I am going mad!

'One day, perhaps, he will disappear as if by magic; but I must know it, if he is to go to some heaven, I must be able to get at least a glimpse of my little friend's assumption!'

Odd couple!

Délires II

Alchimie du verbe

A moi. L'histoire d'une de mes folies.

Depuis longtemps je me vantais de posséder tous les paysages possibles, et trouvais dérisoires les célébrités de la peinture et de la poésie moderne.

J'aimais les peintures idiotes, dessus de portes, décors, toiles de saltimbanques, enseignes, enluminures popularies; la littérature démodée, latin d'église, livres érotiques sans orthographe, romans de nos aïeules, contes de fées, petits livres de l'enfance, opéras vieux, refrains niais, rhythmes naïfs.

Je rêvais croisades, voyages de découvertes dont on n'a pas de relations, républiques sans histories, guerres de religion étouffées, révolutions de mœurs, déplacements de races et de continents: je croyais à tous les enchantements.

J'inventai la couleur des voyelles!—*A* noir, *E* blanc, *I* rouge, *O* bleu, *U* vert.—Je réglai la forme et le mouvement de chaque consonne, et, avec des rhythmes instinctifs, je me flattai d'inventer un verbe poétique accessible, un jour ou l'autre, à tous les sens. Je réservais la traduction.

Ce fut d'abord une étude. J'écrivais des silences, des nuits, je notais l'inexprimable. Je fixais des vertiges.

Loin des oiseaux, des troupeaux, des villageoises,
Que buvais-je, à genoux dans cette bruyère
Entourée de tendres bois de noisetiers,
Dans un brouillard d'après-midi tiède et vert?

Que pouvais-je boire dans cette jeune Oise,
—Ormeaux sans voix, gazon sans fleurs, ciel couvert!—
Boire à ces gourdes jaunes, loin de ma case
Chérie? Quelque liqueur d'or qui fait suer.

Je faisais une louche enseigne d'auberge.
—Un orage vint chasser le ciel. Au soir
L'eau des bois se perdait sur les sables vierges,
Le vent de Dieu jetait des glaçons aux mares;

Pleurant, je voyais de l'or—et ne pus boire.—

Second Delirium

Alchemy of the Word

My turn. The history of one of my madnesses.

For a long time I had boasted that I held every possible scene in my hands, and I thought laughable the great figures of modern painting and poetry.

What I liked were absurd paintings, decorations over doorways, stage scenery, travelling fairs' backcloths, inn-signs, cheap coloured prints; literature gone out of fashion, church Latin, erotic books with bad spelling, novels our grandmothers used to read, fairy-tales, little books for children, old operas, meaningless refrains, crude rhythms.

I dreamed of crusades, unlogged journeys of discovery, republics with no history, wars of religion put down, revolutions in manners, races and continents on the move: I believed in each and every piece of magic.

I invented the colour of vowels!—*A* black, *E* white, *I* red, *O* blue, *U* green.—I organized the shape and movement of every consonant, and by means of instinctive rhythms, flattered myself that I was the inventor of a poetic language, accessible sooner or later to all the senses. Interpretation I kept for myself.

First, I made a study. I wrote down silences, nights, I noted the ineffable. I nailed vertigo.

Far from birds and flocks and village girls
What was I drinking, on my knees in that heather
Surrounded by woods of young hazel
In a warm green mist of afternoon?

What could I be drinking from that young Oise,
—Voiceless elms, flowerless grass, sullen sky!—
Drink what from those yellow gourds, far from
My beloved hut? Some sweat-provoking liquid gold?

I seemed a suspect inn-sign.
—A storm burst and cleared the sky. By evening
Wood-water vanished on virgin sands,
God sent a wind to cast ice over ponds;

Full of tears, I saw gold—and could not drink.

A quatre heures du matin, l'été,
Le sommeil d'amour dure encore.
Sous les bocages s'évapore
  L'odeur du soir fêté.

Là-bas, dans leur vaste chantier
Au soleil des Hespérides,
Déjà s'agitent—en bras de chemise—
    Les Charpentiers.

Dans leurs Déserts de mousse, tranquilles,
Ils préparent les lambris précieux
    Où la ville
  Peindra de faux cieux.

Ô, pour ces Ouvriers charmants
Sujets d'un roi de Babylone,
Vénus! quitte un instant les Amants
Dont l'âme est en couronne.

  Ô Reine des Bergers,
Porte aux travailleurs l'eau-de-vie,
Que leurs forces soient en paix
En attendant le bain dans la mer à midi.

La vieillerie poétique avait une bonne part dans mon alchimie du verbe.

Je m'habituai à l'hallucination simple: je voyais très-franchement une mosquée à la place d'une usine, une école de tambours faite par des anges, des calèches sur les routes du ciel, un salon au fond d'un lac; les monstres, les mystères; un titre de vaudeville dressait des épouvantes devant moi.

Puis j'expliquai mes sophismes magiques avec l'hallucination des mots!

Je finis par trouver sacré le désordre de mon esprit. J'étais oisif, en proie à une lourde fièvre: j'enviais la félicité des bêtes,—les chenilles, qui représentent l'innocence des limbes, les taupes, le sommeil de la virginité!

Mon caractère s'aigrissait. Je disais adieu au monde dans d'espèces de romances:

Four a.m. in summertime
Love stays fast asleep.
In gardens dawn dispels last
        Evening's headiness.

On the enormous site stretching up
Towards the golden apple sun
Already shirt-sleeved carpenters
        Are at their work.

Calm in their deserts of moss
They panel fine ceilings
        Where the town
    Will paint false skies.

For these charming Workers,
These Babylon King's men,
Venus, leave the lovers a moment
        In aureoles of bliss.

        O Queen of Shepherds!
Bring the workers eau-de-vie
To calm their strength
Until they can bathe at noon in the sea.

Old-fashioned notions of poetry played an important part in my alchemy of the word.

I got used to hallucination, pure and simple: I would see, fair and square, a mosque where there was a factory, a drum-corps of angels, coaches on the roads in the sky, a drawing-room at the bottom of a lake; monsters, mysteries; horrors leaped up before me from the titles of some vaudeville.

And then I explained my magic sophisms by turning words into hallucinations!

Finally I came to consider my mind's disorder as sacred. I was idle, prey to oppressive fever; I envied the happiness of beasts—caterpillars, who represent the innocence of limbo; moles, the sleep of virginity!

My character was turning sour. I said my farewells to the world in ballads of a sort:

Chanson de la plus haute tour

Qu'il vienne, qu'il vienne,
Le temps dont on s'éprenne.

J'ai tant fait patience
Qu'à jamais j'oublie.
Craintes et souffrances
Aux cieux sont parties.
Et la soif malsaine
Obscurcit mes veines.

Qu'il vienne, qu'il vienne,
Le temps dont on s'éprenne.

Telle la prairie
A l'oubli livrée,
Grandie, et fleurie
D'encens et d'ivraies,
Au bourdon farouche
Des sales mouches.

Qu'il vienne, qu'il vienne,
Le temps dont on s'éprenne.

J'aimai le désert, les vergers brûlés, les boutiques fanées, les boissons tiédies. Je me traînais dans les ruelles puantes et, les yeux fermés, je m'offrais au soleil, dieu de feu.

'Général, s'il reste un vieux canon sur tes remparts en ruines, bombarde-nous avec des blocs de terre sèche. Aux glaces des magasins splendides! dans les salons! Fais manger sa poussière à la ville. Oxyde les gargouilles. Emplis les boudoirs de poudre de rubis brûlante...'

Oh! le moucheron enivré à la pissotière de l'auberge, amoureux de la bourrache, et que dissout un rayon!

Faim

Si j'ai du goût, ce n'est guère
Que pour la terre et les pierres.
Je déjeune toujours d'air,
De roc, de charbons, de fer.

Song From the Highest Tower

Roll on the day
When love is for real.

I've shown such great patience
That now I forget.
All suffering and fear
Are lost in the air.
And unhealthy thirsting
Is blackening my veins.

Roll on the day
When love is for real.

Like the Great Meadow
Left in neglect,
With blossoming darnel
And rosemary, wild
Savage music
Of fevering flies.

Roll on the day
When love is for real.

I loved empty places, burnt orchards, faded shops, tepid drinks. I hauled myself through stinking lanes, and, eyes shut, gave myself up to the sun, god of fire.

'General, if there's an old cannon left on your ruined ramparts, bombard us with clods of dried earth. Direct your fire at the glass in the most luxurious stores! at drawing-rooms! Make the city eat its own dust. Rust out water-ducts. Fill boudoirs with blazing ruby-powder...'

Oh! the gnat, drunk in the tavern urinal, crazed with borage, dissolved in a shaft of sun-light.

Hunger

What appetite I have
Is for earth and stones.
I feed always on air,
Rock, iron, coals.

Mes faims, tournez. Paissez, faims,
    Le pré des sons.
Attirez le gai venin
    Des liserons.

Mangez les cailloux qu'on brise,
Les vieilles pierres d'églises;
Les galets des vieux déluges,
Pains semés dans les vallées grises.

Le loup criait sous les feuilles
En crachant les belles plumes
De son repas de volailles:
Comme lui je me consume.

Les salades, les fruits
N'attendent que la cueillette;
Mais l'araignée de la haie
Ne manage que des violettes.

Que je dorme! que je bouille
Aux autels de Salomon.
Le bouillon court sur la rouille,
Et se mêle au Cédron.

Enfin, ô bonheur, ô raison, j'écartai du ciel l'azur, qui est du noir, et je vécus, étincelle d'or de la lumière *nature*. De joie, je prenais une expression bouffonne et égarée au possible:

Elle est retrouvée!
Quoi? l'éternité.
C'est la mer mêlée
    Au soleil.

Mon âme éternelle,
Observe ton vœu
Malgré la nuit seule
Et le jour en feu.

Donc tu te dégages
Des humains suffrages,
Des communs élans!
Tu voles selon....

My hungers, turn. Hungers, graze
The fields of bran.
Gather bright poisons
of bindweed.

Eat the stones that they break,
The old church-stones;
Pebbles from old floods,
Bread sown in grey valleys.

The wolf howled in the greenery
Spitting fine feathers,
From his meal of fowl:
Like him, I devour myself.

Salads, fruit
Are ready for picking;
But the hedge spider
Eats only violets.

Let me sleep! Let me boil
On the altars of Solomon.
Boiled liquid spills down the rust
And flows into the Kedron.*

Finally, o reason and happiness, I excised from the sky the blue, which is blackness, and lived as a golden spangle of *natural* light. Full of joy, I put on the wildest, most clownish expression:

Found again!—What?
—Eternity.
The sea lost
   In the sun.

Eternal soul,
Respect your vow
Despite pure night
And burning day.

So you are free
Of people's praise,
Vulgar élan!
Fly where you can...

—Jamais l'espérance.
  Pas d'*orietur*.
Science et patience,
Le supplice est sûr.

Plus de lendemain,
Braises de satin,
  Votre ardeur
  Est le devoir.

Elle est retrouvée!
—Quoi?—l'Éternité.
C'est la mer mêlée
  Au soleil.

Je devins un opéra fabuleux: je vis que tous les êtres ont une fatalité de bonheur: l'action n'est pas la vie, mais une façon de gâcher quelque force, un énervement. La morale est la faiblesse de la cervelle.

A chaque être, plusieurs *autres* vies me semblaient dues. Ce monsieur ne sait ce qu'il fait: il est un ange. Cette famille est une nichée de chiens. Devant plusieurs hommes, je causai tout haut avec un moment d'une de leurs autres vies.—Ainsi, j'ai aimé un porc.

Aucun des sophismes de la folie,—la folie qu'on enferme,—n'a été oublié par moi: je pourrais les redire tous, je tiens le système.

Ma santé fut menacée. La terreur venait. Je tombais dans des sommeils de plusieurs jours, et, levé, je continuais les rêves les plus tristes. J'étais mûr pour le trépas, et par une route de dangers ma faiblesse me menait aux confins du monde et de la Cimmérie, patrie de l'ombre et des tourbillons.

Je dus voyager, distraire les enchantements assemblés sur mon cerveau. Sur la mer, que j'aimais comme si elle eût dû me laver d'une souillure, je voyais se lever la croix consolatrice. J'avais été damné par l'arc-en-ciel. Le Bonheur était ma fatalité, mon remords, mon ver: ma vie serait toujours trop immense pour être dévouée à la force et à la beauté.

Le Bonheur! Sa dent, douce à la mort, m'avertissait au chant du coq,—*ad matutinum*, au *Christus venit*,—dans les plus sombres villes:

—There's never hope.
  No new start.
Truth and patience,
Torture for sure.

No more tomorrow,
Embers of silk,
  Your own ardour
  Must be the task.

Found again!—What?
—Eternity.
The sea lost
  In the sun.

I became a fabulous opera: I saw that happiness is the fate of everyone: action is not life, but a way of destroying a particular strength, a trial of the nerves. Morality is a weakness of the brain.

Several *other* lives, it seemed to me, were owed to every being. This gentleman does not know what he is doing: he is an angel.

That family is a litter of dogs. In front of several men, I chatted very audibly with a moment from one of their other lives.—In this way, I fell in love with a pig.

Not one of the sophistries of madness,—the kind of madness which gets locked away—did I forget: I could repeat them all, I know them inside out.

My health was threatened. Terror was advancing. I fell into sleep which lasted days, and, once I was up again, continued with the saddest dreams. I was ripe for death, and my weakness led me down the perilous path to the utmost edges of the world, and of Cimmeria,* home of shadow and whirlwinds.

I had to travel, to scatter the enchantments gathered on my brain. Over the sea, which I adored as though it was the thing to cleanse me of impurity, I saw the cross of consolation rise. I had been damned by the rainbow. Happiness was my fate, my remorse, my worm: my life would always be too vast for any strength and beauty.

Happiness! Its bite, sweet unto death, called me to attention at cockcrow—'in the morning', at the 'Christ is coming',—in the most sombre cities:

Ô saisons, ô châteaux!
Quelle âme est sans défauts?

J'ai fait la magique étude
Du bonheur, qu'aucun n'élude.

Salut à lui, chaque fois
Que chante le coq gaulois.

Ah! je n'aurai plus d'envie:
Il s'est chargé de ma vie.

Ce charme a pris âme et corps
Et dispersé les efforts.

Ô saisons, ô châteaux!

L'heure de sa fuite, hélas!
Sera l'heure du trépas.

Ô saisons, ô châteaux!

Cela s'est passé. Je sais aujourd'hui saluer la beauté.

L'Impossible

Ah! cette vie de mon enfance, la grande route par tous les temps, sobre surnaturellement, plus désintéressé que le meilleur des mendiants, fier de n'avoir ni pays, ni amis, quelle sottise c'était.—Et je m'en aperçois seulement!

—J'ai eu raison de mépriser ces bonshommes qui ne perdraient pas l'occasion d'une caresse, parasites de la propreté et de la santé de nos femmes, aujourd'hui qu'elles sont si peu d'accord avec nous.

J'ai eu raison dans tous mes dédains: puisque je m'évade!

Je m'évade!

Je m'explique.

Hier encore, je soupirais: 'Ciel! sommes-nous assez de damnés ici-bas! Moi j'ai tant de temps déjà dans leur troupe! Je les connais tous. Nous nous reconnaissons toujours; nous nous dégoûtons. La charité nous est inconnue. Mais nous sommes polis; nos relations avec le

O Seasons, o chateaux!
Which soul is spotless?

I've made the magic study
Of happiness, no one evades.

Salute it then, each time
The Gallic cockerel crows.

Ah! I've finished with wanting;
It's taken my life over.

That spell has taken soul and body,
And wasted every effort.

O seasons, o chateaux!

The hour of its flight, alas!
Will be the hour of death.

O seasons, o chateaux!

All that is finished. Today, I have learned to wave my hand at beauty.*

The Impossible

Ah! that life of my childhood, the high road in all weathers, supernaturally sober, more indifferent than the best of beggars, proud to have neither country, nor friends, what stupidity it all was.—And I've only just seen it!

—I was right to despise those fellows who would never throw up the chance of an embrace, parasites on the cleanliness and health of our women, these days when women are so much at odds with us.

I was right to scorn everything I did: because I'm leaving!

Running away!

I shall explain.

Only yesterday, I sighed: 'God! there are quite enough of our sort down here, the damned! I've been one of their number for far too long! I know them all. We always recognize one another; and we disgust one another. Charity is not in our vocabulary. But we are

monde sont très-convenables.' Est-ce étonnant? Le monde! les marchands, les naïfs!—Nous ne sommes pas déshonorés.—Mais les élus, comment nous recevraient-ils? Or il y a des gens hargneux et joyeux, de faux élus, puisqu'il nous faut de l'audace ou de l'humilité pour les aborder. Ce sont les seuls élus. Ce ne sont pas des bénisseurs!

M'étant retrouvé deux sous de raison—ça passe vite!—je vois que mes malaises viennent de ne m'être pas figuré assez tôt que nous sommes à l'Occident. Les marais occidentaux! Non que je croie la lumière altérée, la forme exténuée, le mouvement égaré... Bon! voici que mon esprit veut absolument se charger de tous les développements cruels qu'a subis l'esprit depuis la fin de l'Orient... Il en veut, mon esprit!

... Mes deux sous de raison sont finis!—L'esprit est autorité, il veut que je sois en Occident. Il faudrait le faire taire pour conclure comme je voulais.

J'envoyais au diable les palmes des martyrs, les rayons de l'art, l'orgueil des inventeurs, l'ardeur des pillards; je retournais à l'Orient et à la sagesse première et éternelle.—Il paraît que c'est un rêve de paresse grossière!

Pourtant, je ne songeais guère au plaisir d'échapper aux souffrances modernes. Je n'avais pas en vue la sagesse bâtarde du Coran.—Mais n'y a-t-il pas un supplice réel en ce que, depuis cette déclaration de la science, le christianisme, l'homme *se joue*, se prouve les évidences, se gonfle du plaisir de répéter ces preuves, et ne vit que comme cela! Torture subtile, niaise; source de mes divagations spirituelles. La nature pourrait s'ennuyer, peut-être! M. Prudhomme est né avec le Christ.

N'est-ce pas parce que nous cultivons la brume! Nous mangeons la fièvre avec nos légumes aqueux. Et l'ivrognerie! et le tabac! et l'ignorance! et les dévouements!—Tout cela est-il assez loin de la pensée de la sagesse de l'Orient, la patrie primitive? Pourquoi un monde moderne, si de pareils poisons s'inventent!

Les gens d'Église diront: C'est compris. Mais vous voulez parler de l'Éden. Rien pour vous dans l'historie des peuples orientaux.—C'est vrai; c'est à l'Éden que je songeais! Qu'est-ce que c'est pour mon rêve, cette pureté des races antiques!

Les philosophes: Le monde n'a pas d'âge. L'humanité se déplace, simplement. Vous êtes en Occident, mais libre d'habiter

polite; our dealings with people are strictly by the book.' Surprising, is it? People? merchants and cretins!—We are not disgraced.—But how would the elect receive us? Now, there are churlish people and happy people, the false elect in fact, since it requires daring or humility to confront them. These are the only elect. They do not give blessings.

Having found some loose change of good sense—soon spent!—I now see that my woes come from not having realized soon enough that we belong to the West. The Western swamps! Not that I think that the light is different, or forms worn out, or movement gone astray... Right! My mind is determined to take on all the cruel developments which the mind has borne since the collapse of the East... Resentful, my mind!

...My small change of reason has run out!—The mind is authority, it demands I be of the West. I would have to silence it if I want things to work out my way.

I used to say, to hell with martyr's palms, the radiancy of art, inventors' pride, plunderers' frenzy; I turned back to the East and to original, eternal wisdom.—It seems that it is a dream of vulgar laziness!

Yet, I was scarcely thinking of the pleasure it would be to escape from modern suffering. I did not have in mind the mongrel wisdom of the Koran.—But isn't there genuine torture in the fact that since that declaration of knowledge, Christianity, man has been *deceiving himself*, proving the obvious, puffed up with the pride of repeating these proofs, the only life he knows! A subtle and crass torture; the source of my spiritual ramblings. Nature might get bored perhaps! Mr Wise-Guy was born with Christ.

Isn't it because we have decided to live in a fog? We ingest fever with our watery vegetables. And drink! tobacco! ignorance! utter blind faith!—Isn't all of that a bit far from the thought and wisdom of the East, our cradle? Why then a modern world, if poisons of this sort are invented!

People of the Church will say: Yes. But you really mean Eden. There is nothing for you in the history of Eastern peoples.—All right, I was thinking of Eden! What does the purity of ancient races have to do with my dream!

Philosophers will say: The world is without age. All that happens is that humanity moves from place to place. You are in the West, but

dans votre Orient, quelque ancien qu'il vous le faille,—et d'y habiter bien. Ne soyez pas un vaincu. Philosophes, vous êtes de votre Occident.

Mon esprit, prends garde. Pas de partis de salut violents. Exerce-toi!—Ah! la science ne va pas assez vite pour nous!

—Mais je m'aperçois que mon esprit dort.

S'il était bien éveillé toujours à partir de ce moment, nous serions bientôt à la vérité, qui peut-être nous entoure avec ses anges pleurant!... —S'il avait été éveillé jusqu'à ce moment-ci, c'est que je n'aurais pas cédé aux instincts délétères, à une époque immémoriale!... —S'il avait toujours été bien éveillé, je voguerais en pleine sagesse!...

Ô pureté! pureté!

C'est cette minute d'éveil qui m'a donné la vision de la pureté!—Par l'esprit on va à Dieu!

Déchirante infortune!

L'Éclair

Le travail humain! c'est l'explosion qui éclaire mon abîme de temps en temps.

'Rien n'est vanité; à la science, et en avant!' crie l'Ecclésiaste moderne, c'est-à-dire *Tout le monde*. Et pourtant les cadavres des méchants et des fainéants tombent sur le cœur des autres... Ah! vite, vite un peu; là-bas, par delà la nuit, ces récompenses futures, éternelles... les échappons-nous?...

—Qu'y puis-je? Je connais le travail; et la science est trop lente. Que la prière galope et que la lumière gronde... je le vois bien. C'est trop simple, et il fait trop chaud; on se passera de moi. J'ai mon devoir, j'en serai fier à la façon de plusieurs, en le mettant de côté.

Ma vie est usée. Allons! feignons, fainéantons, ô pitié! Et nous existerons en nous amusant, en rêvant amours monstres et univers fantastiques, en nous plaignant et en querellant les apparences du monde, saltimbanque, mendiant, artiste, bandit,—prêtre! Sur mon

you are free to live in your East, just as old as you need it to be,—and to live well there. Don't be a defeatist. Philosophers, you belong to your world of the West.

Take care, my mind. No headlong rushes at salvation. Be on your mettle! Ah! Science does not move fast enough for us!

—But I see that my mind sleeps.

If it were properly awake from now on, we would soon arrive at truth, which even now perhaps is all around us with its angels, weeping! If it had been awake up to this moment, then I would not have yielded to pernicious instincts, to time beyond all memory... If it had always been wide awake, I would now be sailing the high seas of wisdom!...

Purity, purity!

It is this minute of wakefulness which has given me the vision of purity!—Through the mind to God!

Harrowing misfortune!

Lightning

Human labour! the explosion which illuminates my abyss from time to time.

'Nothing is vanity: onwards to knowledge!' cries the modern Ecclesiastes, that is, *Everyone.* And yet the corpses of the wicked and the idle still fall on the hearts of others... Ah! quickly, quickly now; over there, the other side of darkness, those future and eternal recompenses... are we going to miss them?...

—What can I do? I know about work; and science is too slow. Let prayers gallop, light rumble... I can see it all quite clearly. It is too simple, and the weather is too hot; they can do without me. I have my duty, I shall be proud of it, the way so many are, putting it to one side.

My life is worn out. So, come on then, let us pretend, let us do nothing, o pity! And we shall live by amusing ourselves, by dreaming of monstrous loves and fantastic universes, by complaining and challenging the way the world appears, clown, beggar, artist, bandit,—and priest! On my hospital bed, the smell of incense came

lit d'hôpital, l'odeur de l'encens m'est revenue si puissante; gardien des aromates sacrés, confesseur, martyr...

Je reconnais là ma sale éducation d'enfance. Puis quoi!... Aller mes vingt ans, si les autres vont vingt ans...

Non! non! à présent je me révolte contre la mort! Le travail paraît trop léger à mon orgueil: ma trahison au monde serait un supplice trop court. Au dernier moment, j'attaquerais à droite, à gauche...

Alors,—oh!—chère pauvre âme, l'éternité serait-elle pas perdue pour nous!

Matin

N'eus-je pas *une fois* une jeunesse aimable, héroïque, fabuleuse, à écrire sur des feuilles d'or,—trop de chance! Par quel crime, par quelle erreur, ai-je mérité ma faiblesse actuelle? Vous qui prétendez que des bêtes poussent des sanglots de chagrin, que des malades désespèrent, que des morts rêvent mal, tâchez de raconter ma chute et mon sommeil. Moi, je ne puis pas plus m'expliquer que le mendiant avec ses continuels *Pater* et *Ave Maria. Je ne sais plus parler!*

Pourtant, aujourd'hui, je crois avoir fini la relation de mon enfer. C'était bien l'enfer; l'ancien, celui dont le fils de l'homme ouvrit les portes.

Du même désert, à la même nuit, toujours mes yeux las se réveillent à l'étoile d'argent, toujours, sans que s'émeuvent les Rois de la vie, les trois mages, le cœur, l'âme, l'esprit. Quand irons-nous, par delà les grèves et les monts, saluer la naissance du travail nouveau, la sagesse nouvelle, la fuite des tyrans et des démons, la fin de la superstition, adorer—les premiers!—Noël sur la terre!

Le chant des cieux, la marche des peuples! Esclaves, ne maudissons pas la vie.

Adieu

L'automne déjà!—Mais pourquoi regretter un éternel soleil, si nous sommes engagés à la découverte de la clarté divine,—loin des gens qui meurent sur les saisons.

so powerfully back to me; keeper of the sacred aromatics, confessor, martyr...

I can see in that my loathsome upbringing. Well, what does it matter?... Reach twenty, if the others are going to...

No! no! for the time being I rebel against death! Work seems too slight a business for pride of my sort: to betray myself to the world would be torture too brief. At the last moment, I would lash out, left and right...

In that event —oh!—my poor dear soul, eternity would not be lost to us, would it!

Morning

Did I not *once* have a pleasant childhood, heroic and fabulous, to be written on leaves of gold,—too much to ask! What crime, what error has led me to my present weakness? You who claim that beasts can weep with grief, the sick abandon hope, the dead have bad dreams, try to tell the story of my fall and my sleeping. For my part, I can no more explain myself than can a beggar with his endless *Pater Nosters* and *Ave Marias. I no longer know how to speak!*

And yet, today, I think I have completed the account of my hell. It was hell indeed; the ancient one whose gates were opened by the Son of Man.

Out of the same desert, on the same night, my weary eyes open always to the silver star, always, without a flicker from the Kings of life, the three wise men, the heart, the soul, the mind. When, beyond the shores and mountains, shall we go to greet the birth of the new work, the new wisdom, the flight of tyrants and demons, the end of superstition, and—the very first!—worship Christmas on earth!

The song of the heavens, nations on the march! We are slaves, but let us not curse life.

Farewell

Autumn this soon! But why hanker after an eternal sun if our quest is divine light, far away from those who die with the seasons.

L'automne. Notre barque élevée dans les brumes immobiles tourne vers le port de la misère, la cité énorme au ciel taché de feu et de boue. Ah! les haillons pourris, le pain trempé de pluie, l'ivresse, les mille amours qui m'ont crucifié! Elle ne finira donc point cette goule reine de millions d'âmes et de corps morts *et qui seront jugés!* Je me revois la peau rongée par la boue et la peste, des vers plein les cheveux et les aisselles et encore de plus gros vers dans le cœur, étendu parmi les inconnus sans âge, sans sentiment... J'aurais pu y mourir... L'affreuse évocation! J'exècre la misère.

Et je redoute l'hiver parce que c'est la saison du comfort!

—Quelquefois je vois au ciel des plages sans fin couvertes de blanches nations en joie. Un grand vaisseau d'or, au-dessus de moi, agite ses pavillons multicolores sous les brises du matin. J'ai créé toutes les fêtes, tous les triomphes, tous les drames. J'ai essayé d'inventer de nouvelles fleurs, de nouveaux astres, de nouvelles chairs, de nouvelles langues. J'ai cru acquérir des pouvoirs surnaturels. Eh bien! je dois enterrer mon imagination et mes souvenirs! Une belle gloire d'artiste et de conteur emportée!

Moi! moi qui me suis dit mage ou ange, dispensé de toute morale, je suis rendu au sol, avec un devoir à chercher, et la réalité rugueuse à étreindre! Paysan!

Suis-je trompé? la charité serait-elle sœur de la mort, pour moi?

Enfin, je demanderai pardon pour m'être nourri de mensonge. Et allons.

Mais pas une main amie! et où puiser le secours?

Oui l'heure nouvelle est au moins très-sévère.

Car je puis dire que la victoire m'est acquise: les grincements de dents, les sifflements de feu, les soupirs empestés se modèrent. Tous les souvenirs immondes s'effacent. Mes derniers regrets détalent,—des jalousies pour les mendiants, les brigands, les amis de la mort, les arriérés de toutes sortes.— Damnés, si je me vengeais!

Il faut être absolument moderne.

Point de cantiques: tenir le pas gagné. Dure nuit! le sang séché fume sur ma face, et je n'ai rien derrière moi, que cet horrible arbrisseau!... Le combat spirituel est aussi brutal que la bataille d'hommes; mais la vision de la justice est le plaisir de Dieu seul.

Cependant c'est la veille. Recevons tous les influx de vigueur et de tendresse réelle. Et à l'aurore, armés d'une ardente patience, nous entrerons aux splendides villes.

Autumn. Our boat, high in the still mists, turns towards the harbour of poverty, the huge city, its filth-stained fire-streaked sky. Ah, the rotted rags, the rain-soaked bread, the drunkenness, the thousand loves that crucified me! Will she never have done, this queen of the night, monarch of a million dead *who will now be judged!* I see once more my filthy pestilential skin, my hair and armpits rank with worms, and bigger worms still in my heart, me, stretched out among ageless unknown people who feel nothing... I could have died there... Nightmare thought! I hate poverty.

How I fear winter, season of slippers!

Sometimes I see in the sky beaches without end, swarming with enraptured white nations. Above me a great golden ship flutters flags of every colour in the morning breeze. I have created every carnival, every triumph, every drama. I have sought to invent new flowers, new stars, new bodies, new tongues. I thought I could acquire supernatural powers. Well no, I must lay my memories and imaginings in the earth! No fame, no glory, artist and storyteller manqué!

Me,—ha!—who thought myself a magus, an angel, above morality. I am back on the ground, looking out a task, with raw reality to embrace. Peasant!

Am I deceived? Could charity be for me the sister of death?

Ah well, I shall seek forgiveness for a life of lies. Onwards.

But no helping hand! and where to search for help?

Yes, the new era is certainly hard.

For I can say that victory is mine: grinding teeth, hissing fire, pestilential sighs are on the wane. All vile memories dissolve. My last regrets make themselves scarce; let beggars, brigands, those in love with death, the retarded of every kind, squabble over them—And they would know damnation, should I take revenge.

It is necessary to be absolutely modern.

No hymns of thanksgiving; yield not one inch. A tough night! Dried blood smokes on my face and there is nothing behind me save that small, terrible tree!... The spiritual fight is as brutal as men in battle; but the vision of justice is for God's pleasure alone.

Yet this is the eve. Accept every wave of strength and true tenderness. And at dawn, armed with scorching patience, we shall enter the cities of splendour.

Que parlais-je de main amie! Un bel avantage, c'est que je puis rire des vieilles amours mensongères, et frapper de honte ces couples menteurs,—j'ai vu l'enfer des femmes là-bas;—et il me sera loisible de *posséder la vérité dans une âme et un corps.*

Avril–août, 1873.

Why did I speak of a helping hand! My great advantage now is that I can laugh at all the old mendacities of love, I can strike shame into that charade known as The Couple—I have seen down there the hell of women—and now I shall be free to *possess truth in one soul and one body*.

April–August 1873

Illuminations

Après le Déluge

Aussitôt après que l'idée du Déluge se fut rassise,

Un lièvre s'arrêta dans les sainfoins et les clochettes mouvantes et dit sa prière à l'arc-en-ciel à travers la toile de l'araignée.

Oh! les pierres précieuses qui se cachaient,—les fleurs qui regardaient déjà.

Dans la grande rue sale les étals se dressèrent, et l'on tira les barques vers la mer étagée là-haut comme sur les gravures.

Le sang coula, chez Barbe-Bleue,—aux abattoirs,—dans les cirques, où le sceau de Dieu blêmit les fenêtres. Le sang et le lait coulèrent.

Les castors bâtirent. Les 'mazagrans' fumèrent dans les estaminets.

Dans la grande maison de vitres encore ruisselante les enfants en deuil regardèrent les merveilleuses images.

Une porte claqua, et sur la place du hameau, l'enfant tourna ses bras, compris des girouettes et des coqs des clochers de partout, sous l'éclatante giboulée.

Madame *** établit un piano dans les Alpes. La messe et les premières communions se célébrèrent aux cent mille autels de la cathédrale.

Les caravanes partirent. Et le Splendide Hôtel fut bâti dans le chaos de glaces et de nuit du pôle.

Depuis lors, la Lune entendit les chacals piaulant par les déserts de thym,—et les églogues en sabots grognant dans le verger. Puis, dans la futaie violette, bourgeonnante, Eucharis me dit que c'était le printemps.

—Sourds, étang,—Écume, roule sur le pont, et par-dessus les bois;—draps noirs et orgues,—éclairs et tonnerre;—montez et roulez;—Eaux et tristesses, montez et relevez les Déluges.

Car depuis qu'ils se sont dissipés,—oh les pierres précieuses s'enfouissant, et les fleurs ouvertes!—c'est un ennui! et la Reine, la Sorcière qui allume sa braise dans le pot de terre, ne voudra jamais nous raconter ce qu'elle sait, et que nous ignorons.

Illuminations

After the Flood

As soon as the idea of the Flood had subsided,

A hare stopped among the clover and the moving flower-bells and said its prayer to the rainbow through the spider's web.

Oh! the precious stones hiding—the flowers looking round already.

In the dirty main street the stalls were set up, and the boats were dragged towards the sea moving up in shelves, as in old prints.

At Bluebeard's, blood flowed—in abattoirs—in circuses, where the seal of God blanched the windows. Blood and milk flowed.

Beavers built. In bars and cafés, fierce coffees steamed.

In the great house of window-panes still running with water, the children in mourning looked at the marvellous pictures.

A door slammed shut, and, on the village square, the child whirled his arms, recognized by weathervanes and steeplecocks everywhere, under the brilliant sudden shower.

Madame *** installed a piano in the Alps. Mass and first communions were celebrated at the cathedral's hundred thousand altars.

The caravans departed. And the Hotel Splendide was built in the chaos of ice and polar night.

From then on, the Moon heard jackals howling across the deserts of thyme—and eclogues in their wooden shoes grumbling in the orchard. Then, in the violet, budding grove, Eucharis* told me it was Spring.

Surge up, pond,—Foam, roll across the bridge, over the woods;—black drapes and organs;—lightnings, thunder;—rise and roll;—Waters and sorrows, rise and heighten the Floods.

For since they have dispersed,—oh, the precious stones burying themselves, and the opened flowers!—all excitement has gone! and the Queen, the Witch who lights her charcoal fire in the earthen pot, will never deign to tell us what she knows, and we do not.

Enfance

I

Cette idole, yeux noirs et crin jaune, sans parents ni cour, plus noble que la fable, mexicaine et flamande; son domaine, azur et verdure insolents, court sur des plages nommées, par des vagues sans vaisseaux, de noms férocement grecs, slaves, celtiques.

A la lisière de la forêt—les fleurs de rêve tintent, éclatent, éclairent,—la fille à lèvre d'orange, les genoux croisés dans le clair déluge qui sourd des prés, nudité qu'ombrent, traversent et habillent les arcs-en-ciel, la flore, la mer.

Dames qui tournoient sur les terrasses voisines de la mer; enfantes et géantes, superbes noires dans la mousse vert-de-gris, bijoux debout sur le sol gras des bosquets et des jardinets dégelés—jeunes mères et grandes sœurs aux regards pleins de pèlerinages, sultanes, princesses de démarche et de costume tyranniques, petites étrangères et personnes doucement malheureuses.

Quel ennui, l'heure du 'cher corps' et 'cher cœur'.

II

C'est elle, la petite morte, derrière les rosiers.—La jeune maman trépassée descend le perron—La calèche du cousin crie sur le sable—Le petit frère— (il est aux Indes!) là, devant le couchant, sur le pré d'œillets.—Les vieux qu'on a enterrés tout droits dans le rempart aux giroflées.

L'essaim des feuilles d'or entoure la maison du général. Ils sont dans le midi.—On suit la route rouge pour arriver à l'auberge vide. Le château est à vendre; les persiennes sont détachées.—Le curé aura emporté la clef de l'église.—Autour du parc, les loges des gardes sont inhabitées. Les palissades sont si hautes qu'on ne voit que les cimes bruissantes. D'ailleurs il n'y a rien à voir là-dedans.

Les prés remontent aux hameaux sans coqs, sans enclumes. L'écluse est levée. O les calvaires et les moulins du désert, les îles et les meules.

Des fleurs magiques bourdonnaient. Les talus *le* berçaient. Des

Childhood

I

This idol, dark eyes, yellow mane, no family or court, nobler than fables, Mexican and Flemish: his domain, insolent azure and green, runs over beaches bearing fierce Greek and Slav and Celtic names, given them by waves with no ships.

At the forest edge—dream flowers tinkle, splinter, flare—the orange-lip girl, knees crossed in the clear flood welling from the meadows, nakedness shaded, traversed and costumed by the rainbows, flora, sea.

Ladies promenading on terraces next to the sea; little girls and giantesses, superb black women in grey-green moss, jewels tall on the rich soil of the unfrozen little gardens and groves—young mothers, big sisters, their eyes deep with pilgrimage, Sultans' wives, princesses of tyrannical demeanour and dress, little foreign girls, people full of soft unhappiness.

Wearisome, the hour of feeling and fondnesses.

II

That's her, the little dead girl, behind the rose-bushes.—The deceased young mamma descends the flight of steps.—The cousin's carriage grates along the sand—the little brother (away in the Indies!) there, against the sunset, in the meadow of pinks—the old people, buried upright in the wallflower rampart.

The swarm of golden leaves rings the general's residence. They are in the South—You take the red road to find the deserted inn. The chateau is up for sale; shutters hanging off—The priest no doubt has removed the key to the church—Around the estate, the wardens' lodges are unoccupied. The fences are so high you see only the bustling tree-tops. Anyway, there is nothing to see in there.

The meadows reach up to hamlets where no cockerels are, no anvils. The sluice-gate is raised. Oh, the Calvaries, and the mills of emptiness, the islands, the haystacks.

Magic flowers were humming. The slopes cradled *him*. Fabulously

bêtes d'une élégance fabuleuse circulaient. Les nuées s'amassaient sur la haute mer faite d'une éternité de chaudes larmes.

III

Au bois il y a un oiseau, son chant vous arrête et vous fait rougir.

Il y a une horloge qui ne sonne pas.

Il y a une fondrière avec un nid de bêtes blanches.

Il y a une cathédrale qui descend et un lac qui monte.

Il ya une petite voiture abandonnée dans le taillis, ou qui descend le sentier en courant, enrubannée.

Il y a une troupe de petits comédiens en costumes, aperçus sur la route à travers la lisière du bois.

Il y a enfin, quand l'on a faim et soif, quelqu'un qui vous chasse.

IV

Je suis le saint, en prière sur la terrasse,—comme les bêtes pacifiques paissent jusqu'à la mer de Palestine.

Je suis le savant au fauteuil sombre. Les branches et la pluie se jettent à la croisée de la bibliothèque.

Je suis le piéton de la grand'route par les bois nains; la rumeur des écluses couvre mes pas. Je vois longtemps la mélancolique lessive d'or du couchant.

Je serais bien l'enfant abandonné sur la jetée partie à la haute mer, le petit valet suivant l'allée dont le front touche le ciel.

Les sentiers sont âpres. Les monticules se couvrent de genêts. L'air est immobile. Que les oiseaux et les sources sont loin! Ce ne peut être que la fin du monde, en avançant.

V

Qu'on me loue enfin ce tombeau, blanchi à la chaux avec les lignes du ciment en relief—très loin sous terre.

Je m'accoude à la table, la lampe éclaire très vivement ces journaux que je suis idiot de relire, ces livres sans intérêt.

elegant beasts moved about. The clouds were gathering over the high sea, an eternity of warm tears.

III

In the wood, there is a bird, its song makes you stop and blush.

There is a clock which never strikes.

There is a hollow in the ground with a nest of white animals.

There is a cathedral which goes down and a lake which rises.

There is a little vehicle abandoned in the copse, or running down the lane, covered in ribbons.

There is a troupe of little costumed actors, glimpsed on the road through the limits of the wood.

And finally, when you are hungry or thirsty, there is someone who chases you off.

IV

I am the saint, at prayer on the terrace,—as the gentle beasts graze their way down to the Sea of Palestine.

I am the scholar in the dark armchair. The rain and branches crash against the windows of the library.

I am the one who walks the high road through the stunted woods; the noise of the sluice-gates drowns out my footsteps. For a good while, I can see the melancholy golden wash of sunset.

I might well be the child abandoned on the jetty heading out to sea, the little farmboy following the lane which rises up to touch the sky.

The paths are rough. The knolls are covered with broom. The air is still. How the birds and springs are far away! It can only be the end of the world, if you go on.

V

Let me rent this tomb in the end, whitewashed, cement-lines in relief—deep underground.

I lean my elbows on the table, the lamp casts fierce light on these newspapers I am stupid enough to reread, these books empty of interest.

A une distance énorme au-dessus de mon salon souterrain, les maisons s'implantent, les brumes s'assemblent. La boue est rouge ou noire. Ville monstrueuse, nuit sans fin!

Moins haut, sont des égouts. Aux côtés, rien que l'épaisseur du globe. Peut-être les gouffres d'azur, des puits de feu. C'est peut-être sur ces plans que se rencontrent lunes et comètes, mers et fables.

Aux heures d'amertume je m'imagine des boules de saphir, de métal. Je suis maître du silence. Pourquoi une apparence de soupirail blêmirait-elle au coin de la voûte?

Conte

Un Prince était vexé de ne s'être employé jamais qu'à la perfection des générosités vulgaires. Il prévoyait d'étonnantes révolutions de l'amour, et soupçonnait ses femmes de pouvoir mieux que cette complaisance agrémentée de ciel et de luxe. Il voulait voir la vérité, l'heure du désir et de la satisfaction essentiels. Que ce fût ou non une aberration de piété, il voulut. Il possédait au moins un assez large pouvoir humain.

Toutes les femmes qui l'avaient connu furent assassinées. Quel saccage du jardin de la beauté! Sous le sabre, elles le bénirent. Il n'en commanda point de nouvelles.—Les femmes réapparurent.

Il tua tous ceux qui le suivaient, après la chasse ou les libations.—Tous le suivaient.

Il s'amusa à égorger les bêtes de luxe. Il fit flamber les palais. Il se ruait sur les gens et les taillait en pièces.—La foule, les toits d'or, les belles bêtes existaient encore.

Peut-on s'extasier dans la destruction, se rajeunir par la cruauté! Le peuple ne murmura pas. Personne n'offrit le concours de ses vues.

Un soir il galopait fièrement. Un Génie apparut, d'une beauté ineffable, inavouable même. De sa physionomie et de son maintien ressortait la promesse d'un amour multiple et complexe! d'un bonheur indicible, insupportable même! Le Prince et le Génie s'anéantirent probablement dans la santé essentielle. Comment n'auraient-ils pas pu en mourir? Ensemble donc ils moururent.

Mais ce Prince décéda, dans son palais, à un âge ordinaire. Le prince était le Génie. Le Génie était le Prince.

La musique savante manque à notre désir.

A huge distance above my subterranean sitting-room, houses plant themselves down, mists assemble. The mud is red or black. Monstrous city, night without end!

Not quite so high are drains. All around, just the thickness of the globe. Perhaps the azure gulfs, wells of fire. It is on these planes perhaps that moons and comets meet, seas and fables.

In my bitter hours, I imagine balls of sapphire, metal. I am master of the silence. Why should something which resembles a tunnel of light gleam weakly at the corner of the arch?

Tale

A Prince was vexed that he had only ever spent his time perfecting acts of banal generosity. He envisaged astounding revolutions in love, and suspected his wives of being able to do better than their usual accommodations enhanced by heaven and luxury. He wanted to see the truth, the hour of essential desire and gratification. Whether or not this was an aberration of piety, he wanted. At least he had sufficient human power.

All the women he had known were done to death. What havoc in the garden of beauty! As the blade fell, they blessed him. He summoned no further women.—Women reappeared.

He killed everyone who followed him, after the hunt or after drink.—Still the hordes, the golden rooftops, the fine beasts continued to exist.

Is it possible to be delirious with destruction, to find youth again in cruelty! There was not a murmur from the people. No one offered to endorse his views.

One evening he was galloping along proudly. A Genie appeared, of ineffable beauty, too much even to admit. From his look, his bearing, there emerged the promise of a multiple and complex love! of happiness beyond words, unbearable even! The Prince and the Genie probably blotted themselves out in essential health. How could they not have died of it? So, together they died.

But this Prince passed away in his palace at a normal age. The Prince was the Genie. The Genie was the Prince.

Our desire lacks knowing music.

Parade

Des drôles très solides. Plusieurs ont exploité vos mondes. Sans besoins et peu pressés de mettre en œuvre leurs brillantes facultés et leur expérience de vos consciences. Quels hommes mûrs! Des yeux hébétés à la façon de la nuit d'été, rouges et noirs, tricolores, d'acier piqué d'étoiles d'or; des facies déformés, plombés, blêmis, incendiés; des enrouements folâtres! La démarche cruelle des oripeaux!— Il y a quelques jeunes,—comment regardaient-ils Chérubin?—pourvus de voix effrayantes et de quelques ressources dangereuses. On les envoie prendre du dos en ville, affublés d'un *luxe* dégoûtant.

Ô le plus violent Paradis de la grimace enragée! Pas de comparaison avec vos Fakirs et les autres bouffonneries scéniques. Dans des costumes improvisés avec le goût du mauvais rêve ils jouent des complaintes, des tragédies de malandrins et de demi-dieux spirituels comme l'histoire ou les religions ne l'ont jamais été. Chinois, Hottentots, bohémiens, niais, hyènes, Molochs, vieilles démences, démons sinistres, ils mêlent les tours populaires, maternels, avec les poses et les tendresses bestiales. Ils interpréteraient des pièces nouvelles et des chansons 'bonnes filles'. Maîtres jongleurs, ils transforment le lieu et les personnes, et usent de la comédie magnétique. Les yeux flambent, le sang chante, les os s'élargissent, les larmes et des filets rouges ruissellent. Leur raillerie ou leur terreur dure une minute, ou des mois entiers.

J'ai seul la clef de cette parade sauvage.

Antique

Gracieux fils de Pan! Autour de ton front couronné de fleurettes et de baies tes yeux, des boules précieuses, remuent. Tachées de lies brunes, tes joues se creusent. Tes crocs luisent. Ta poitrine ressemble à une cithare, des tintements circulent dans tes bras blonds. Ton cœur bat dans ce ventre où dort le double sexe. Promène-toi, la nuit, en mouvant doucement cette cuisse, cette seconde cuisse et cette jambe de gauche.

Parade

Weird-looking, sturdy types. Many of them have exploited your worlds. Wanting for nothing, and in no haste to bring into play their brilliant abilities and their knowledge of how you think. What mature men! Eyes bewildered like summer night, red and black, three-coloured, steel pricked out with golden stars; deformed features, like lead, blanched, on fire; caprices of hoarseness! The cruel swagger of flashy rags—There are some young people—what would they make of Cherubino?*—endowed with frightening voices and dangerous resources. They are sent into town to parade themselves, got up in disgusting *luxury*.

O most violent Paradise of the furious grimace! No comparison with your Fakirs and the other buffooneries of the stage. In costumes as if in an improvised bad dream, they act out sad stories, tragedies of brigands and demigods more spirited than history or religion ever were. Chinese, Hottentots, gypsies, dimwits, hyenas, Molochs, antique lunacies, sinister demons, they mix popular turns, stories heard at mother's knee, with bestial poses and blandishments. They would happily do new plays, sentimental songs. Master-jugglers that they are, they transform place and person, using hypnotic make-believe. Eyes flame, blood sings, bones expand, tears run, and strands of red. Their jeers, their terror last a few seconds, or months and months.

I alone have the key to this wild parade.

Antique

Graceful son of Pan! Around your head crowned with little flowers and berries your eyes, precious spheres, move. Stained with brown dregs, your cheeks grow hollow. Your fangs gleam. Your chest is like a cithara, a trickle of notes runs round your blond arms. Your heart beats in that belly where the double sex lies still. Walk, at night, gently moving that thigh, that second thigh, and that left leg.

Being Beauteous

Devant une neige un Être de Beauté de haute taille. Des sifflements de mort et des cercles de musique sourde font monter, s'élargir et trembler comme un spectre ce corps adoré; des blessures écarlates et noires éclatent dans les chairs superbes. Les couleurs propres de la vie se foncent, dansent, et se dégagent autour de la Vision, sur le chantier. Et les frissons s'élèvent et grondent et la saveur forcenée de ces effets se chargeant avec les sifflements mortels et les rauques musiques que le monde, loin derrière nous, lance sur notre mère de beauté,—elle recule, elle se dresse. Oh! nos os sont revêtus d'un nouveau corps amoureux.

'Ô la face cendrée...'

Ô la face cendrée, l'écusson de crin, les bras de cristal! Le canon sur lequel je dois m'abattre à travers la mêlée des arbres et de l'air léger!

Vies

I

Ô les énormes avenues du pays saint, les terrasses du temple! Qu'a-t-on fait du brahmane qui m'expliqua les Proverbes? D'alors, de là-bas, je vois encore même les vieilles! Je me souviens des heures d'argent et de soleil vers les fleuves, la main de la campagne sur mon épaule, et de nos caresses debout dans les plaines poivrées.—Un envol de pigeons écarlates tonne autour de ma pensée.—Exilé ici j'ai eu une scène où jouer les chefs-d'œuvre dramatiques de toutes les littératures. Je vous indiquerais les richesses inouïes. J'observe l'histoire des trésors que vous trouvâtes. Je vois la suite! Ma sagesse est aussi dédaignée que le chaos. Qu'est mon néant, auprès de la stupeur qui vous attend?

Being Beauteous

Against snow a tall Being of Beauty. Hisses of death and circles of muted music make this worshipped body rise, expand, and tremble like a ghost; black and scarlet wounds burst in superb flesh. The colours, clearly those of life, grow dark, dance, stand out against the Vision taking shape. And the shudders rise and rumble, and the frenzied flavour of these effects as they accept deadly hisses and raucous music which the world, far behind us, hurls at our mother of beauty—she moves back, makes herself tall. Oh! our bones now wear a new and loving body.

'O the ashen face...'

O the ashen face, the horsehair escutcheon, the crystal arms! The cannon on which I must fall through the fray of trees and buoyant air!

Lives

I

O the enormous avenues of the holy land, the temple terraces! What has become of the Brahmin who explained to me the Proverbs? Of that time, that place, I still see even the old women! I remember hours of silver and sun towards the river, the landscape's hand on my shoulder and our caresses as we stood on the spiced plains.—A flight of scarlet pigeons clamours round my thoughts.—Exiled here, once I had a stage on which to perform the great dramatic works of all literatures. I would show you unbelievable riches. I observe the history of the treasures which once you found. I can see what will follow! My wisdom is as despised as chaos. What is my nothingness compared to the stupor which awaits you?

II

Je suis un inventeur bien autrement méritant que tous ceux qui m'ont précédé; un musicien même, qui ai trouvé quelque chose comme la clef de l'amour. A présent, gentilhomme d'une campagne aigre au ciel sobre, j'essaie de m'émouvoir au souvenir de l'enfance mendiante, de l'apprentissage ou de l'arrivée en sabots, des polémiques, des cinq ou six veuvages, et quelques noces où ma forte tête m'empêcha de monter au diapason des camarades. Je ne regrette pas ma vieille part de gaîté divine: l'air sobre de cette aigre campagne alimente fort activement mon atroce scepticisme. Mais comme ce scepticisme ne peut désormais être mis en œuvre, et que d'ailleurs je suis dévoué à un trouble nouveau,—j'attends de devenir un très méchant fou.

III

Dans un grenier où je fus enfermé à douze ans j'ai connu le monde, j'ai illustré la comédie humaine. Dans un cellier j'ai appris l'histoire. A quelque fête de nuit dans une cité du Nord j'ai rencontré toutes les femmes des anciens peintres. Dans un vieux passage à Paris on m'a enseigné les sciences classiques. Dans une magnifique demeure cernée par l'Orient entier j'ai accompli mon immense œuvre et passé mon illustre retraite. J'ai brassé mon sang. Mon devoir m'est remis. Il ne faut même plus songer à cela. Je suis réellement d'outre-tombe, et pas de commissions.

Départ

Assez vu. La vision s'est rencontrée à tous les airs.
Assez eu. Rumeurs des villes, le soir, et au soleil, et toujours.
Assez connu. Les arrêts de la vie.—Ô Rumeurs et Visions!
Départ dans l'affection et le bruit neufs!

II

I am an inventor with quite different virtues from all those who have gone before me, a musician in fact, who has found something like the keynote of love. At present, a country gentleman in a harsh stretch of land under sober sky, I try to be moved by the memory of a beggar childhood, of apprenticeship or arrival in clogs, of polemics, of my five or six widowhoods, and of a few orgies of alcohol, when a strong head stopped me reaching the same fever-pitch as my drinking-companions. I do not regret my erstwhile share of divine gaiety: the sober air of that harsh landscape feeds most actively my atrocious scepticism. But, as this scepticism cannot be put to use any longer, and as anyway I am engrossed in a new uneasiness,—I expect to go mad in a particularly vicious way.

III

In an attic where I was locked up when I was twelve, I came to know the world, I illustrated the human comedy. In a store-cupboard, I learnt history. At some night-time festival in a city of the North, I met all the women of the old painters. In an ancient Paris passage-way, I was taught the classical sciences. In a magnificent dwelling ringed round by the whole Orient, I finished my huge work and spent my illustrious retirement. I brewed my blood. I have been exempted from my duty. No need to think of it any more even. I am truly from beyond the grave, and completely unbeholden.

Departure

Enough seen. The vision has been met in every air.

Enough had. Distant sounds of cities, in the evening, and in the sun, and always.

Enough known. Life's injunctions. O Sounds and Visions!

Departure in new affection and new noise.

Royauté

Un beau matin, chez un peuple fort doux, un homme et une femme superbes criaient sur la place publique. 'Mes amis, je veux qu'elle soit reine!' 'Je veux être reine!' Elle riait et tremblait. Il parlait aux amis de révélation, d'épreuve terminée. Ils se pâmaient l'un contre l'autre.

En effet ils furent rois toute une matinée où les tentures carminées se relevèrent sur les maisons, et toute l'après-midi, où ils s'avancèrent du côté des jardins de palmes.

A une Raison

Un coup de ton doigt sur le tambour décharge tous les sons et commence la nouvelle harmonie.

Un pas de toi. C'est la levée des nouveaux hommes et leur en-marche.

Ta tête se détourne: le nouvel amour! Ta tête se retourne,—le nouvel amour!

'Change nos lots, crible les fléaux, à commencer par le temps', te chantent ces enfants. 'Élève n'importe où la substance de nos fortunes et de nos vœux' on t'en prie.

Arrivée de toujours, qui t'en iras partout.

Matinée d'ivresse

Ô *mon* Bien! ô *mon* Beau! Fanfare atroce où je ne trébuche point! chevalet féerique! Hourra pour l'œuvre inouïe et pour le corps merveilleux, pour la première fois! Cela commença sous les rires des enfants, cela finira par eux. Ce poison va rester dans toutes nos veines même quand, la fanfare tournant, nous serons rendu à l'ancienne inharmonie. Ô maintenant nous si digne de ces tortures! rassemblons fervemment cette promesse surhumaine faite à notre corps et à notre âme créés: cette promesse, cette démence! L'élégance, la science, la violence! On nous a promis d'enterrer dans l'ombre l'arbre du bien et du mal, de déporter les honnêtetés tyranniques,

Royalty

One beautiful morning, in a country of very gentle people, a magnificent man and woman were shouting in the public square: 'My friends, I want her to be queen!' 'I want to be queen!' She was laughing and trembling. He was telling their friends about a revelation, an ordeal completed. They were swooning one against the other.

And indeed, monarchs they were, for a whole morning during which crimson hangings were raised up the house façades, and for the entire afternoon of their progress towards the gardens of palms.

To a Reason

One touch of your finger on the drum sets off every sound and starts the new harmony.

You take one step, new men rise and start to march.

Your head turns away: new love! Your head turns back,—new love!

'Change our lot, wipe out plagues, starting with time', these children chant at you. 'Cherish and nurture the substance of our fortunes and our desires where you please', they beg.

You who have arrived from all time, and will leave for everywhere.

Morning of Drunkenness

Oh *my* Good, *my* Beauty! Atrocious fanfare in which I do not waver! magical torture-rack! Salute the unheard-of work and the marvellous body, for the first time! It began amid the laughter of the children, it will finish with them. This poison will stay in all our veins even when the fanfare changes and brings us back to the old disharmony. O now, let us who so deserve these tortures fervently gather that superhuman promise made to our created bodies; that promise, that madness! Elegance, knowledge, violence! We have the promise that the tree of good and evil shall be buried in darkness, that tyrannical

afin que nous amenions notre très pur amour. Cela commença par quelques dégoûts et cela finit,—ne pouvant nous saisir sur-le-champ de cette éternité,—cela finit par une débandade de parfums.

Rire des enfants, discrétion des esclaves, austérité des vierges, horreur des figures et des objets d'ici, sacrés soyez-vous par le souvenir de cette veille. Cela commençait par toute la rustrerie, voici que cela finit par des anges de flamme et de glace.

Petite veille d'ivresse, sainte! quand ce ne serait que pour le masque dont tu nous as gratifié. Nous t'affirmons, méthode! Nous n'oublions pas que tu as glorifié hier chacun de nos âges. Nous avons foi au poison. Nous savons donner notre vie tout entière tous les jours.

Voici le temps des *Assassins*.

Phrases

Quand le monde sera réduit en un seul bois noir pour nos quatre yeux étonnés,—en une plage pour deux enfants fidèles,—en une maison musicale pour notre claire sympathie,—je vous trouverai.

Qu'il n'y ait ici-bas qu'un vieillard seul, calme et beau, entouré d'un 'luxe inouï',—et je suis à vos genoux.

Que j'aie réalisé tous vos souvenirs,—que je sois celle qui sait vous garrotter,—je vous étoufferai.

Quand nous sommes très forts,—qui recule? très gais, qui tombe de ridicule? Quand nous sommes très-méchants, que ferait-on de nous.

Parez-vous, dansez, riez,—Je ne pourrai jamais envoyer l'Amour par la fenêtre.

Ma camarade, mendiante, enfant monstre! comme ça t'est égal, ces malheureuses et ces manœuvres, et mes embarras. Attache-toi à nous avec ta voix impossible, ta voix! unique flatteur de ce vil désespoir.

decencies shall be exiled, so that we may introduce our love of utmost purity. It began in some disgust and it finished—unable as we are to seize this eternity here and now—it finished in a riot of scents.

Laughter of the children, discretion of the slaves, the virgins' austerity, the horror of the faces and objects which belong here, may you be hallowed by the memory of this wake. It began in utter boorishness, here it is ending in angels of fire and ice.

Small drunken wake, holy! if only for the mask you have bestowed on us. Method, we confirm you! We do not forget that yesterday you glorified each of our ages. We have faith in the poison. We know how to give our life whole, every day.

This is the time of the ASSASSINS.*

Phrases

When the world has been reduced to a single dark wood for our four astonished eyes,—to a beach for two faithful children,—to a house of music for our manifest sympathy,—I shall find you.

Let there remain here below just a single old man, calm and beautiful, surrounded by 'untold riches',—and I shall be at your feet.

Let me have accomplished all your memories,—let me be the woman who knows how to bind you hand and foot,—I shall suffocate you.

When we are very strong,—who pulls back? when we sparkle so, who falls down in ridicule? When we are full of malice, what would they do to us?

Put on finery, dance, laugh,—I shall never be able to send Love out of the window.

My companion, beggar-girl, monster child! how these unfortunate women and these manoeuvres and my difficulties leave you unmoved. Attach yourself to us with your impossible voice, your voice! the one emollient for this vile despair.

[Phrases]

Une matinée couverte, en Juillet. Un goût de cendres vole dans l'air;—une odeur de bois suant dans l'âtre,—les fleurs rouies—le saccage des promenades—la bruine des canaux par les champs—pourquoi pas déjà les joujoux et l'encens?

J'ai tendu des cordes de clocher à clocher; des guirlandes de fenêtre à fenêtre; des chaînes d'or d'étoile à étoile, et je danse.

Le haut étang fume continuellement. Quelle sorcière va se dresser sur le couchant blanc? quelles violettes frondaisons vont descendre?

Pendant que les fonds publics s'écoulent en fêtes de fraternité, il sonne une cloche de feu rose dans les nuages.

Avivant un agréable goût d'encre de Chine une poudre noire pleut doucement sur ma veillée,—Je baisse les feux du lustre, je me jette sur le lit, et tourné du côté de l'ombre je vous vois, mes filles! mes reines!

Ouvriers

Ô cette chaude matinée de février. Le Sud inopportun vint relever nos souvenirs d'indigents absurdes, notre jeune misère.

Henrika avait une jupe de coton à carreau blanc et brun, qui a dû être portée au siècle dernier, un bonnet à rubans, et un foulard de soie. C'était bien plus triste qu'un deuil. Nous faisions un tour dans la banlieue. Le temps était couvert et ce vent du Sud excitait toutes les vilaines odeurs des jardins ravagés et des prés desséchés.

[Phrases]

An overcast morning in July. A taste of ashes wafts through the air;—the smell of smoke seeping in the hearth,—well-soaked flowers,—the wrecked walks,—the drizzle of canals across the fields—indeed, why not toys and incense now?

I have hung ropes from belfry to belfry; garlands from window to window; golden chains from star to star, and I dance.

The pond, high up, does not stop steamimg. What witch will set herself up against the white sunset? What violet foliage will fall?

While public funds are being squandered on festivals of brotherhood, a bell of rose-coloured fire tolls in the clouds.

Sharpening a pleasant flavour of India ink, a mist of black powder falls gently on my vigil,—I lower the gas-mantle, I throw myself on the bed, and, turned towards the shadow, I see you, my girls! my queens!

Workers

O that warm February morning! The inopportune South wind came to rekindle the memories of our absurdly penniless condition, our juvenile destitution.

Henrika was wearing a brown-and-white check cotton shirt, the sort of thing which must have been in fashion last century, a bonnet with ribbons, and a silk scarf. It was sadder than a funeral. We were strolling round the outskirts of the city. The sky was overcast, and the South wind conjured all the ugly smells of the ravaged gardens and dried-up fields.

Cela ne devait pas fatiguer ma femme au même point que moi. Dans une flache laissée par l'inondation du mois précédent à un sentier assez haut elle me fit remarquer de très petits poissons.

La ville, avec sa fumée et ses bruits de métiers, nous suivait très loin dans les chemins. Ô l'autre monde, l'habitation bénie par le ciel et les ombrages! Le sud me rappelait les misérables incidents de mon enfance, mes désespoirs d'été, l'horrible quantité de force et de science que le sort a toujours éloignée de moi. Non! nous ne passerons pas l'été dans cet avare pays où nous ne serons jamais que des orphelins fiancés. Je veux que ce bras durci ne traîne plus *une chère image*.

Les Ponts

Des ciels gris de cristal. Un bizarre dessin de ponts, ceux-ci droits, ceux-là bombés, d'autres descendant ou obliquant en angles sur les premiers, et ces figures se renouvelant dans les autres circuits éclairés du canal, mais tous tellement longs et légers que les rives chargées de dômes s'abaissent et s'amoindrissent. Quelques-uns de ces ponts sont encore chargés de masures. D'autres soutiennent des mâts, des signaux, de frêles parapets. Des accords mineurs se croisent, et filent, des cordes montent des berges. On distingue une veste rouge, peut-être d'autres costumes et des instruments de musique. Sont-ce des airs populaires, des bouts de concerts seigneuriaux, des restants d'hymnes publics? L'eau est grise et bleue, large comme un bras de mer.—Un rayon blanc, tombant du haut du ciel, anéantit cette comédie.

Ville

Je suis un éphémère et point trop mécontent citoyen d'une métropole crue moderne parce que tout goût connu a été éludé dans les ameublements et l'extérieur des maisons aussi bien que dans le plan de la ville. Ici vous ne signaleriez les traces d'aucun monument de superstition. La morale et la langue sont réduites à leur plus simple expression, enfin! Ces millions de gens qui n'ont pas besoin de se connaître amènent si pareillement l'éducation, le métier et la

It cannot have wearied my wife as much as it did me. In a little pool left behind by last month's floods on a path quite high up, she pointed out to me some tiny fish.

The city, with its smoke and the bustle of its workplaces, followed us far along our path. O the other world, the abode blessed by the sky and the shade of trees! The South wind brought back to me the wretched incidents of childhood, my summer despairs, the horrifying quantity of strength and knowledge from which fate has always kept me at arm's length. No! we shall not spend the summer in this mean land where we can never be anything but betrothed orphans. I want this hardened arm no more to drag *a cherished image.*

The Bridges

Grey crystal skies. A bizarre pattern of bridges, some straight, some curved, yet others sloping down or angled in obliquely at the first, and these figures repeated in the other lit-up stretches of canal, but all so long and light that the banks, heavy with domes, sink and grow smaller. Some of these bridges are still crowded with hovels. Others sprout masts, signals, frail parapets. Minor chords meet and melt; strands of rope rise from the banks. A red coat can be discerned, other costumes too, perhaps, and musical instruments. Are these well-known airs, snatches of lordly concerts, remnants of public anthems? The water is grey and blue, wide as an arm of the sea.—A ray of white light, falling from high up in the sky, clears away this charade.

City

I am an ephemeral and none-too-discontented citizen of a metropolis thought to be modern because all established taste has been avoided in the furnishings and on the outsides of houses as well as in the city plan. Here you will find no trace of any monument to superstition. So, morals and language finally have been reduced to their simplest expression! These myriad people who have no need to know one another carry on in such similar ways their education, their work

vieillesse, que ce cours de vie doit être plusieurs fois moins long que ce qu'une statistique folle trouve pour les peuples du continent. Aussi comme, de ma fenêtre, je vois des spectres nouveaux roulant à travers l'épaisse et éternelle fumée de charbon,—notre ombre des bois, notre nuit d'été!—des Erinnyes nouvelles, devant mon cottage qui est ma patrie et tout mon cœur puisque tout ici ressemble à ceci,—la Mort sans pleurs, notre active fille et servante, un Amour désespéré, et un joli Crime piaulant dans la boue de la rue.

Ornières

A droite l'aube d'été éveille les feuilles et les vapeurs et les bruits de ce coin du parc, et les talus de gauche tiennent dans leur ombre violette les mille rapides ornières de la route humide. Défilé de féeries. En effet: des chars chargés d'animaux de bois doré, de mâts et de toiles bariolées, au grand galop de vingt chevaux de cirque tachetés, et les enfants et les hommes sur leurs bêtes les plus étonnantes;—vingt véhicules, bossés, pavoisés et fleuris comme des carrosses anciens ou de contes, pleins d'enfants attifés pour une pastorale suburbaine;—Même des cercueils sous leur dais de nuit dressant les panaches d'ébène, filant au trot des grandes juments bleues et noires.

Villes [I]

L'acropole officielle outre les conceptions de la barbarie moderne les plus colossales. Impossible d'exprimer le jour mat produit par le ciel immuablement gris, l'éclat impérial des bâtisses, et la neige éternelle du sol. On a reproduit dans un goût d'énormité singulier toutes les merveilles classiques de l'architecture. J'assiste à des expositions de peinture dans des locaux vingt fois plus vastes qu'Hampton-Court. Quelle peinture! Un Nabuchodonosor norwégien a fait construire les escaliers des ministères; les subalternes que j'ai pu voir sont déjà plus fiers que des Brahmas et j'ai tremblé à l'aspect des gardiens de colosses et officiers de constructions. Par le groupement des bâtiments en squares, cours et terrasses fermées, on a évincé les cochers.

and their old age that their life-span must be many times shorter than certain wild statistics show about the people of the continent. And so I see from my window new spectres rolling through the thick, eternal coal-smoke—our woodland shade, our summer night!—new Erinyes,* in front of the cottage which is my country and all my heart as everything here looks like this,—dry-eyed Death, our busy daughter and servant, a desperate Love and a nice Crime whimpering in the muck of the street.

Ruts

To the right the summer dawn wakes the leaves and mists and sounds of this corner of the park, and the slopes to the left keep in their violet shadow the thousand rapid ruts on the moistened road. Parade of enchantments. And yes: carts laden with animals of golden wood, poles and multicoloured canvas, the galloping stride of twenty dappled circus horses, and the children and men on their most extraordinary mounts;—twenty vehicles, sculpted, hung with flags and decorated with flowers like the coaches of old or out of fairy tales, full of children got up for suburban pastorals;—Even coffins under their canopy of night flourishing ebony plumes, passing by to the trot of the great tall blue-black mares.

Cities [I]

The official acropolis surpasses the most colossal conceptions of modern barbarity. Impossible to describe the flat light produced by the grey unchanging sky, the imperial glare of the buildings, and the eternal snow on the ground. With singularly outrageous taste, all the marvels of classical architecture have been reproduced. I visit exhibitions of painting in places twenty times the size of Hampton Court.* What painting! A Norwegian Nebuchadnezzar has had made the staircases of the ministries; the underlings I managed to see are prouder than Brahmins* as it is, and the look of the men guarding the colossi and of the building officials made me tremble. The grouping of buildings into squares, enclosed courtyards, and terraces,

Les parcs représentent la nature primitive travaillée par un art superbe. Le haut quartier a des parties inexplicables: un bras de mer, sans bateaux, roule sa nappe de grésil bleu entre des quais chargés de candélabres géants. Un pont court conduit à une poterne immédiatement sous le dôme de la Sainte-Chapelle. Ce dôme est une armature d'acier artistique de quinze mille pieds de diamètre environ.

Sur quelques points des passerelles de cuivre, des plates-formes, des escaliers qui contournent les halles et les piliers, j'ai cru pouvoir juger la profondeur de la ville! C'est le prodige dont je n'ai pu me rendre compte: quels sont les niveaux des autres quartiers sur ou sous l'acropole? Pour l'étranger de notre temps la reconnaissance est impossible. Le quartier commerçant est un circus d'un seul style, avec galeries à arcades. On ne voit pas de boutiques. Mais la neige de la chaussée est écrasée; quelques nababs aussi rares que les promeneurs d'un matin de dimanche à Londres, se dirigent vers une diligence de diamants. Quelques divans de velours rouge: on sert des boissons polaires dont le prix varie de huit cents à huit mille roupies. A l'idée de chercher des théâtres sur ce circus, je me réponds que les boutiques doivent contenir des drames assez sombres. Je pense qu'il y a une police; mais la loi doit être tellement étrange, que je renonce à me faire une idée des aventuriers d'ici.

Le faubourg aussi élégant qu'une belle rue de Paris est favorisé d'un air de lumière. L'élément démocratique compte quelque cent âmes. Là encore les maisons ne se suivent pas; le faubourg se perd bizarrement dans la campagne, le 'Comté' qui remplit l'occident éternel des forêts et des plantations prodigieuses où les gentilshommes sauvages chassent leurs chroniques sous la lumière qu'on a créée.

Vagabonds

Pitoyable frère! Que d'atroces veillées je lui dus! 'Je ne me saisissais pas fervemment de cette entreprise. Je m'étais joué de son infirmité. Par ma faute nous retournerions en exil, en esclavage.' Il me supposait un guignon et une innocence très bizarres, et il ajoutait des raisons inquiétantes.

has displaced the cabmen. The parks exemplify primitive nature shaped with marvellous art. The better district of the town has inexplicable details: an arm of the sea, empty of boats, unfolds its gauze sheet of blue hail between quays stacked with giant candelabra. A short bridge leads to a postern right underneath the dome of the Sainte-Chapelle.* This dome is an armature of artistically worked steel some fifteen thousand feet in diameter.

At certain points on the copper footbridges, the platforms, the stairs which run round the covered markets and the pillars, I thought I could judge the depth of the city! This is the prodigy I was not able to pin down: how far below or above the acropolis are the other districts? For the stranger of our time reconnaissance is impossible. The commercial district is a circus done in a single style, with arched galleries. No shops to be seen. But the snow on the streets has been trampled; a handful of nabobs, as rare as a Sunday-morning stroller in London, make their way towards a carriage of diamonds. A few divans of red velvet: polar drinks are served, whose prices go from eight hundred to eight thousand rupees. I consider searching out some theatres in this circus, but tell myself that the shops themselves must house some decidedly murky dramas. I think there exists a police force; but the laws must be so strange that I give up trying to imagine what the city's shady characters are like.

Away from the centre, it is as elegant as a fine Parisian street, and graced by an air of light. The democratic element numbers about one hundred souls. Here again, the houses are not arranged in rows; the last part of the city dissolves strangely into the countryside, the 'County' which fills the unending west with the forests and colossal plantations where savage gentlefolk hunt down its newspaper columns by man-made light.

Tramps

Pitiful brother! What atrocious nights of wakefulness I owed him! 'I was not mad to embark on this venture. I scoffed at his infirmity. If we went back into exile, into slavery, it would be my fault.' He attributed to me the strangest ill-luck and innocence, and added worrying explanations.

Je répondais en ricanant à ce satanique docteur, et finissais par gagner la fenêtre. Je créais, par-delà la campagne traversée par des bandes de musique rare, les fantômes du futur luxe nocturne.

Après cette distraction vaguement hygiénique je m'étendais sur une paillasse. Et, presque chaque nuit, aussitôt endormi, le pauvre frère se levait, la bouche pourrie, les yeux arrachés,—tel qu'il se rêvait!—et me tirait dans la salle en hurlant son songe de chagrin idiot.

J'avais en effet, en toute sincérité d'esprit, pris l'engagement de le rendre à son état primitif de fils du soleil,—et nous errions, nourris du vin des cavernes et du biscuit de la route, moi pressé de trouver le lieu et la formule.

Villes [II]

Ce sont des villes! C'est un peuple pour qui se sont montés ces Alleghanys et ces Libans de rêve! Des chalets de cristal et de bois qui se meuvent sur des rails et des poulies invisibles. Les vieux cratères ceints de colosses et de palmiers de cuivre rugissent mélodieusement dans les feux. Des fêtes amoureuses sonnent sur les canaux pendus derrière les chalets. La chasse des carillons crie dans les gorges. Des corporations de chanteurs géants accourent dans des vêtements et des oriflammes éclatants comme la lumière des cimes. Sur les plates-formes au milieu des gouffres les Rolands sonnent leur bravoure. Sur les passerelles de l'abîme et les toits des auberges l'ardeur du ciel pavoise les mâts. L'écroulement des apothéoses rejoint les champs des hauteurs où les centauresses séraphiques évoluent parmi les avalanches. Au-dessus du niveau des plus hautes crêtes une mer troublée par la naissance éternelle de Vénus, chargée de flottes orphéoniques et de la rumeur des perles et des conques précieuses,—la mer s'assombrit parfois avec des éclats mortels. Sur les versants des moissons de fleurs grandes comme nos armes et nos coupes, mugissent. Des cortèges de Mabs en robes rousses, opalines, montent des ravines. Là-haut, les pieds dans la cascade et les ronces, les cerfs tètent Diane. Les Bacchantes des banlieues sanglotent et la lune brûle et hurle. Vénus entre dans les cavernes des forgerons et des ermites. Des groupes de beffrois chantent les idées des peuples.

I replied by sneering at this satanic man of learning, and ended up moving to the window. I created, beyond the tract of land traversed by ribbons of distant music, the phantoms of the luxury to come, by night.

After this vaguely hygienic diversion, I stretched out on a straw mattress. And, almost every night, as soon as sleep had come, the poor brother got up, his mouth stinking, his eyes mere sockets,—just as he saw himself in his dreams!—and dragged me into the room, howling his dream of idiot pain.

Indeed, in all sincerity of mind, I had made the commitment to restore him to his original state as a child of the sun,—so we wandered, nourished on the wine of caverns and the traveller's crust, with me hurrying to find the place and the key.

Cities [II]

These are cities! This is a people for whom these dream Alleghenies* and these Lebanons* have risen into being! Chalets of glass and wood which move on invisible rails and pulleys. The ancient craters ringed round by colossi and copper palms roar mellifluously in the flames. Festivals of love echo over the canals suspended behind the chalets. The chase of chiming bells reverberates around the gorges. Guilds of giant singers hurry in, draped in robes and oriflammes as brilliant as the light from mountain-tops. On the platforms deep in the gulfs the Rolands* trumpet their defiance. On the footbridges of the abyss and the roofs of the inns the heat of the heavens unfurls flags on the poles. The collapse of apotheoses spreads to the highest fields where seraphic centauresses move among the avalanches. Above the level of the tallest summits, a sea agitated by the endless birth of Venus, shouldering choral fleets, singing with precious pearls and conches,—sea sometimes darkening with deadly shards of light. From the slopes comes the bellow of harvested flowers as big as our weapons and goblets. Processions of Mabs* in opaline and russet robes climb out of the ravines. Up there, feet in the waterfall and the brambles, Diana* suckles the deer. The Bacchantes* of the suburbs sob and the moon burns and howls. Venus enters the blacksmiths' and the hermits' caves. Clusters of bell-towers sing out the ideas of the

Des châteaux bâtis en os sort la musique inconnue. Toutes les légendes évoluent et les élans se ruent dans les bourgs. Le paradis des orages s'effondre. Les sauvages dansent sans cesse la fête de la nuit. Et une heure je suis descendu dans le mouvement d'un boulevard de Bagdad où des compagnies ont chanté la joie du travail nouveau, sous une brise épaisse, circulant sans pouvoir éluder les fabuleux fantômes des monts où l'on a dû se retrouver.

Quels bons bras, quelle belle heure me rendront cette région d'où viennent mes sommeils et mes moindres mouvements?

Veillées

I

C'est le repos éclairé, ni fièvre ni langueur, sur le lit ou sur le pré.

C'est l'ami ni ardent ni faible. L'ami.

C'est l'aimée ni tourmentante ni tourmentée. L'aimée.

L'air et le monde point cherchés. La vie.

—Était-ce donc ceci?

—Et le rêve fraîchit.

II

L'éclairage revient à l'arbre de bâtisse. Des deux extrémités de la salle, décors quelconques, des élévations harmoniques se joignent. La muraille en face du veilleur est une succession psychologique de coupes de frises, de bandes atmosphériques et d'accidences géologiques.—Rêve intense et rapide de groupes sentimentaux avec des êtres de tous les caractères parmi toutes les apparences.

III

Les lampes et les tapis de la veillée font le bruit des vagues, la nuit, le long de la coque et autour du steerage.

La mer de la veillée, telle que les seins d'Amélie.

nations. From castles of bone unknown music comes. Every legend circulates and waves of impulse pour into the settlements. The paradise of storms is breaking up. The savages celebrate the night in endless dance. And in an hour I have come down into the life of a Baghdad boulevard where gathered people have sung the joy of the new work, in a heavy breeze, moving about, unable to avoid the fabulous phantoms of the mountains which must have been their meeting place.

What kind arms, what auspicious hour will restore to me this region from which come my sleeping and my merest movements?

Vigils

I

This is enlightened repose, neither fever nor languor, on the bed or in the meadow.

This is the friend, neither urgent nor lukewarm. The friend.

This is the loved one, neither tormentor nor tormented. The loved one.

The air and world not looked for. Life.

—So, was it this?

—And the dream grows cold.

II

Light returns to the central beam. From the two ends of the room, unremarkable scenes, harmonic elevations connect. The wall facing the watcher is a psychological succession of cross-sections of friezes, atmospheric layers, and geological strata.—Intense and fleeting dream of sentimental groups with every kind of being in every possible manifestation.

III

The lamps and carpets of the vigil make the sound of waves, at night, along the hull and down below.

The sea of the vigil, like Amélie's breasts.

Les tapisseries, jusqu'à mi-hauteur, des taillis de dentelle, teinte d'émeraude, où se jettent les tourte-relles de la veillée.

. . . .

La plaque du foyer noir, de réels soleils des grèves: ah! puits des magies; seule vue d'aurore, cette fois.

Mystique

Sur la pente du talus les anges tournent leurs robes de laine dans les herbages d'acier et d'émeraude.

Des prés de flammes bondissent jusqu'au sommet du mamelon. A gauche le terreau de l'arête est piétiné par tous les homicides et toutes les batailles, et tous les bruits désastreux filent leur courbe. Derrière l'arête de droite la ligne des orients, des progrès.

Et tandis que la bande en haut du tableau est formée de la rumeur tournante et bondissante des conques des mers et des nuits humaines,

La douceur fleurie des étoiles et du ciel et du reste descend en face du talus, comme un panier, contre notre face, et fait l'abîme fleurant et bleu là-dessous.

Aube

J'ai embrassé l'aube d'été.

Rien ne bougeait encore au front des palais. L'eau était morte. Les camps d'ombres ne quittaient pas la route du bois. J'ai marché, réveillant les haleines vives et tièdes, et les pierreries regardèrent, et les ailes se levèrent sans bruit.

La première entreprise fut, dans le sentier déjà empli de frais et blêmes éclats, une fleur qui me dit son nom.

Je ris au wasserfall blond qui s'échevela à travers les sapins: à la cime argentée je reconnus la déesse.

Alors je levai un à un les voiles. Dans l'allée, en agitant les bras. Par la plaine, où je l'ai dénoncée au coq. A la grand'ville elle fuyait parmi les clochers et les dômes, et courant comme un mendiant sur les quais de marbre, je la chassais.

En haut de la route, près d'un bois de lauriers, je l'ai entourée avec

The wall-hangings, the lower half, thickets of lace, emerald-tinted, where the doves of the vigil swirl.

. . . .

The backplate of the blackened heath, real suns on strands: ah! wells of many magics; dawn sighted only once this time.

Mystical

On the slope of the bank angels turn their robes of wool in pastures of steel and emerald.

Meadows of flame leap up to the top of the knoll. To the left the vegetable-mould on the ridge is trampled by every homicide and every battle, and all the noises of disaster curve away. Behind the ridge to the right, the line of orients, of progress.

And whereas the strip at the top of the picture is formed by the spinning, leaping whisper of conches and human nights,

The flower-strewn softness of the stars and the sky and of everything else drifts down opposite the slope, like a basket, against our face, and makes the flowering blue abyss below.

Dawn

I have been dawn's summer lord.*

Utter stillness on the palace fronts. Lifeless water. The shadow-camps on the woodland road had not yet been struck. I walked awakening warm and living breaths, and the precious stones looked, and the wings lifted without a sound.

The first enterprise was, on the path already live with shards of clean, cool light, a flower which told me its name.

I laughed at the wasserfall which tossed its blond cascade down through the pines: at the silver summit I recognized the goddess.

Then one by one I raised the veils. Down the path, my arms flailing. Across the levels, where I denounced her to the cock. In the city she flitted from belfry to dome, and running like a beggar across the marble quays, I kept up the chase.

At the top of the road, by a laurel grove, her veils gathered, I

ses voiles amassés, et j'ai senti un peu son immense corps. L'aube et l'enfant tombèrent au bas du bois.

Au réveil il était midi.

Fleurs

D'un gradin d'or,—parmi les cordons de soie, les gazes grises, les velours verts et les disques de cristal qui noircissent comme du bronze au soleil,—je vois la digitale s'ouvrir sur un tapis de filigranes d'argent, d'yeux et de chevelures.

Des pièces d'or jaune semées sur l'agate, des piliers d'acajou supportant un dôme d'émeraudes, des bouquets de satin blanc et de fines verges de rubis entourent la rose d'eau.

Tels qu'un dieu aux énormes yeux bleus et aux formes de neige, la mer et le ciel attirent aux terrasses de marbre la foule des jeunes et fortes roses.

Nocturne vulgaire

Un souffle ouvre des brèches operadiques dans les cloisons,—brouille le pivotement des toits rongés,—disperse les limites des foyers,—éclipse les croisées.—Le long de la vigne, m'étant appuyé du pied à une gargouille,—je suis descendu dans ce carrosse dont l'époque est assez indiquée par les glaces convexes, les panneaux bombés et les sophas contournés—Corbillard de mon sommeil, isolé, maison de berger de ma niaiserie, le véhicule vire sur le gazon de la grande route effacée: et dans un défaut en haut de la glace de droite tournoient les blêmes figures lunaires, feuilles, seins;—Un vert et un bleu très foncés envahissent l'image. Dételage aux environs d'une tache de gravier.

—Ici, va-t-on siffler pour l'orage, et les Sodomes, et les Solymes,—et les bêtes féroces et les armées,

—(Postillon et bêtes de songe reprendront-ils sous les plus suffocantes futaies, pour m'enfoncer jusqu'aux yeux dans la source de soie).

—Et nous envoyer, fouettés à travers les eaux clapotantes et les boissons répandues, rouler sur l'aboi des dogues...

—Un souffle disperse les limites du foyer.

enfolded her, and got some sense of her enormous body. In the depths of the wood, dawn and the child fell.

On waking, it was noon.

Flowers

From a golden tier—among the silk ropes, grey gauzes, green velvets, and crystal discs darkening like bronze in the sun,—I see foxgloves open on a carpet of silver filigree, eyes and hair.

Yellow gold coins sown on agate, mahogany columns supporting a dome of emeralds, bunches of white satin and fine stems of rubies surround the water-rose.

Like a god with enormous blue eyes the shapes of snow, the sky and the sea draw to the marble terraces the host of vigorous young roses.

Vulgar Nocturne

One breath opens operatic breaches in the walls,—blurs the pivoting motion of the worn-down roofs,—scatters the limits of the hearths,—eclipses the windows.—The length of the vine, one foot resting on a gargoyle,—I have travelled down in this carriage whose vintage is shown clearly enough by the convex window-glass, the bulging panels, and elaborately-designed seating—Hearse of my sleep, alone, shepherd's hut of my empty-headedness, the vehicle swerves along the grass of the buried highway: and in a flaw high up on the right-hand window, pale lunar figures, leaves and breasts spin round;—Deepest green and blue invade the picture. Unharnessing near a patch of gravel.

—Here, we will whistle up the storms and the Sodoms and Solymas,*—and the wild beasts and the armies,

—(Coachmen and dream-beasts will continue through the most suffocating thickets, and make me sink up to the eyes in the source of silk.)

—And send us, whipped across the choppy waters and the spilled drinks, to roll on the bulldogs' bark...

—One breath scatters the limits of the hearth.

Marine

Les chars d'argent et de cuivre—
Les proues d'acier et d'argent—
Battent l'écume,—
Soulèvent les souches des ronces.
Les courants de la lande
Et les ornières immenses du reflux
Filent circulairement vers l'est,
Vers les piliers de la forêt,—
Vers les fûts de la jetée,
Dont l'angle est heurté par des
tourbillons de lumière.

Fête d'hiver

La cascade sonne derrière les huttes d'opéra-comique. Des girandoles prolongent, dans les vergers et les allées voisins du Méandre,—les verts et les rouges du couchant. Nymphes d'Horace coiffées au Premier Empire,—Rondes Sibériennes, Chinoises de Boucher.—

Angoisse

Se peut-il qu'Elle me fasse pardonner les ambitions continuellement écrasées,—qu'une fin aisée répare les âges d'indigence,—qu'un jour de succès nous endorme sur la honte de notre inhabileté fatale,

(Ô palmes! diamant!—Amour! force!—plus haut que toutes joies et gloires!—de toutes façons, partout,—Démon, dieu—Jeunesse de cet être-ci; moi!)

Que des accidents de féerie scientifique et des mouvements de fraternité sociale soient chéris comme restitution progressive de la franchise première?...

Mais la Vampire qui nous rend gentils commande que nous nous

Seascape

Silver chariots, and copper—
Steel prows, and silver—
Smack the foam—
Heave the thorn-stumps out.
The currents of the great expanse
Huge lines scored by back-tracking tides
Circle away to the East,
Towards the limbs of the forest—
Towards the piers of the jetty,
A salient whipped by whirlpool-light.

Winter Festival

The waterfall sounds behind huts out of a comic opera. Wheeling fireworks in the orchards and avenues alongside the Meander,*—prolong the greens and reds of sunset. Nymphs out of Horace,* wearing their hair in First Empire* style,—Round Siberian women, Chinese women à la Boucher.*—

Anguish

Can it be that She might forgive my continually ruined ambitions,—that a comfortable end might compensate the ages of poverty,—that one day's success might lull us into forgetting the shame of our fatal incompetence,

(O palms! diamond!—Love! strength!—higher than any joy or glory!—of every kind, everywhere,—Demon, god—Youth of this being, here and now: myself!)

That accidents of scientific magic and movements of social brotherhood might be cherished as the progressive restitution of first freedom?...

But the Vampire who makes us behave correctly commands

amusions avec ce qu'elle nous laisse, ou qu'autrement nous soyons plus drôles.

Rouler aux blessures, par l'air lassant et la mer; aux supplices, par le silence des eaux et de l'air meurtriers; aux tortures qui rient, dans leur silence atrocement houleux.

Métropolitain

Du détroit d'indigo aux mers d'Ossian, sur le sable rose et orange qu'a lavé le ciel vineux viennent de monter et de se croiser des boulevards de cristal habités incontinent par de jeunes familles pauvres qui s'alimentent chez les fruitiers. Rien de riche.—La ville!

Du désert de bitume fuient droit en déroute avec les nappes de brumes échelonnées en bandes affreuses au ciel qui se recourbe, se recule et descend, formé de la plus sinistre fumée noire que puisse faire l'Océan en deuil, les casques, les roues, les barques, les croupes.—La bataille!

Lève la tête: le pont de bois, arqué; les derniers potagers de Samarie; ces masques enluminés sous la lanterne fouettée par la nuit froide; l'ondine niaise à la robe bruyante, au bas de la rivière; les crânes lumineux dans les plans de pois—et les autres fantasmagories—la campagne.

Des routes bordées de grilles et de murs, contenant à peine leurs bosquets, et les atroces fleurs qu'on appellerait cœurs et sœurs, Damas damnant de longueur,—possessions de fériques aristocraties ultra-Rhénanes, Japonaises, Guaranies, propres encore à recevoir la musique des anciens—et il y a des auberges qui pour toujours n'ouvrent déjà plus—il y a des princesses, et si tu n'es pas trop accablé, l'étude des astres—Le ciel.

Le matin où avec Elle, vous vous débattîtes parmi les éclats de neige, les lèvres vertes, les glaces, les drapeaux noirs et les rayons bleus, et les parfums pourpres du soleil des pôles,—ta force.

Barbare

Bien après les jours et les saisons, et les êtres et les pays,

Le pavillon en viande saignante sur la soie des mers et des fleurs arctiques; (elles n'existent pas.)

us to amuse ourselves with what she leaves us, or else be more amusing.

To roll towards wounds, through the fatiguing air and the sea; towards torments, through the silence of the murderous waters and air; towards tortures which laugh, in their hideously surging silence.

Metropolitan

From the indigo straits to Ossian's* seas, on the orange-pink sand which the wine-sky has washed, crystal boulevards have just risen and met, settled straightaway by poor young families who get their food from the fruiterer's. No riches here.—The city!

From the bitumen desert flee, in headlong disarray with sheets of fog spread out in ghastly layers in the curving, receding, falling sky, formed by the most sinister black smoke which the grieving Ocean can produce, the helmets, the wheels, the boats, the rumps. Battle!

Raise your eyes: the wooden bridge, arched; the last vegetable gardens of Samaria;* those masks lit up the lantern lashed by the cold night; the mindless water-nymph in the noisy dress, deep in the river; the luminous skulls in the rows of peas—and the other phantasmagoria—the countryside.

Roads lined with railings and walls, able hardly to contain their clumps of trees, and the atrocious flowers which might be called hearts and sisters, Damascus damning with tiresomeness,—the property of fairy-tale aristocracies from beyond the Rhine, Japanese, Guaranis,* still fit to receive the music of the old traditions—and there are inns which have already closed their doors, and which will not reopen—there are princesses, and if you are not too overwhelmed, the study of the stars—the sky.

The morning when, with Her, you fought together in the sparkle of snow, the green lips, the ice, the black flags and the blue rays, and the purple perfume of the polar sun,—your strength.

Barbaric

Long after the days and seasons, and the creatures and countries, the pavilion of bleeding meat on the silk of the seas and Arctic flowers; (they do not exist.)

Remis des vieilles fanfares d'héroïsme—qui nous attaquent encore le cœur et la tête—loin des anciens assassins—

Oh! Le pavillon en viande saignante sur la soie des mers et des fleurs arctiques; (elles n'existent pas)

Douceurs!

Les brasiers pleuvant aux rafales de givre,—Douceurs!—les feux à la pluie du vent de diamants jetée par le cœur terrestre éternellement carbonisé pour nous.—Ô monde!—

(Loin des vieilles retraites et des vieilles flammes, qu'on entend, qu'on sent,)

Les brasiers et les écumes. La musique, virement des gouffres et choc des glaçons aux astres.

Ô Douceurs, ô monde, ô musique! Et là, les formes, les sueurs, les chevelures et les yeux, flottant. Et les larmes blanches, bouillantes,—ô douceurs!—et la voix féminine arrivée au fond des volcans et des grottes arctiques.

Le pavillon...

Solde

A vendre ce que les Juifs n'ont pas vendu, ce que noblesse ni crime n'ont goûté, ce qu'ignorent l'amour maudit et la probité infernale des masses: ce que le temps ni la science n'ont pas à reconnaître:

Les Voix reconstituées; l'éveil fraternel de toutes les énergies chorales et orchestrales et leurs applications instantanées; l'occasion, unique, de dégager nos sens!

A vendre les Corps sans prix, hors de toute race, de tout monde, de tout sexe, de toute descendance! Les richesses jaillissant à chaque démarche! Solde de diamants sans contrôle!

A vendre l'anarchie pour les masses; la satisfaction irrépressible pour les amateurs supérieurs; la mort atroce pour les fidèles et les amants!

A vendre les habitations et les migrations, sports, féeries et comforts parfaits, et le bruit, le mouvement et l'avenir qu'ils font!

A vendre les applications de calcul et les sauts d'harmonie inouïs. Les trouvailles et les termes non soupçonnés, possession immédiate,

Élan insensé et infini aux splendeurs invisibles, aux délices

Restored from the old fanfares of heroism—which still attack our hearts and heads—far from the old assassins—

Oh! The pavilion of bleeding meat on the silk of the seas and Arctic flowers; (they do not exist)

Sweetness!

Blazing coals raining squalls of frost,—Sweetness!—the fires in the wind's rain of diamonds thrown out by the earth's entrails eternally burnt for us to cinders—O world!—

(Far from the old retreats and the old flames, which are heard, which are felt,)

Blaze and foam. Music, twisting gulfs, collision of icicles and stars.

O sweetness, o world, o music! And there, the shapes, sweats, heads of hair, the eyes, floating. And the white tears, boiling,—o sweetness!—and the female voice reaching the volcanoes' fundament and the Arctic caves.

The pavilion...

Sale

For sale: what the Jews have not sold, what neither nobility nor crime has tasted, what cursed love and the damnable integrity of the masses do not know; what neither time nor knowledge needs to recognize:

The Voices reconstituted; the brotherly awakening of every choral and orchestral energy and their instantaneous application; the opportunity, the only one, to free our senses!

For sale: the priceless bodies, belonging to no race, no world, no sex, no lineage! Riches gushing forth at every step! Unrestricted sale of diamonds!

For sale: anarchy for the masses; irrepressible satisfaction for true connoisseurs; atrocious death for the faithful and for lovers!

For sale: dwelling-places and migrations, sports, perfect magic, perfect comforts, and the noise, the movement and the future they create!

For sale: applications of calculus and harmonic ranges never heard before. Unsuspected finds and terms, immediate possession,

A senseless and infinite impetus towards invisible splendours,

insensibles,—et ses secrets affolants pour chaque vice—et sa gaîté effrayante pour la foule—

A vendre les Corps, les voix, l'immense opulence inquestionable, ce qu'on ne vendra jamais. Les vendeurs ne sont pas à bout de solde! Les voyageurs n'ont pas à rendre leur commission de si tôt!

Fairy

Pour Hélène se conjurèrent les sèves ornamentales dans les ombres vierges et les clartés impassibles dans le silence astral. L'ardeur de l'été fut confiée à des oiseaux muets et l'indolence requise à une barque de deuils sans prix par des anses d'amours morts et de parfums affaissés.

—Après le moment de l'air des bûcheronnes à la rumeur du torrent sous la ruine des bois, de la sonnerie des bestiaux à l'écho des vals, et des cris des steppes.—

Pour l'enfance d'Hélène frissonnèrent les fourrures et les ombres,—et le sein des pauvres, et les légendes du ciel.

Et ses yeux et sa danse supérieurs encore aux éclats précieux, aux influences froides, au plaisir du décor et de l'heure uniques.

Jeunesse

I
Dimanche

Les calculs de côté, l'inévitable descente du ciel, la visite des souvenirs et la séance des rhythmes occupent la demeure, la tête et le monde de l'esprit.

—Un cheval détale sur le turf suburbain, et le long des cultures et des boisements, percé par la peste carbonique. Une misérable femme de drame, quelque part dans le monde, soupire après des abandons improbables. Les desperadoes languissent après l'orage, l'ivresse et les blessures. De petits enfants étouffent des malédictions le long des rivières.—

Reprenons l'étude au bruit de l'œuvre dévorante qui se rassemble et remonte dans les masses.

imperceptible delights,—and its hair-raising secrets for every vice—and its frightening gaiety for the crowd—

For sale: the Bodies, the voices, the huge unquestionable opulence; what will never be sold. The vendors still have goods to clear! Travellers will not have to settle up just yet!

Fairy

For Helen the ornamental saps conspired in the virgin shades and the impassive brightness in the silence of stars. The summer heat was entrusted to mute birds and the required indolence to a funeral barge beyond price in among bays of dead loves and faded perfumes.

—After the time of the woodcutter women's tunes sung to the sound of the torrent beneath the ruin of the wood, of the bells of the cattle in the valley's echo, and of the cries from the steppes.—

For Helen's childhood the furs and shadows shivered,—and the breast of the poor, and the legends of the sky.

And her eyes and her dancing still superior to the precious bursts of light, to the effects of the cold, to the pleasure of the unique scene and moment.

Youth

I

Sunday

Calculations set to one side, the inevitable descent from the sky, the visit paid by memories and the seance of rhythms take over the house, the head and the world of the mind.

—A horse charges off on the suburban race-course, away through the fields and woodlands, riddled with carbonic plague. A sorry woman out of some drama, somewhere in the world, sighs for improbable surrenders to love. The desperadoes long for storms, drunkenness, and wounds. Little children, along river-banks, utter curses under their breath.—

Back to our studies, to the noise of the consuming work which gathers and swells again among the masses.

II
Sonnet

Homme de constitution ordinaire, la chair
n'était-elle pas un fruit pendu dans le verger;—ô
journées enfantes!—le corps un trésor à prodiguer;—ô
aimer, le péril ou la force de Psyché? La terre
avait des versants fertiles en princes et en artistes,
et la descendance et la race vous poussaient aux
crimes et aux deuils: la monde votre fortune et votre
péril. Mais à présent, ce labeur comblé; toi, tes calculs,
—toi, tes impatiences—ne sont plus que votre danse et
votre voix, non fixées et point forcées, quoique d'un double
événement d'invention et de succès + une raison,
—en l'humanité fraternelle et discrète par l'univers
sans images;—la force et le droit réfléchissent la
danse et la voix à présent seulement appréciées.

III
Vingt ans

Les voix instructives exilées.... L'ingénuité physique amèrement rassise.... —Adagio—Ah! l'égoïsme infini de l'adolescence, l'optimisme studieux: que le monde était plein de fleurs cet été! Les airs et les formes mourant.... —Un chœur, pour calmer l'impuissance et l'absence! Un chœur de verres, de mélodies nocturnes.... En effet les nerfs vont vite chasser.

IV

Tu en es encore à la tentation d'Antoine. L'ébat du zèle écourté, les tics d'orgueil puéril, l'affaissement et l'effroi.

Mais tu te mettras à ce travail: toutes les possibilités harmoniques et architecturales s'émouvront autour de ton siége. Des êtres parfaits, imprévus, s'offriront à tes expériences. Dans tes environs affluera rêveusement la curiosité d'anciennes foules et de luxes oisifs. Ta mémoire et tes sens ne seront que la nourriture de ton impulsion

II

Sonnet

Man of ordinary constitution, was not the flesh
a fruit hanging in the orchard;—oh
days of childhood!—the body a treasure to waste;—oh
loving, the peril or the strength of Psyche?* The earth
had slopes rich in princes and artists,
and lineage and race drove us to
crimes and bereavements: the world your fortune and your
peril. But now, that toil rewarded; you, your calculations,
—you, your fits of impatience—are no more than your dancing
and your voice, not fixed and certainly not forced, although an
added reason for a double consequence of inventiveness + success,
—in brotherly and discreet humanity throughout the universe
devoid of images;—force and justice reflect the
dancing and the voices which are only now esteemed.

III

Twenty years old

The voices of instruction in exile... The body's ingenuousness bitterly put in its place... —Adagio—Ah! the infinite egotism of adolescence, the studious optimism: how full of flowers the world was that summer! Tunes and forms fading... —A choir, to calm down impotence and absence! A choir of glass pieces, of nocturnal melodies... *Soon, indeed*, the nerves will slip their moorings.

IV

You have not yet left behind the temptation of St Anthony.* Wild energy curtailed, the tics of puerile pride, the collapse and the terror.

But you will apply yourself to this task: all harmonic and architectural possibilities will move about your seat. Perfect, unforeseen beings will offer themselves for your experiments. Around you there will gather dreamily the curiosity of ancient crowds and of idle luxuries. Your memory and your senses will be no more than the nourishment of your creative impetus. And the world, when you move

créatrice. Quant au monde, quand tu sortiras, que sera-t-il devenu? En tout cas, rien des apparences actuelles.

Guerre

Enfant, certains ciels ont affiné mon optique: tous les caractères nuancèrent ma physionomie. Les Phénomènes s'émurent.—A présent l'inflexion éternelle des moments et l'infini des mathématiques me chassent par ce monde où je subis tous les succès civils, respecté de l'enfance étrange et des affections énormes.—Je songe à une Guerre, de droit ou de force, de logique bien imprévue.

C'est aussi simple qu'une phrase musicale.

Promontoire

L'aube d'or et la soirée frissonnante trouvent notre brick en large en face de cette Villa et de ses dépendances, qui forment un promontoire aussi étendu que l'Épire et le Péloponnèse ou que la grande île du Japon, ou que l'Arabie! Des fanums qu'éclaire la rentrée des théories, d'immenses vues de la défense des côtes modernes; des dunes illustrées de chaudes fleurs et de bacchanales; de grands canaux de Carthage et des Embankments d'une Venise louche; de molles éruptions d'Etnas et des crevasses de fleurs et d'eaux des glaciers; des lavoirs entourés de peupliers d'Allemagne; des talus de parcs singuliers penchant des têtes d'Arbres du Japon; les façades circulaires des 'Royal' ou des 'Grand' de Scarbro' ou de Brooklyn; et leurs railways flanquent, creusent, surplombent les dispositions de cet Hôtel, choisies dans l'histoire des plus élégantes et des plus colossales constructions de l'Italie, de l'Amérique et de l'Asie, dont les fenêtres et les terrasses à présent pleines d'éclairages, de boissons et de brises riches, sont ouvertes à l'esprit des voyageurs et des nobles—qui permettent, aux heures du jour, à toutes les tarentelles des côtes,—et même aux ritournelles des vallées illustres de l'art, de décorer merveilleusement les façades du Palais. Promontoire.

on, what will it have become? At all events, it will not remotely resemble the way it is now.

War

As a child, certain skies sharpened the way I saw: every character very subtly changed my features. Phenomena were moved.—Now, the unending inflection of moments and the infinity of mathematics send me scurrying through this world where I endure every civil success, respected by strange childhood and by vast affection.—I dream of a War, of justice or of might, of logic quite unforeseen.

It is as simple as a musical phrase.

Promontory

Golden dawn and trembling dusk find our brig lying off the coast opposite that villa and its outbuildings, a promontory as long as Epirus and the Peloponnese or the great island of Japan, or Arabia! Shrines lit up by returning processions; huge views of modern coastal defences; dunes coloured by incandescent flowers and bacchanals; great Carthaginian canals, Embankments of a shifty Venice; feeble eruptions of Etnas; crevasses of flowers and glacier water; wash-houses ringed with German poplars; slopes of strange parks where Trees of Japan hang their heads; the curving frontage of *Royals* and *Grands* in Scarborough* and Brooklyn; their railways run beside and under and over the planes and surfaces of this Hotel, chosen from the history of the most elegant, most colossal buildings of Italy, America, Asia; its windows and terraces, bathed now in precious lights, drinks, sweet air, are open to the spirit of the travellers and the nobility—and they permit, in daylight hours, every tarantella of the coasts, and even the ritornelli of art's illustrious valleys, to cover in splendour the façades of the Palace. Promontory.

Scènes

L'ancienne Comédie poursuit ses accords et divise ses Idylles:

Des boulevards de tréteaux.

Un long pier en bois d'un bout à l'autre d'un champ rocailleux où la foule barbare évolue sous les arbres dépouillés.

Dans des corridors de gaze noire suivant le pas des promeneurs aux lanternes et aux feuilles.

Des oiseaux des mystères s'abattent sur un ponton de maçonnerie mû par l'archipel couvert des embarcations des spectateurs.

Des scènes lyriques accompagnées de flûte et de tambour s'inclinent dans des réduits ménagés sous les plafonds, autour des salons de clubs modernes ou des salles de l'Orient ancien.

La féerie manœuvre au sommet d'un amphithéâtre couronné par les taillis,—Ou s'agite et module pour les Béotiens, dans l'ombre des futaies mouvantes sur l'arête des cultures.

L'opéra-comique se divise sur une scène à l'arête d'intersection de dix cloisons dressées de la galerie aux feux.

Soir historique

En quelque soir, par exemple, que se trouve le touriste naïf, retiré de nos horreurs économiques, la main d'un maître anime le clavecin des prés; on joue aux cartes au fond de l'étang, miroir évocateur des reines et des mignonnes, on a les saintes, les voiles, et les fils d'harmonie, et les chromatismes légendaires, sur le couchant.

Il frissonne au passage des chasses et des hordes. La comédie goutte sur les tréteaux de gazon. Et l'embarras des pauvres et des faibles sur ces plans stupides!

A sa vision esclave,—l'Allemagne s'échafaude vers des lunes; les déserts tartares s'éclairent—les révoltes anciennes grouillent dans le centre du Céleste Empire, par les escaliers et les fauteuils de rois—un petit monde blême et plat, Afrique et Occidents, va s'édifier. Puis

Scenes

The ancient Comedy follows its conventions and shares out its idylls;

Boulevards of stage-planks.

A long wooden pier from one end to the other of a rock-strewn field where the crowd of barbarians moves about beneath the bare trees.

In corridors of black gauze following the footsteps of the walkers, with their lanterns and leaves.

Birds from mystery plays alight on a stone pontoon moved by the archipelago teeming with boatloads of spectators.

Lyrical scenes, to the accompaniment of flute and drum, slope down into recesses worked in under the ceilings, round the meeting-rooms of modern clubs or the great rooms of the ancient East.

The magic event plays at the top of an ampitheatre crowned with thickets,—Or gets busy and alters itself to suit the Boeotians,* in the shadow of the waving clumps of trees at the top of the cultivated land.

The comic opera is divided on a stage at the angle where ten partitions intersect, built from the gallery down to the footlights.

Historic Evening

On some evening, shall we say, when the innocent tourist, away from our economic horrors, the hand of a master touches into life the harpsichord of the meadows; there a card game is going on at the bottom of the pond, a mirror which evokes queens and favourites, there are the women saints, the veils, the threads of harmony, and the legendary chromatics against the sunset.

He gives a shudder as the hunts and hordes go past. The play drips onto the grass staging. And the embarrassment of the poor and the frail on these stupid levels!

To his enslaved sight,—Germany scaffolds up towards moons; the Tartar deserts light up—the ancient revolts seethe in the heart of the Celestial Empire, in the stairways and the armchairs of kings—a little world, pale and flat, Africa and Occidents, is going to be built.

un ballet de mers et de nuits connues, une chimie sans valeur, et des mélodies impossibles.

La même magie bourgeoise à tous les points où la malle nous déposera! Le plus élémentaire physicien sent qu'il n'est plus possible de se soumettre à cette atmosphère personnelle, brume de remords physiques, dont la constatation est déjà une affliction.

Non!—Le moment de l'étuve, des mers enlevées, des embrasements souterrains, de la planète emportée, et des exterminations conséquentes, certitudes si peu malignement indiquées dans la Bible et par les Nornes et qu'il sera donné à l'être sérieux de surveiller.—Cependant ce ne sera point un effet de légende!

Bottom

La réalité étant trop épineuse pour mon grand caractère,—je me trouvai néanmoins chez ma dame, en gros oiseau gris bleu s'essorant vers les moulures du plafond et traînant l'aile dans les ombres de la soirée.

Je fus, au pied du baldaquin supportant ses bijoux adorés et ses chefs-d'œuvre physiques, un gros ours aux gencives violettes et au poil chenu de chagrin, les yeux aux cristaux et aux argents des consoles.

Tout se fit ombre et aquarium ardent. Au matin,—aube de juin batailleuse,—je courus aux champs, âne, claironnant et brandissant mon grief, jusqu'à ce que les Sabines de la banlieue vinrent se jeter à mon poitrail.

H

Toutes les monstruosités violent les gestes atroces d'Hortense. Sa solitude est la mécanique érotique, sa lassitude, la dynamique amoureuse. Sous la surveillance d'une enfance elle a été, à des époques nombreuses, l'ardente hygiène des races. Sa porte est ouverte à la misère. Là, la moralité des êtres actuels se décorpore en sa passion ou en son action—Ô terrible frisson des amours novices sur le sol sanglant et par l'hydrogène clarteux! trouvez Hortense.

Then a ballet of known seas and nights, a worthless chemistry, and impossible melodies.

The same bourgeois magic wherever the packet-boat happens to put us ashore! The most elementary physicist can feel that it is possible no longer to submit oneself to this private atmosphere, this fog of physical remorse, to recognize which is in itself an affliction.

No!—The day of the steam-room, of seas removed, of underground conflagrations, of the planet borne away, and the resultant exterminations, certainties indicated so mildly by the Bible and the Norns,* and which it will be the serious person's lot to watch over.—But in no way will this be the stuff of legend!

Bottom

Reality being too thorny for my my great character,—I found myself nevertheless at my lady's, in the guise of a big blue-grey bird soaring towards the mouldings on the ceiling and dragging my wings among the shadows of the evening.

I was, at the foot of the canopy supporting her adored jewels and her physical masterpieces, a huge bear with violet gums and fur, shagreened by suffering, my eyes on the crystal and the silver on the console-tables.

All became dark and burning aquarium. In the morning,—a quarrelsome June dawn,—I ran into the fields, an ass, trumpeting and brandishing my grievance, until the Sabine women* from the suburbs arrived and threw themselves on my breast.

H

All that is unnatural violates the atrocious gestures of Hortense. Her solitude is erotic mechanics, her weariness, love's dynamic. Under a childhood's supervision she has been, in several eras, the ardent hygiene of the races. Her door is open to destitution. There, the morality of present beings is disembodied in her passion or her action—O terrible trembling of novice loves on the blood-soaked ground and in the milky hydrogen! work out who is Hortense.

Mouvement

Le mouvement de lacet sur la berge des chutes du fleuve,
Le gouffre à l'étambot,
La célérité de la rampe,
L'énorme passade du courant,
Mènent par les lumières inouïes
Et la nouveauté chimique
Les voyageurs entourées des trombes du val
Et du strom.

Ce sont les conquérants du monde
Cherchant la fortune chimique personnelle;
Le sport et le comfort voyagent avec eux;
Ils emmènent l'éducation
Des races, des classes et des bêtes, sur ce Vaisseau.
Repos et vertige
A la lumière diluvienne,
Aux terribles soirs d'étude.

Car de la causerie parmi les appareils,—le sang,
  les fleurs, le feu, les bijoux,—
Des comptes agités à ce bord fuyard,
—On voit, roulant comme une digue au-delà de
  la route hydraulique motrice,
Monstrueux, s'éclairant sans fin,—leur stock d'études;—
Eux chassés dans l'extase harmonique
Et l'héroïsme de la découverte.

Aux accidents atmosphériques les plus surprenants
Un couple de jeunesse s'isole sur l'arche,
—Est-ce ancienne sauvagerie qu'on pardonne?
Et chante et se poste.

Movement

The swaying movement by the tumbling riverside,
The vortex at the sternpost,
The speed of the ramp
The vast to-and-fro of the current,
Among outlandish lights
And chemical invention
Steer the travellers through the valley's waterspouts
And the riptide.

These are the conquerors of the world
Seeking their own chemical fortune:
Sport and comfort travel with them;
They bear away the education
Of races, classes, beasts, on this Vessel.
Rest and vertigo
In the diluvian light,
On terrible nights of study.

For, from the talk among the machinery,—the blood,
the flowers, the fire, the jewels,—
From the agitated reckonings on these fugitive boards,
—Can be seen, rolling like a dyke beyond the
roads hydraulic motive power,
Monstrous, endlessly illuminated,—their stock of studies;—
Themselves driven into harmonic ecstasy
And the heroism of discovery.

Amid the most astonishing atmospheric activity,
Standing apart on the ark, two young people,
—Past savagery pardoned perhaps?—
And sing and take up their stations.

Dévotion

A ma sœur Louise Vanaen de Voringhem:—Sa cornette bleue tournée à la mer du Nord.—Pour les naufragés.

A ma sœur Léonie Aubois d'Ashby. Baou—l'herbe d'été bourdonnante et puante.—Pour la fièvre des mères et des enfants.

A Lulu,—démon—qui a conservé un goût pour les oratoires du temps des Amies et de son éducation incomplète. Pour les hommes!—A madame ***.

A l'adolescent que je fus. A ce saint vieillard, ermitage ou mission.

A l'esprit des pauvres. Et à un très haut clergé.

Aussi bien à tout culte en telle place de culte mémoriale et parmi tels événements qu'il faille se rendre, suivant les aspirations du moment ou bien notre propre vice sérieux,

Ce soir à Circeto des hautes glaces, grasse comme le poisson, et enluminée comme les dix mois de la nuit rouge,—(son cœur ambre et spunk),—pour ma seule prière muette comme ces régions de nuit et précédant des bravoures plus violentes que ce chaos polaire.

A tout prix et avec tous les airs, même dans des voyages métaphysiques.—Mais plus *alors*.

Démocratie

'Le drapeau va au paysage immonde, et notre patois étouffe le tambour.

'Aux centres nous alimenterons la plus cynique prostitution. Nous massacrerons les révoltes logiques.

'Aux pays poivrés et détrempés!—au service des plus monstrueuses exploitations industrielles ou militaires.

'Au revoir ici, n'importe où. Conscrits du bon vouloir, nous aurons la philosophie féroce; ignorants pour la science, roués pour le confort; la crevaison pour le monde qui va. C'est la vraie marche. En avant, route!'

Devotions

To my sister Louise Vanaen de Voringhem:*—her blue coif turned towards the North Sea.—For the shipwrecked.

To my sister Léonie Aubois d'Ashby.* Baou—the buzz and stench of summer grass.—For the fevers of mothers and children.

To Lulu—a demon—who has preserved her taste for the oratories of the days of Girlfriends and her incomplete education. For men!—To Madame ***.

To the adolescent I once was. To that old holy man, hermitage or mission.

To the spirit of the poor. And to a very high clergy.

Equally to all denominations in whatever place of memorial worship and among whatever events it might be necessary to witness, depending on the aspirations of the moment or our own major vice,

This evening, to Circeto* of the heights of ice, fat as fish, and illuminated like the ten months of the red night,—(her heart amber and spunk), for my only prayer, silent as these regions of night, and preceding deeds of daring more violent than this polar chaos.

Whatever the cost, whatever shape or form, even on metaphysical journeys.—But no more *then*.

Democracy

'The flag moves through a disgusting landscape, and our patois drowns out the drum.

'In the interior, we shall fuel the most cynical prostitution. We shall massacre every revolt which makes sense.

'Hello, sodden lands of spices!—serving the most monstrous industrial or military exploitation.

'Goodbye to here, anywhere will do. Conscripts of good will, our attitude will be ferocious; knowing nothing about science, everything about comforts; the world and its ways can go hang. This is the true way forward. Quick march!'

Génie

Il est l'affection et le présent puisqu'il a fait la maison ouverte à l'hiver écumeux et à la rumeur de l'été, lui qui a purifié les boissons et les aliments, lui qui est le charme des lieux fuyants et le délice surhumain des stations. Il est l'affection et l'avenir, la force et l'amour que nous, debout dans les rages et les ennuis, nous voyons passer dans le ciel de tempête et les drapeaux d'extase.

Il est l'amour, mesure parfaite et réinventée, raison merveilleuse et imprévue, et l'éternité: machine aimée des qualités fatales. Nous avons tous eu l'épouvante de sa concession et de la nôtre: ô jouissance de notre santé, élan de nos facultés, affection égoïste et passion pour lui, lui qui nous aime pour sa vie infinie...

Et nous nous le rappelons et il voyage... Et si l'Adoration s'en va, sonne, sa promesse sonne: 'Arrière ces superstitions, ces anciens corps, ces ménages et ces âges. C'est cette époque-ci qui a sombré!'

Il ne s'en ira pas, il ne redescendra pas d'un ciel, il n'accomplira pas la rédemption des colères de femmes et des gaîtés des hommes et de tout ce péché: car c'est fait, lui étant, et étant aimé.

Ô ses souffles, ses têtes, ses courses; la terrible célérité de la perfection des formes et de l'action.

Ô fécondité de l'esprit et immensité de l'univers!

Son corps! Le dégagement rêvé, le brisement de la grâce croisée de violence nouvelle!

Sa vue, sa vue! tous les agenouillages anciens et les peines *relevés* à sa suite.

Son jour! l'abolition de toutes souffrances sonores et mouvantes dans la musique plus intense.

Son pas! les migrations plus énormes que les anciennes invasions.

Ô lui et nous! l'orgueil plus bienveillant que les charités perdues.

Ô monde! et le chant clair des malheurs nouveaux!

Il nous a connus tous et nous a tous aimés. Sachons, cette nuit d'hiver, de cap en cap, du pôle tumultueux au château, de la foule à la plage, de regards en regards, forces et sentiments las, le héler et le voir, et le renvoyer, et sous les marées et au haut des déserts de neige, suivre ses vues, ses souffles, son corps, son jour.

Genie

He is affection and the present since he has opened the house to frothy winter and the murmur of summer, he who has purified drink and food, he who has charmed elusive places, who has been the superhuman delight of resting-places. He is affection and the future, the strength and love which we, standing in rage and ennui, see pass through the stormy sky and among the pennants of ecstasy.

He is love, perfectly measured and reinvented, marvellous and unforeseen reason, and eternity: machine beloved of everything inevitable. We have all known the terror of his concession and of ours: our health, pleasure, free flight of our faculties, selfish affection and passion for him, for him who loves us, will love us for all of his endless life...

And we recall him and he travels on... And if Adoration moves off, rings, his promise rings: 'Away with these superstitions, these erstwhile bodies, this home-making, these ages. These are the times that have gone under!'

He will not go away, he will not come down again from any heaven, he will not address the redemption of women's anger or men's joys and all that sin: it is done, because he is, and because he is loved.

His breaths, his heads, his flights: the terrible swiftness taking forms and action to perfection!

Fecundity of mind, vastness of the universe!

His body! the dreamt release, the smashing of grace crossed with new violence!

The sight, the sight of him! all the old kneeling, the sorrows *lifted* in his wake.

The light that he is! the abolition of all heard and shifting suffering in a music more intense.

His step! migrations more enormous than ancient invasions.

Him, us! pride more kindly than all that wasted charity.

World! and the limpid song of fresh unhappiness!

He has known us all and loved us all. Let us know, this winter night, from cape to cape, from the tumultuous pole to the chateau, from the crowd to the shore, from glance to glance, wearied strength and feelings, how to greet him and see him, send him away, and, beneath the tides and at the crest of the snow-deserts, follow his eyes, his breathing, his body, his light.

EXPLANATORY NOTES

Poems, 1869–1871

Orphans' New Year Gifts

Rimbaud's first published poem of January 1870. The influences are felt here—and in a number of Rimbaud's early verse poems—of Victor Hugo (1802–85), Charles Baudelaire (1821–67), François Coppée (1842–1908), and other poets of the nineteenth century. The theme is similar to that of 'Seven-year-old Poets'.

The Blacksmith

The allusion is to the invasion of Louis XVI's palace by revolutionaries in August 1792, one of whom, a butcher called Legendre, scared the king into voluntarily donning the red revolutionary bonnet.

21 *red of Revolution*: a reference to Phrygian bonnet adopted by revolutionaries. Rimbaud has the blacksmith crown the king with it, although in fact Louis XVI placed it on his own head.

Sun and Skin

As well as the Latin poet Lucretius (98–53 BC), the influences of Hugo, Théodore de Banville (1823–91), and Charles Leconte de Lisle (1818–94) are felt in this classically minded long poem. Although he was soon to reject Banville, Rimbaud respectfully sent a number of his own poems to the older man.

27 *Ariadne*: daughter of King Minos, she helped Theseus to kill the Minotaur, but was then abandoned by him on the island of Naxos.

Lysios... Phrygian: Lysios is another name for Bacchus, god of wine. Phrygia was an ancient country situated in Western Turkey.

Europa: daughter of Agenor, king of Tyre, whom Zeus abducted in the form of a white bull.

Leda: wife of Tyndareus, king of Sparta. Zeus seduced her in the form of a swan.

Cypris: name for Aphrodite, goddess of love, worshipped on Cyprus.

29 *Endymion*: in Greek mythology a hunter, the most beautiful of men, who was loved by Selene (the moon).

Ophelia

Rimbaud's starting-point is Ophelia's suicide by drowning in Shakespeare's *Hamlet*, IV. viii: 'Her clothes spread wide, and, mermaid-like, awhile they bore her up.'

31 *visions*: a pre-echo of the *voyant* theme of the poet as seer or visionary. Rimbaud implies that her visionary power was too much for Ophelia to bear.

Hanged Men Dance

Reminiscent of the well-known 'Ballad of the Hanged Men' by François Villon (?1431–89).

33 *Paladins*: knights-errant.

Tartufe's Punishment

Tartufe is the hypocritical *dévot* in Molière's eponymous comedy of 1664. Rimbaud's pseudo-priest is more sinister-looking than Molière's, highlighting Rimbaud's fierce anticlericalism. The final line is a wry re-working of two lines spoken by Dorine in Molière: 'I could see you naked head to toe, | And still your skin would leave me cold.'

Venus Emerging

This sonnet wilfully inverts normal aesthetic expectations concerning the goddess, especially in the final stanza.

37 *CLARA VENUS*: *clara* (Latin) = 'renowned'.

Nina Answers Back

The theme of free imagination versus flat reality is central both to Rimbaud's work and his life. The identification of imagination with the male principle and harsh realism with the female is far from exclusive to this poem.

To Music

Rimbaud's characteristic contempt for the complacencies of comfortable living, as well as his erotic daydreams, form the basis of one of his sharpest social satires.

'The dead of '92 and '93...'

Le Pays, a Republican journal, after the declaration of the Franco-Prussian War on 10 July 1870 published stirring lines by Paul de Cassagnac, reminding readers of some glorious successes of the Revolutionary Armies a century earlier. Mazas Prison was an infamous and grim place, now vanished. It stood near the Pont d'Austerlitz, in the east part of Paris.

53 *Valmy . . . Italy*: the Battle of Valmy, 20 September 1792, in which *va-nu-pieds* ('barefoot soldiers') pushed back the invading German forces. Fleurus is a town in Belgium, where General Jourdan routed the Austrian army in 1794. Napoleon's campaign in Italy of 1791–6 paved the way for Italian republicanism.

Evil

Here God has been seen by commentators either as championing the poor

against the rich, or as being indifferent to everything except the wealth and trappings of religion.

55 *sneering king*: French troops (scarlet) and German (green) are treated with equal contempt by their respective heads of state.

Caesars' Rage

A mocking portrait of Napoleon III who, having capitulated in 1870 at Sedan, was held prisoner by the Germans in Wilhelmshöhe Castle.

Tuileries: the Tuileries Palace in Paris was burnt down by Communards in May 1871.

57 *old bespectacled Confederate*: Émile Ollivier, who announced the declaration of the Franco-Prussian War on 19 July 1870 with 'a light heart'.

St Cloud: one of Napoleon III's residences, just west of Paris. Burnt down by the Germans in 1871.

Asleep in the Valley

One of Rimbaud's most celebrated poems, this anti-war sonnet, in which death is not once named directly, was inspired by the Franco-Prussian War.

At the Green Inn, five p.m.

Rimbaud associates green, in 'Vowels', with peace; towards the end of 'Comedy of Thirst' he makes another reference to 'the Green Inn'.

59 *Charleroi*: a Belgian town close to Rimbaud's home town of Charleville.

Cunning

Like 'At the Green Inn', this poem is set in Charleroi. Compare also 'First Night.'

61 *come over*: deliberately bad grammar, to mirror a similar deliberate error in French ('*une* froid').

'Centre: the Emperor...'

Sarrebrück, on the French–German border, is the site of the first battle of the Franco-Prussian War (2 August 1870), a victory for Napoleon III, but so unspectacular as to prompt Rimbaud's sarcastic adjective. The engraving referred to is a so-called *Image d'Épinal*, popular eighteenth- and nineteenth-century prints depicting scenes of French life.

Pitou: an affectionate sobriquet for the good-hearted ordinary soldier (cf. the British 'Tommy').

Dumanet: a sobriquet for a stupid, gullible private soldier.

Boquillon: a reference to the simple, bewildered main figure in the satirical journal *La Lanterne de Boquillon*.

My Bohemia (Fantasy)

An autobiographical allusion, probably to Rimbaud's flight to Charleroi and then Paris at the end of August 1870.

Crows

65 *dead of yesterdays*: possibly an allusion to those who died in the fierce fighting in Paris during the last days of the Commune (May 1871).

Seated

One of Rimbaud's cruellest caricatures. The strength and originality of his poetic language are now most marked.

69 *And they stir into life* . . .: the meaning of this final line is obviously sexual.

The Customs Men

Another typically anti-authoritarian poem.

Tariff Soldiers: customs men have obtained jobs thanks to the creation of new, seemingly arbitrary national frontiers.

Fausts: Faust, the man of science of German legend who made a pact with the devil, whereby he obtained earthly riches and power in exchange for his soul, fascinated generations of writers, particularly in the nineteenth century.

Diavolos: Fra Diavolo was a celebrated Italian brigand who fought against domination of Naples by French. He was captured by them and hanged in 1806.

Tortured Heart

Four versions exist of this haunted triolet (a fixed-form poem constructed on pattern of repetitions). It appears to be about rites of passage performed by sailors, but alternatively it may concern the degrading behaviour of soldiers in barracks during the Commune in May 1871. This was the time when Rimbaud announced his concept of the *voyant*, the poet as seer.

Paris War-Cry

The background to this sequence of eight linked quatrains is the removal, on 18 March 1871, of the French government from Paris to Versailles, 30 km. west of the capital. The Commune took control of Paris, and in response, from April, the Versailles government bombarded the suburbs. Whether Rimbaud was in Paris during the Commune is not certain, but his strong Communard sympathies are clear from this angry poem.

73 *Thiers and Picard*: Adolphe Thiers (1797–1877), head of the Executive from February 1871, removed the government to Versailles then brutally crushed the Paris Commune. Ernest Picard (1821–77), was a government minister with Thiers. Together, they controlled the regular troops.

Sèvres . . . Asnières: all suburbs of Paris, heavily shelled by Versailles artillery.

they've ne... ne... never been to sea: allusion to a traditional French children's song with a grim storyline about sailors adrift on a boat, and casting lots to see who will be eaten.

P(r)ic-Ard: expansion to render important pun in French (Eros/Zeros).

Corots: a reference to strong use of reds in the landscape paintings of Jean-Baptiste Corot (1796–1875).

Favre: Jules Favre (1809–80), a hugely unpopular foreign minister, negotiated the French surrender to Bismark and signed the Treaty of Frankfurt (May 1871).

75 *fat cats*: in the National Assembly of early 1871 the *Ruraux* represented the interests of anti-republican property-owning classes.

Squatting Down

In its contempt for the easy, complacent life, this poem can be compared to 'Seated'.

79 *Milotus*: possibly a Latin back-formation from [Ernest] Millot, a friend of Rimbaud's.

Parisian Orgy, or Paris Filling Up Again

This bitter anti-Versailles poem laments the reappearance in the capital of all the old, reactionary values after the suppression of the Commune.

81 *barbarians*: the German army had entered Paris, having starved the city into submission after a lengthy blockade.

The Hands of Jeanne-Marie

A poem celebrating not only the valiant resistance of the Communards to the superior Versailles forces but also—somewhat uncharacteristically for Rimbaud—the heroism of women on the barricades during the notorious 'Week of Blood' of 21–8 May 1871.

87 *Khenghavars*: possible corruption of Kengawer, a Persian town.

Sions: Jerusalem.

89 *Eleison*: allusion to the first words of the Mass, *Kyrie eleison* ('Lord have mercy . . .'). Rimbaud opposes a secular Republican anthem to religious incantations.

The Just Man

In this incomplete poem—up to twenty lines appear to be missing—commentators have seen the Just Man as either Christ or Victor Hugo. Many of the obscure allusions make some sense in terms of the latter. Rimbaud's cynicism and fury are extreme.

93 *Breton bard*: usually considered to be Hugo, who spent part of a nineteen-year exile in the Channel Islands, off the Brittany coast. But it could refer to Ossian, a legendary Gaelic bard, whose name was used in 1760 by the Scottish writer James McPherson for his own, pre-Romantic poems.

95 *Pater famili-ass*: to render the French pun (*barbe* means both 'beard' and 'bore').

Socrates: Greek philosopher (468–?399 BC), here castigated presumably for his serene acceptance of death.

Seven-year-old-Poets

A celebrated poem of childhood without innocence. The tensions between the precocious child-poet and the constraining world form the poem's argument, reaching its climactic point in the prophetic final line.

97 *Paul Demeny*: an aspiring poet and friend of Rimbaud's in the Charleville days, to whom one of the two 'Letters of the visionary' is addressed.

the Mother: the use of the definite article, pointedly impersonal, and a capital letter renders 'the Mother' a universal (and negative) symbol.

101 *getting under sail*: this vivid final image heralds such great poems of the sea and new life as 'Drunken Boat'.

Poor People in Church

Another poem expressing both Rimbaud's contempt for the conformities of religious ritual, and disgust at the poor—possibly surprising in view of his hatred of authority—the rich, and the comfortable life.

103 *noses scavenging old prayer-books*: grammatical freedom to parallel the French neologism (*fringalant*).

What the Poet is Told on the Subject of Flowers

The sarcasm of the dedication to an unadmired poet prepares the way for this sustained parody of the themes and conventions of Parnassian poetry as exemplified by Banville, starting with the over-used lily. Parnassianism, which flourished in mid-nineteenth-century France, favoured dispassionate, so-called objective poetry. It also liked to use the names of exotic flora.

105 *Kerdrel*: elected to National Assembly in 1871; defender of the Royalist cause; the fleur-de-lis is France's royal emblem.

107 *Asoka*: a tree found in India.

Grandville: minor artist (1803–47) whose *Fleurs animées* depicted a series of fantasy flowers.

109 *Oise*: a river in north-eastern France.

111 *Phoebus*: Greek god of the sun.

Sea of Sorrento: the Gulf of Naples, a symbol of sentimentality in Parnassian poetry.

113 *Renan*: Ernest Renan, author of a celebrated *Life of Jesus* (1863).

Tomcat Murr: from the novel *Lebenansichten des Kater Murr* (*Life and Opinions of Tomcat Murr*) by E. T. A. Hoffmann (1760–1822).

Thyrsuses: the thyrsus was a staff tipped with a pine-cone, carried in Bacchic celebrations.

115 *Tréguier*: a Breton town, birthplace of Renan (see note above).

Paramaribo: port, and capital of Surinam.

Figuier: author of several books in the mid-nineteenth century on marvels of nature and science.

Hachette: major French publisher.

Alcide Bava: this pseudonym has been decoded as the 'brave man' (Alcide, associated with Hercules) 'spitting ink' (Bava, from verb 'to dribble').

First Communions

Rimbaud addresses the nefarious, mystical influences of Christianity, seen as significant causes of 'weakness' and 'confusion' in women.

119 *Queen of Sion*: Virgin Mary

121 *little bride*: i.e. the bride of Christ

Drunken Boat

One of finest and most celebrated of Rimbaud's poems. Written (1871) when he had not seen the ocean, this astonishing evocation of exotic seascapes and voyages far from Europe is usually read as a metaphor prophetic of the poet's own journey into *voyance*, the realms of vision. It is remarkable for its explosive language. See the Introduction for a discussion of the poem.

Evening Prayers

This lavatorial sonnet is one of several in which Rimbaud increases the shock value by linking an excremental vision with the performance of religious devotions.

135 *Lord of Cedar and Hyssop*: i.e. God. In the Old Testament cedar is often noted as a precious and fragrant wood, while 'hyssop' is valuable for purifying properties.

Vowels

This is one of Rimbaud's most celebrated and discussed poems. Commentators have sought to find the keys to the colour symbolism, often linking it to Rimbaud's known interest in alchemy. The most obvious *literary* analogy is Baudelaire's *Correspondances* sonnet, whose synaesthesia—the correspondence of sensory impressions so that an auditory impression, say, can be a visual one (thus, 'the *green* note of a flute')—sets up a mystical pattern of hidden meanings.

135 *Those Eyes*: in the French there is ambiguity here: as possessive article '*Ses* [Yeux]' could mean 'his', 'her', 'its'. Rimbaud might mean God's eyes, or those of 'the young girl with violet eyes' whom he once followed in Paris. I have adopted the solution proposed by the English poet Harry Guest in one of his versions of 'Vowels'.

'The star's wept...'

A quatrain in which the central position given to a series of colours relates it to 'Vowels'.

Album Zutique

The 'Album' is a product of the informal gatherings of certain poets in Paris to discuss poetry, compose facetious verses, smoke, and drink extravagantly. 'Zut', a mild expletive, normally means 'damn', but here, in its adjectival form, it is stronger, and corresponds to the insulting gestures made with either the middle finger or with two fingers. Among the poets Rimbaud frequented in Paris, it was common practice to parody certain respected or fashionable contemporary poets, whose false signatures appear throughout this collection.

Lilies

137 *lillicrap*: family name chosen to parallel the pun in *balançoir*, which can mean both 'children's swing' and 'hoax'.

'I was sitting...'

This is the first of a number of poems in the *Album Zutique* to parody the *dizains* (ten-line poems) of François Coppée. A contemporary of Rimbaud, Coppée was given to comfortable, flat realism, and was the frequent butt of Rimbaud's and Verlaine's invective (see note to *Orphans' New Year Gifts*).

Stupidities II. Paris

141 *Godillot*: this and the following are all names of commercial businesses or of literary figures of the time.

Old Lady's Old Men!

145 *18th March*: wrong date for the birth of the son of Napoleon III and the Empress Eugénie, the subject of this mock-celebration. He was actually born on 16 March 1856.

Damned Cherub

147 *holey*: to render 'saintly' and 'vacant', which meanings are both present in the French.

'To my bedside reading...'

This poem abounds in references to books and writers (Senancour, Madame de Genlis, Gresset, Boileau) of a learned stamp.

149 *Dr Venetti*: Nicolas Venette, who lived in the seventeeth century, wrote an influential treatise on conjugal love.

Saturnian hypotyposes

'Hypotyposis' is the vivid description of a scene, event, or situation, its effects heightened by imitation and association. 'Saturnian' refers to a type of Latin verse; it also brings to mind the *Poèmes saturniens* of Verlaine. Louis Belmontet (1799–1879) was a very minor, if prolific, poet.

Remembrances of Senility

Given the sexual content of the poem, 'remembrances' has been preferred to, say, 'souvenir'. The poem is obviously about the poet's father and the part he may have played in Arthur's sexual development.

Recollection

See note to 'Old Lady's Old Men!'

155 *snow-white Ns*: decorations denoting 'Napoleon'.

'The child who picked up bullets...'

This poem was not originally in the *Album Zutique*, but most editors now include it. The sarcastic allusion in the title is to the Prince Imperial and the 'courage' he showed during his first experience of warfare in 1870.

The Stupra

The title, from Latin, means 'obscenities'. These three sonnets are contemporaneous with the *Album Zutique*, but were not published until 1923—and then only in a limited, de-luxe edition.

'Once, animals spewed...'

161 *Kléber*: a celebrated army general during years of the French Revolution. Died 1800.

Last Poems

'What do they mean to us...'

A fiercely revolutionary poem, it contains many allusions to acts of violence during the last days of the Commune.

163 *It's nothing . . . here*: bitter resignation to abject reality of this single, final line calls to mind similar construction in such poems as 'Nina Answers Back'.

Memory

A celebrated poem which might be about Rimbaud's flight from home, or about his father's abandonment of his family in 1860.

167 *My boat*: this image of a boat tied up and stuck fast is in sharp contrast with the movement of the 'Drunken Boat'.

Tear

This poem, with some changes, is repeated in the 'Alchemy of the Word' section of *A Season in Hell*.

167 *Oise*: see note to p. 109.

Blackcurrant River

Possibly an allusion to the Semois, a small tributary of the River Meuse flowing near Charleville.

Comedy of Thirst

Rimbaud opposes his own spiritual needs to the different urgings of parents and friends, but ends apparently as desirous of oblivion as in 'Drunken Boat'.

173 *Hydra*: poisonous, multi-headed water-snake in Greek mythology; slain by Hercules.

175 *Green Inn*: cf. the poem title 'At the Green Inn'.

Lovely Morning Thought

This poem is repeated, with changes, in the *Alchemy of the Word* section of *A Season in Hell.*

177 *golden apple sun*: 'Hespérides' is metaphor for the West, a surprising choice here, as the poem is about sunrise. The Garden of the Hesperides was the source of golden apples in Greek mythology.

Babylon King's men: Nebuchadnezzar, king of Babylon, presided over a city famed as much for its cruelty as for its hanging gardens.

Queen of Shepherds: 'Reine des Bergers' means Venus (invoked in the previous stanza). Rimbaud is playing on Venus as both goddess and planet (the 'morning star').

Festivals of Patience

This sequence of four poems demonstrates Rimbaud's tendency in his later verse towards somewhat shorter lines and elliptical, enigmatic pronouncements. The sequence has been subjected to much critical scrutiny and speculative interpretation. The two middle poems, with changes, are repeated in the 'Alchemy of the Word' section of *A Season in Hell.*

Young Couple

The couple is Rimbaud and Verlaine, though Verlaine and his wife Mathilde also come to mind.

Michael and Christine

This dense poem, not susceptible to clear interpretation, appears to be a sustained hallucination in the *voyant* tradition. It has been the subject of several commentaries.

189 *Sologne*: area of Central France through which the river Loire flows, characterized by flat expanses of unspoilt land.

'Flowerbeds of amaranth...'

A poem containing several difficult allusions, not wholly explicable.

191 *palace of Jupiter*: possibly the Palais des Académies, Brussels.

'O seasons, o chateaux...'

This is a much anthologized, obscure poem. Is 'season' life on earth, and 'chateau' the soul? What is the 'spell'? The poem has attracted much commentary. A changed version closes the 'Alchemy of the Word' section of *A Season in Hell.*

'Hear the bellow'

This short-line, enigmatic poem is close in spirit to the verse sections of *A Season in Hell* and to all of *Illuminations*.

Shame

Rimbaud talks of himself, conjuring up the woes and misery which others (his mother? Verlaine?) might wish him to suffer.

199 *He*: probably Verlaine.

Rocky Mountain cat: the 'mountains' could be the hills near Roche, north-eastern France, where Rimbaud spent time on a family farm.

Mess-room by Night

It is likely that this is Rimbaud's last poem in verse, dating from October 1875. Despite references to particular people (e.g. Lefêbvre, someone in Charleville), the intended target of this parodic poem could be rhyme, over-used and much abused.

The Deserts of Love

These fragments of 1871 or 1872 give some idea of how Rimbaud's mind was working at the time of the composition of *A Season in Hell* and *Illuminations*. The dream-like imagery seems to contain allusions to the homosexual part of Rimbaud's life.

Fragments According to the Gospel

These pieces are usually taken to be linked either to *A Season in Hell* or to *Illuminations*. However, some critics now feel that they should be read as an autonomous group. They are difficult to date. Rimbaud's hostility to Christianity is here more sustained than in his other anti-religious poems. The starting-point is St John's Gospel (John 4: 41), and the city of Samaria, emblem of heresy and stupidity.

A Season in Hell

For a more general view of *A Season*, see Introduction. The following notes are explanations of detail, and are not intended primarily to be interpretative.

Bad Blood

213 *Declaration of the Rights of Man*: this declaration of certain fundamental rights—to own property, have protection from oppression, to be free, to be safe—dates from the French Revolution, and lies at the heart of the Republican ideal.

Swabian plain: a region of south-western Germany.

Solyma: a poetic name for Jerusalem.

217 *De profundis Domine*: Psalm 30, 'Out of the depths have I cried unto thee, O Lord'.

219 *children of Ham*: Ham was a son of the biblical Noah, and is usually regarded as the ancestor of black races.

First Delirium: The Foolish Virgin

The allusion is to the biblical parable of the Wise and Foolish Virgins (Matthew, 25: 1–3). The virgins await the Heavenly Bridegroom; five are wise, and prepared; five are foolish, and unprepared. The latter are thereby denied the Kingdom of Heaven. Rimbaud relocates the story to Hell. His text is also a metaphor for his relationship with Verlaine.

Second Delirium: Alchemy of the Word

Rimbaud reproduces here some of the poems from 'Derniers Vers', but slightly altered, usually to their detriment, as if to emphasize the self-disgust which runs through *A Season in Hell*.

241 *Kedron*: a river which flows into the Dead Sea.

243 *Cimmeria*: classical name for the lands at the limits of the known world, associated with the dead.

245 *wave my hand at beauty*: the French verb means both 'greet' and 'bid farewell'. The English keeps that ambiguity.

Illuminations

For a more general view of *Illuminations*, see Introduction. The following notes are explanations of detail, and are not intended primarily to be interpretative.

After the Flood

257 *Eucharis*: a nymph, the companion of Calypso; her name connotes grace.

Parade

265 *Cherubino*: the charming, naïve, and very young man in Beaumarchais's play (and Mozart's opera) *The Marriage of Figaro*.

Being Beauteous

The title is in English in the original.

Morning of Drunkenness

273 *ASSASSINS*: usually taken to mean not only murderers, but also users of hashish. 'Hashish' and 'assassin' have the same etymological derivation.

City

279 *Erinyes*: Greek name for the Furies, who pursued and punished wrongdoers.

Cities [I]

Hampton Court: the English royal palace, just outside London.

Brahmins: the manuscript is very difficult to decipher here. I have opted for Treharne's reading (see Bibliography). The Indian term is consonant with several other references in the poem.

281 *Sainte-Chapelle*: the imposing Gothic church in the heart of Paris which, ironically, has no dome.

Cities [II]

283 *Alleghenies*: a mountain range in the United States.

Lebanons: plural suggests mountains in Lebanon, not the country itself.

Rolands: Roland is the hero of the eleventh-century French epic, *The Song of Roland.*

Mabs: Mab is queen of the fairies in English folklore. See Shakespeare, *Romeo and Juliet*, I. iv.

Diana: goddess of hunting.

Bacchantes: ecstatic followers of Bacchus, god of wine.

Dawn

287 *I have been dawn's summer lord*: a slightly free translation, to echo the tightly organized sounds of the French line. Rimbaud's poem is most carefully structured. Note, for example, that the first and final lines in French have eight syllables each.

Vulgar Nocturne

289 *Solymas*: see note to p. 213.

Winter Festival

291 *Meander*: a winding river in Asia Minor.

Horace: Latin poet (65–8 BC).

First Empire: created by Napoleon Bonaparte, the First Empire lasted from 1804 to 1814.

Boucher: François Boucher (1703–70), painter and engraver.

Metropolitan

293 *Ossian*: see note to p. 93.

Samaria: see headnote to *Fragments According to the Gospel.*

Guaranis: South American Indians.

Youth

299 *Psyche*: warned by Eros, her lover, not to look at him, Psyche disobeyed and so lost him; but the pair were eventually reunited. The story is told in Apuleius, *The Golden Ass.*

St Anthony: a hermit tormented by temptations of the Devil; despite wild visions and fantasies, he did not succumb.

Promontory

301 *Scarborough*: Rimbaud visited this seaside town in north-eastern England in 1874. The hotel names are authentic.

Scenes

303 *Boeotians*: a people of Ancient Greece, regarded as dull-witted and lacking sophistication.

Historic Evening

305 *Norns*: in Norse mythology, the Fates.

Bottom

The reference is to Nick Bottom the weaver in Shakespeare's *A Midsummer Night's Dream*. Bottom is changed into an ass.

Sabine women: according to Roman legend, these women were abducted to serve as wives to the early inhabitants of Rome.

Devotions

309 *Louise Vanaen de Voringhen*: possibly a nurse who looked after Rimbaud in a Brussels hospital in 1873.

Léonie Aubois d'Ashby: seemingly an invented name and person.

Circeto: possibly a fusion of Circe, the enchantress in Homer's *Odyssey*, and Ceto, in Greek mythology the mother of the hideous Graiae and Gorgons. However *cetus* is also Latin for 'whale'.

INDEX OF TITLES

INDEX OF FIRST LINES

A SELECTION OF **OXFORD WORLD'S CLASSICS**

APOLLINAIRE, ALFRED JARRY, and MAURICE MAETERLINCK	**Three Pre-Surrealist Plays**
HONORÉ DE BALZAC	**Cousin Bette** **Eugénie Grandet** **Père Goriot**
CHARLES BAUDELAIRE	**The Flowers of Evil** **The Prose Poems and Fanfarlo**
DENIS DIDEROT	**This is Not a Story and Other Stories**
ALEXANDRE DUMAS (PÈRE)	**The Black Tulip** **The Count of Monte Cristo** **Louise de la Vallière** **The Man in the Iron Mask** **La Reine Margot** **The Three Musketeers** **Twenty Years After**
ALEXANDRE DUMAS (FILS)	**La Dame aux Camélias**
GUSTAVE FLAUBERT	**Madame Bovary** **A Sentimental Education** **Three Tales**
VICTOR HUGO	**The Last Day of a Condemned Man and Other Prison Writings** **Notre-Dame de Paris**
J.-K. HUYSMANS	**Against Nature**
JEAN DE LA FONTAINE	**Selected Fables**
PIERRE CHODERLOS DE LACLOS	**Les Liaisons dangereuses**
MME DE LAFAYETTE	**The Princesse de Clèves**
GUY DE MAUPASSANT	**A Day in the Country and Other Stories** **Mademoiselle Fifi**
PROSPER MÉRIMÉE	**Carmen and Other Stories**

A SELECTION OF OXFORD WORLD'S CLASSICS

Ludovico Ariosto	**Orlando Furioso**
Giovanni Boccaccio	**The Decameron**
Matteo Maria Boiardo	**Orlando Innamorato**
Luís Vaz de Camões	**The Lusíads**
Miguel de Cervantes	**Don Quixote de la Mancha** **Exemplary Stories**
Dante Alighieri	**The Divine Comedy** **Vita Nuova**
Benito Pérez Galdós	**Nazarín**
Leonardo da Vinci	**Selections from the Notebooks**
Niccolò Machiavelli	**Discourses on Livy** **The Prince**
Michelangelo	**Life, Letters, and Poetry**
Petrarch	**Selections from the *Canzoniere* and Other Works**
Giorgio Vasari	**The Lives of the Artists**

A SELECTION OF **OXFORD WORLD'S CLASSICS**

Jane Austen	**Catharine and Other Writings**
	Emma
	Mansfield Park
	Northanger Abbey, Lady Susan, The Watsons, and Sanditon
	Persuasion
	Pride and Prejudice
	Sense and Sensibility
Anne Bront	**Agnes Grey**
	The Tenant of Wildfell Hall
Charlotte Bront	**Jane Eyre**
	The Professor
	Shirley
	Villette
Emily Bront	**Wuthering Heights**
Wilkie Collins	**The Moonstone**
	No Name
	The Woman in White
Charles Darwin	**The Origin of Species**
Charles Dickens	**The Adventures of Oliver Twist**
	Bleak House
	David Copperfield
	Great Expectations
	Hard Times
	Little Dorrit
	Martin Chuzzlewit
	Nicholas Nickleby
	The Old Curiosity Shop
	Our Mutual Friend
	The Pickwick Papers
	A Tale of Two Cities

A SELECTION OF **OXFORD WORLD'S CLASSICS**

George Eliot	**Adam Bede** **Daniel Deronda** **Middlemarch** **The Mill on the Floss** **Silas Marner**
Elizabeth Gaskell	**Cranford** **The Life of Charlotte Brontë** **Mary Barton** **North and South** **Wives and Daughters**
Thomas Hardy	**Far from the Madding Crowd** **Jude the Obscure** **The Mayor of Casterbridge** **A Pair of Blue Eyes** **The Return of the Native** **Tess of the d'Urbervilles** **The Woodlanders**
Walter Scott	**Ivanhoe** **Rob Roy** **Waverley**
Mary Shelley	**Frankenstein** **The Last Man**
Robert Louis Stevenson	**Kidnapped and Catriona** **The Strange Case of Dr Jekyll and Mr Hyde and Weir of Hermiston** **Treasure Island**
Bram Stoker	**Dracula**
William Makepeace Thackeray	**Barry Lyndon** **Vanity Fair**
Oscar Wilde	**Complete Shorter Fiction** **The Picture of Dorian Gray**

A SELECTION OF OXFORD WORLD'S CLASSICS

Ann Radcliffe	The Castles of Athlin and Dunbayne The Italian The Mysteries of Udolpho The Romance of the Forest A Sicilian Romance
Frances Sheridan	Memoirs of Miss Sidney Bidulph
Tobias Smollett	The Adventures of Roderick Random The Expedition of Humphry Clinker Travels through France and Italy
Laurence Sterne	The Life and Opinions of Tristram Shandy, Gentleman A Sentimental Journey
Jonathan Swift	Gulliver's Travels A Tale of a Tub and Other Works
Horace Walpole	The Castle of Otranto
Gilbert White	The Natural History of Selborne
Mary Wollstonecraft	Mary and The Wrongs of Woman

MORE ABOUT **OXFORD WORLD'S CLASSICS**

American Literature

British and Irish Literature

Children's Literature

Classics and Ancient Literature

Colonial Literature

Eastern Literature

European Literature

History

Medieval Literature

Oxford English Drama

Poetry

Philosophy

Politics

Religion

The Oxford Shakespeare
